CHRISTIANITY:
LINEAMENTS OF A
SACRED TRADITION

By the Author

Orientation and Descent (poems)
The Marble Threshing Floor: Studies in Modern Greek Poetry
The Greek East and the Latin West: A Study in the
Christian Tradition
Athos: The Mountain of Silence
Six Poets of Modern Greece (with Edmund Keeley)
Constantinople: The Iconography of a Sacred City
The Pursuit of Greece (editor)
Byzantium
George Seferis: Collected Poems (1925-1955) (with
Edmund Keeley)
Modern Greece (with John Campbell)
C. P. Cavafy: Selected Poems (with Edmund Keeley)
W. B. Yeats and the Search for Tradition (essay)
C. P. Cavafy: Collected Poems (with Edmund Keeley)
Christianity and Eros: Essays on the Theme of Sexual Love
Church, Papacy and Schism: A Theological Enquiry
The Wound of Greece: Studies in Neo-Hellenism
The Philokalia (with G. E. H. Palmer and Kallistos Ware)
Motets for a Sunflower (poems)
Angelos Sikelianos: Selected Poems (with Edmund Keeley)
Odysseus Elytis: Selected Poems (with Edmund Keeley)
The Rape of Man and Nature: An Enquiry into the Origins and
Consequences of Modern Science
Edward Lear: The Corfu Years (editor)
The Sacred in Life and Art
Human Image: World Image. The Death and Resurrection
of Sacred Cosmology
In the Sign of the Rainbow: Selected Poems 1940-1989
George Seferis: Complete Poems (with Edmund Keeley)
For Every Thing That Lives is Holy (essay)

Philip Sherrard

Christianity:
Lineaments
of a
Sacred Tradition

Foreword by
Kallistos Ware

HOLY CROSS ORTHODOX PRESS
Brookline, Massachusetts

© 1998 by Holy Cross Orthodox Press
Published by Holy Cross Orthodox Press
50 Goddard Avenue
Brookline, MA 02445 USA

ISBN 1-885652-05-4

"The Revival of Hesychast Spirituality" by Philip Sherrard, [Chapter 13]
*Christian Spirituality; Post-Reformation and Modern, Volume 18 of World Spiritu-
ality: An Encyclopedic History of the Religious Quest*, edited by Louis Dupré and
Don E. Saliers in collaboration with John Meyendorff. Copyright © 1989 by
the Crossroad Publishing Company, New York. Used with permission of the
publisher.

"The Revival of Hesychast Spirituality" by Philip Sherrard from Christian
Spirituality Vol. III, edited by Louis Dupré and Don E. Saliers in collaboration
with John Meyendorff. Copyright © 1989 by SCM Press, Ltd. London. Used
with permission of the publisher.

Library of Congress Cataloging-in-Publication Data
Sherrard, Philip.
Christianity: lineaments of a sacred tradition / Philip Sherrard; with a
foreword by Kallistos Ware.
p. cm.
Includes bibliographical references.
ISBN 1-885652-05-4 (pbk.)
1. Christianity—Essence, genius, nature. I. Title.
BT60.S45   1997
230'.19dc—21   97-38450
                                                          CIP

Acknowledgments

The writing and compilation of this book was completed shortly before the author's death on 30th May 1995 and thus he did not have the opportunity of emending or revising the final typescript which, in the normal course of the gestation of a book, an author would do. Therefore, in the preparation of the present text, the help and contribution of a number of people has been enlisted; in this respect I would like to thank most warmly Fr John Chryssavgis, John Dillon, Garth and Elizabeth Fowden, Irene Hoenig, Brian Keeble, Andrew Louth, Marcus Plested, Fr Vincent Rossi, Sheila Stern, Bishop Kallistos Ware, Graham Whitaker, Fr Alexander and Julie Williams and, particularly, Liadain Sherrard with whom the responsibility of the final editorial decisions in all cases was shared. Philip Sherrard was not an 'academic' writer in the common sense of the word, and tended to eschew the use of what he considered superfluous footnotes. For this present edition every attempt has been made to give references for quotations cited but in some instances the source has not been located.

I also wish to thank Selga Sherrard, Efthymia Provata and, especially, George Provatas for their generous and unstinting contribution in the practical realm of the typing and the word processing of the final text.

Finally, acknowledgments and thanks are due to The Temenos Academy, London, for permission to reproduce the text of Chapter 9, which was a paper first given at the Academy in 1994 and published by them, with the title "Every Thing That Lives is Holy", in 1995, The Crossroad Publishing Company of New York for permission to reproduce what forms the substantial part of Chapter 11, published as "The Revival of Hesychast Spirituality" in Volume 18 of their *World Spirituality: An Encyclopedic History of the Religious Quest* (1989) and the editors of *Studies in Comparative Religion* in which earlier and shorter versions of some of the other chapters first appeared.

Denise Sherard
Katounia, Limni
Spring, 1998

Contents

Foreword   ix

Chapter One
The Meaning and Necessity of Sacred Tradition   1

Chapter Two
Christianity and Christendom   27

Chapter Three
Christianity and Other Sacred Traditions   53

Chapter Four
Christianity and the Metaphysics of Logic   76

Chapter Five
Christianity and the Challenge of
Georgios Gemistos Plethon
and Friedrich Nietzsche   114

Chapter Six
Christianity and the Religious Thought
of C. G. Jung   134

Chapter Seven
The Presence of Evil:
Christian and Neoplatonic Views   158

Chapter Eight
On Death and Dying: A Christian Approach   180

Chapter Nine
Christianity and the Desecration of the Cosmos   200

Chapter Ten
The Meaning of Creation *ex nihilo*   232

Chapter Eleven
The Renewal of the Tradition
of Contemplative Spirituality   245

Index   269

Foreword

Greece and Orthodoxy: A Double Vocation

Philip Sherrard was working on the present book, *Christianity: Lineaments of a Sacred Tradition,* during the final months before his death on 30 May 1995. He was well aware at the time that he might not live much longer. He incorporated articles and lectures composed over a period of many years, but at the same time he revised the whole text, making several significant additions. In this manner, although the book cannot be termed in the strict sense his 'last will and testament', it reflects nevertheless his considered viewpoint at the conclusion of his life, and all the pieces contained in it are things that he himself wished to preserve. He arranged the material in such a way as to confer on the book as a whole a unifying theme, despite the diversity of its contents. Above all the opening chapter on 'The Meaning and Necessity of Sacred Tradition' possesses a programmatic character, summing up in concise form the vision of truth that inspired Philip during his forty years as writer, teacher, and personal guide.

Philip Sherrard will long be remembered for his work in two related fields: as a translator and expositor of modern Greek poetry, and as a creative and sometimes prophetic interpreter of the living tradition of the Orthodox Church. In both spheres his literary and scholarly work was the expression of a deep personal commitment. He did not merely write books about Greece, but chose to make his home there; he did not simply study Orthodoxy with academic detachment, but took the decision to become himself a member of the Orthodox communion, at a time when such a step was altogether exceptional. Poetry, theology, and life formed for him a single unity.

From Oxford to Katounia

Philip Owen Arnould Sherrard was born in Oxford on 23 September 1922. His father, Raymond Sherrard, from an Anglo-Irish family, was an agricultural economist who, after some years of farming, took up a position at the Agricultural Research Institute in the University of Oxford. His mother Brynhild was a daughter of Sydney Olivier, colonial administrator, one-time Governor of Jamaica, Secretary of State in Ramsay Macdonald's Labour government of 1924, and an early member of the left-wing Fabian Society. Brynhild was at the centre of the circle dubbed 'the neo-pagans' by her friend Virginia Woolf; this included Rupert Brooke, Lytton Strachey, and others associated with the Bloomsbury Group. But, as Patrick Leigh Fermor observes, although Philip inherited strong literary leanings, in the end 'it was neither the Fabians nor Bloomsbury which were to influence his life; in many ways – in his rejection of agnosticism, for instance – he was opposed to them'.[1]

Philip grew up in the English countryside. The poet Kathleen Raine, whose friendship with him began in the mid-1940s, says that 'Philip's childhood was unusually fortunate in uniting patrician standards with "progressive" values'. She goes on to quote his own words in later life, 'I could not have had a better childhood, and have always been extremely grateful for it.'[2] He belonged to a large family of eight children in all, taking into account stepsisters and stepbrothers. His mother Brynhild had two sons and a daughter from a first marriage before she married Philip's father; she and Raymond then had three children, Philip and two daughters. Brynhild died when Philip was twelve, and his father remarried and had two more daughters by his second wife. In Kathleen Raine's words, 'It was his father who held together his family, moving from one dilapidated but beautiful farmhouse to another, with little money, but sustained by his free spirit.... The relationship between

---

[1] *The Daily Telegraph* (London), 12 June 1995.
[2] Kathleen Raine, *Philip Sherrard (1922-1995): A Tribute* (The Delos Press, Birmingham, The Redlake Press, Clun, 1996), pp. 6-7. This is a perceptive and sympathetic account, to which I am much indebted.

Philip and his father was one of equality, of shared love of poetry and things of the mind.'[3]

Philip's daughter Liadain has written of his early years: 'He would speak with sheer delight and nostalgia about his farm up-bringing, the early rising, the milking, the harvest in an England still rural and to a large extent unmechanized. His love and knowledge of nature had its roots in that childhood, as did his practical acquaintance with the land and his deep need of it. His later violent reaction against England may have been – unconsciously – activated by those profound and beautiful memories of it as it used to be, as he had experienced it in childhood before the war, and as it would never be again.'[4] Richard Jefferies, author of *The Story of My Heart* and other books on nature, was among Philip's favorite writers.

Philip was educated at Dauntsey's, a minor but 'progressive' English public school, and then in October 1940 he entered Peterhouse, Cambridge. Here he started to work on the History Tripos. He was also a successful athlete, excelling in rowing, cricket and other sports, a 'half-blue' for squash. His studies were cut short after two years when in 1942 he volunteered to fight in the Second World War. He was offered a commission but chose to join the army as a private, although he later became an officer in the Royal Artillery, rising to the rank of captain. After active service in Italy and Austria, he was sent to Greece. This was his first visit there, and it marked the beginning of a life-long love of the Greek land, of its history, culture, and religious faith.

Philip's character was in fact profoundly non-violent and un-military, and this was apparent even in his years of army service. His God-daughter Julie du Boulay – whose book *Portrait of a Greek Mountain Village*, published in 1974, emphasizes many of the characteristics that Philip himself found significant in the traditional Greek way of life – tells the story of how he was once receiving the surrender of a German officer in Italy. He asked for the German's

---

[3] Raine, *Philip Sherrard*, p. 7.
[4] Quoted in Raine, *Philip Sherrard*, p. 7.

weapon. The officer refused, saying, 'What would you do in my place?' Philip responded by taking his own revolver from his holster, and laying it on the table. It was made of wood, for he had not wanted to carry a real one. 'This story', Julie du Boulay comments, 'reveals some of Philip's most endearing characteristics – a willingness to risk himself, a love of peace, an utter lack of pomposity, an ability to be just slightly out of step with more conventional thinking. These qualities endured for much of the rest of his life.'[5]

Philip's independence of judgement, and his dislike of coercion and brutality, were evident in his reaction to the forced 'repatriation' of Ukrainian and other East European soldiers who had surrendered to the British at the end of the war. I can recall him describing his indignation when he discovered that they were being systematically handed over to the Communists, even though the British authorities had no illusions about the grim fate that awaited them. Philip for his part refused to co-operate with this evil policy. From what he said, I gathered that he came close to directly disobeying orders from his superiors.

While in Athens at the end of the war Philip met his future wife Anna Mirodia, whom he married in 1946. They had two daughters, Selga and Liadain, but the marriage was eventually dissolved.

During his time in Greece, Philip also encountered the Orthodox Church, and this proved a decisive turning-point in his life. Abandoning his non-religious upbringing, he became Orthodox in 1956. He was received through the sacrament of baptism, for he had never been baptized in childhood. For Philip, entry into the Orthodox communion meant that he was embracing the Christian faith in its true and complete form. But this was not all. He also felt that he was entering a Church which, despite its failings, had none the less preserved an organic and life-giving connection between human beings and the natural world. As the years passed, he saw this organic connection as more and more important – indeed, as essential for the future survival of humankind – and he made it the central theme of his later writings.

[5] *The Guardian* (London), 8 June 1995.

Some years before his entry into Orthodoxy, Philip had embarked upon an academic career. He spent the year 1947-48 at King's College, London, reading modern Greek literature and commencing work on his doctoral dissertation for London University. At a time when most western Hellenophiles turned to Classical Greece, Philip preferred the living culture that he found in the Greek poets of the nineteenth and twentieth centuries, Solomos, Palamas, Cavafy, Sikelianos, and Seferis. His study of them eventually appeared in 1956 under the title *The Marble Threshing Floor: Studies in Modern Greek Poetry*. The remarkable flowering of modern Greek poetry was as yet little appreciated in the West, and Philip played a decisive part in making it known to the English-speaking public.

Philip occupied a variety of academic posts. During 1951-52 he was Assistant Director of the British School of Archaeology in Athens. He was attached during 1954-57 to the research staff of the Royal Institute of International Affairs, and during 1957-58 he was a research fellow at St Antony's College, Oxford. At Oxford he became a friend of Maurice Bowra, one of the few literary critics whom he admired. During 1958-62 he was back at the British School in Athens as Assistant Director and Librarian. Finally, during 1970-77 he taught in London University as Lecturer in the History of the Orthodox Church, a post attached jointly to King's College and to the School of Slavonic and Eastern European Studies. There is little doubt that, had he wished, he could have successfully pursued a normal university career. But he was too much of a 'free spirit' – his interests were too wide-ranging, and his approach too unconventional – for him to feel totally at home in academia. He was a born teacher in the Socratic sense, but he did not really enjoy giving instruction under the formal conditions of university life. He preferred the greater liberty, and the greater insecurity, of working in rural Greece as a freelance author and translator.

Philip's links with the Greek soil were greatly strengthened when in 1959 he was fortunate enough to come across a disused magnesite mine for sale near Limni on the island of Evia (Euboea).

Katounia – 'half-logger's camp, half-Arcady', in the words of Patrick Leigh Fermor, who lived there for a time – occupied a remote and little-frequented site between the sea and a steeply-rising pine forest. It comprised a group of houses, at that time largely in ruins, which had been built for the manager and staff of the mine, and there was also ample land. Although expecting the property to be far beyond his limited resources, Philip went nonetheless to see the estate agent, who promptly named a price. At first Philip imagined that the figure quoted (which seemed surprisingly small) must be in gold pounds, but to his astonishment he discovered that it was in paper pounds – no more than a relatively small fraction of what he had anticipated. So Katounia became his home.

When St Antony of Egypt moved to his final retreat at the 'Inner Mountain', his biographer St Athanasios records that at once 'he fell in love with the place'.[6] Of Philip too the same may be said: he came to feel a deep, even passionate, love for his retreat at Katounia. Here he lived permanently in his later years, after resigning from his London University post in 1977. His time was spent in reading, writing and translating, in building, in watering his orange and lemon trees, and in dispensing generous hospitality to a few chosen friends. To some of these he became a spiritual guide, a true *geronta* or lay 'elder', although he himself would have disclaimed any such title. He and his second wife, the publisher Denise Harvey, enjoyed a close and happy relationship. Denise's publishing house, based initially in Athens and then at Katounia, reissued several of Philip's books, along with other studies on modern Greece, in the 'Romiosyni Series', as it is called. Particularly successful in the series were two volumes of Edward Lear's Greek journals, both beautifully illustrated with Lear's own water-colours and sketches – *The Cretan Journal* (1984) and *The Corfu Years* (1988) – the second of these with Philip himself as editor.

Philip and Denise lived in their home at Katounia with a simplicity that was almost monastic. They had no telephone and no electricity, and heating was provided by firewood. Near to their house, in the last years of Philip's life they constructed a tiny church,

[6] St Athanasios of Alexandria, *The Life of St Antony* 40.

largely with their own hands, using building techniques and an architectural style that were strictly traditional. With an approach that was ascetic and yet civilized, Philip succeeded in reducing his life to the primary essentials, both spiritual and material.

Tall and slim, Philip continued until his early seventies to be physically agile and mentally alert. But around 1993 cancer was diagnosed and, although he enjoyed a remission in 1994, it returned during the following year in a much more virulent form. He came to London for treatment and here, somewhat suddenly, he died on 30 May 1995. He was fortunate to be spared a prolonged and painful illness. His body was flown back to Greece and on 3 June, in a spot chosen by himself, he was buried at Katounia beside the chapel that he and Denise had built. In his wife's words, his body was 'consigned to the hands of God, to the living breathing earth in an embrace of cypress trees next to a running stream'. On the third anniversary of his death, 30 May 1998, I had the great joy of taking part in the consecration of this chapel.

Orthodoxy and the Philosophia Perennis

An important part in Philip's experience of Orthodoxy was played by the Holy Mountain of Athos. Here he went frequently on pilgrimage, coming in particular under the influence of a remarkable Russian hermit, Fr Nikon of Karoulia (1875-1963), who instructed him in the practice of the Jesus Prayer. Philip knew the Athonite peninsula from end to end, walking indefatigably along the steep upland paths which intersect that sacred territory. It disturbed him profoundly to observe, in his later years, how the monks and pilgrims preferred to travel by motor vehicles along the newly-made roads, with the result that the ancient pathways became overgrown and impassable. He saw this as a symptom of grave spiritual sickness, indicating as it did the tragic loss of living communion with the world of nature.[7] On one winter's afternoon as he walked alone through the woods above Karyes, so he told

[7] See his trenchant article, even more timely today than when first written over twenty years ago, 'The Paths of Athos', *Eastern Churches Review* 9 (1977), pp. 100-107.

me, he was suddenly engulfed in a snowstorm and lost his way, narrowly escaping death from exposure.

Philip's love of the Holy Mountain is evident in his book *Athos: The Mountain of Silence* (1960), which was reissued in revised form as *Athos the Holy Mountain* (1982). In comparison with most Western accounts of the Mountain, this has the huge advantage of being written by someone who not only belonged to the Orthodox Church but who also, without being himself a monk, possessed a real understanding of the reasons why others choose the monastic vocation. Philip's links with the Holy Mountain were strengthened by his collaboration, during his last twenty years, on the English translation of that classic expression of Athonite spirituality *The Philokalia*.

While firm in his loyalty to the Orthodox Church, Philip's spiritual vision extended at the same time beyond Orthodoxy and, indeed, beyond the Christian faith. He considered that there is, in Kathleen Raine's words, 'a universal and unanimous wisdom underlying all sacred traditions'.[8] For reasons that he advances in Chapter 3 of this present book, he rejected the view that Christianity possesses an exclusive monopoly of the truth. Without wishing to detract from the historical reality of the Incarnation of the Logos from the Virgin Mary, he also believed that there is a broader revelation of the Divine Logos to every human heart. As St Paul affirmed to the Athenians in his speech on the Areopagus, 'God is not far from each one of us, for in Him we live and move and in Him we exist' (Acts 17:27-28). Philip saw Christ the Logos as 'the true light that illumines everyone who comes into the world' (Jn. 1:9). For Philip, as for the second-century Apologist Justin Martyr, Christ is the cosmic Sower who has implanted *logoi spermatikoi*, seeds of the truth, in all human persons without exception. From this it follows that, in Philip's words, the Divine is 'disclosed at every point of time and in every creature…. the Logos in His *kenosis*, His self-emptying, is hidden everywhere.'[9] Christians need therefore to acknowledge that 'sacred traditions other

[8] Raine, *Philip Sherrard*, p. 5.
[9] Quotations from Philip Sherrard, not otherwise identified, are taken from the present work.

than their own are divinely instituted ways of spiritual realization'. The one truth of the Logos is present in all the great world religions: 'It is the Logos who is received in the spiritual illumination of a Brahmin, a Buddhist or a Moslem.'

Yet, although upholding in this way the reality of a universal sacred wisdom or *Philosophia Perennis*, Philip was firmly opposed to syncretism or eclecticism. Only through attachment to a particular religious tradition can we come to a genuine vision of the universal truth. 'Our primary loyalty and faith', he says, 'must of course be directed towards our own tradition and to deepening experience of that.' For Western people the normative tradition is the Christian faith: 'Christianity is *the* spiritual tradition of the West.'[10] In this emphasis upon the need to adhere to an established tradition, Philip was clearly influenced by the ideas of René Guénon, for whom indeed he expresses a warm admiration at the start of Chapter 4 in this book (but whom he also criticizes in the same chapter).

Philip's appreciation of a universal wisdom underlying the various sacred traditions of the world was reinforced by his long-standing friendship with a remarkable Greek, Marco Pallis, whose visits to Tibetan monasteries in Sikkim and Ladak – recounted in his work *Peaks and Lamas* – led him to become a Buddhist. Marco was also active in the revival of early English music, being one of the founders of the English Consort of Viols. When approached by religious 'seekers', Philip used to recommend to them Marco's second book *The Way and the Mountain*.

This belief in an all-embracing spiritual wisdom led Philip, in collaboration with Kathleen Raine, Keith Critchlow and Brian Keeble, in 1981 to found *Temenos*, 'A Review of the Arts of the Imagination', as it was called. Although they thought it prudent not to allude explicitly to 'the sacred' in the title of the review, that in fact was where their real concern lay. At the same time the reference to the imagination deserves to be noted. Influenced by the Sufi understanding of the imagination, as expounded by Henri

---

[10] *The Greek East and the Latin West*, p. 196.

Corbin, Philip deeply valued the imaginative faculty, which he saw as corresponding in some measure to what the Greek Fathers styled the *nous* or spiritual intellect. Philip was a regular contributor to the thirteen issues of *Temenos* that appeared between 1981 and 1993. The review itself ceased publication for a number of years, but has now been revived as the *Temenos Academy Review*; closely linked to it is the Temenos Academy, founded in 1991.

5/28/12

Those who encountered Philip exclusively in an Orthodox context have been surprised and even disturbed by his openness to non-Christian religious traditions. Did he perhaps go too far? Some readers of the present book may ask: In the opening chapter on Sacred Tradition, why does he not speak more clearly about the New Testament, the Church and the sacraments, about Christ's Incarnation, Crucifixion and Resurrection? In Chapter 3, on non-Christian faiths, how far does he uphold the uniqueness of Jesus Christ as the *only* incarnate Son of God? Is he right in this same chapter to describe the Incarnation as a 'consequence of our ignominy'? Surely it is the supreme expression of God's eternal love. When discussing death in Chapter 8, might he not have said more about the distinctively Christian belief in the second coming of Christ and the resurrection of the body?

To appreciate Philip's approach, we need to allow first for the hermeneutic task which he was attempting. Much of what he wrote is addressed in the first instance, not to an exclusively Christian audience, and still less to members of the Orthodox Church, but to a mixed readership that included adherents of different faiths, as well as 'seekers' who had not yet found a home in any particular tradition. Had he commenced with a terminology that was exclusively and, indeed, aggressively Christian, would he not have risked alienating many who might otherwise be prepared to listen attentively to his message?

In the second place, and more importantly, Philip's writings form a unity, and each particular chapter or book has to be read in the context of his total *oeuvre*. As soon as this is done, it becomes overwhelmingly clear that he does not regard Christ's Incarnation as secondary or peripheral. On the contrary, his entire understanding of the relationship between the uncreated and the created – between God, humankind and the world – is based upon one foundation or paradigm, and upon one alone: upon the 'union without confusion' between divine and human nature that came to pass in the single, undivided person of Christ incarnate. Almost everything contained in his theological and ecological writings is nothing else than an extended commentary upon the Chalcedonian Definition. Faithful to St Paul's message on the Areopagus, Philip insisted upon the common ground shared by Christians and non-Christians, but this did not lead him to disavow his own Christian patrimony.

Philip was genuinely Orthodox, but his vision of Orthodox Christianity was generous and wide-ranging, not defensive or timidly parochial. All too many Orthodox Christians today understand their faith as negation rather than affirmation. Philip rebelled against this. The breadth of his sympathies is apparent from the list of thinkers whose influence he acknowledges at the beginning of his book *Human Image: World Image* (1992). This includes not only Justin Martyr, Irenaeus, Clement of Alexandria, Origen, the author of the *Corpus Dionysiacum*, and Maximos the Confessor, but also Eckhart, Ruysbroeck, Plotinus, Rumi, Boehme, and Blake, and, among twentieth-century masters, Yeats (whom he held in high regard), Corbin, Titus Burckhardt, Coomaraswamy, Gershom Scholem, R.G. Collingwood, and C.S. Lewis.

The Pursuit of Greece

Philip was a prolific writer, and the full list of his works, covering both Greek poetry and Orthodox theology, is striking and extensive. As a translator from the Greek, he enjoyed a long and productive collaboration with the American scholar Edmund Keeley. Together they prepared *Six Poets of Modern Greece* (1960) and the Penguin volume *Four Greek Poets* (1966). This was followed by joint translations of the collected poems of Seferis (1967) and Cavafy (1975), and of selected poems by Sikelianos (1979) and Elytis (1981), together with an anthology of modern Greek poetry entitled *The Dark Crystal* (1981). So close was the co-operation between the two of them, so extensive were the revisions that each made in the work of the other, that by the time a book went to press it was no longer possible to know which of them had done the first draft of any particular poem. In the case of Seferis, the poet himself took an occasional hand in the work of translation. The renderings by Sherrard and Keeley remain to this day the best versions of modern Greek poetry in the English language. What made Philip particularly effective as a translator was the fact that he was himself a gifted poet in his own right. His love of poetry runs as a unifying thread through his whole life. It is certainly appropriate that his earliest published work was a book of poems, *Orientation and Descent* (1953), while the last publication to appear in his lifetime was the collection of his selected poems, *In The Sign of the Rainbow* (1994), covering the years 1940-89. All his poems are basically autobiographical, an immediate expression of his inner life.

What mattered to Philip, when he wrote about Greek poetry, was above all the 'world-view' of the writers whom he discussed, the vision of primary truth that they strove to articulate. This is evident at once in his earliest study of Greek poetry, *The Marble Threshing Floor*, published in 1956. This book is remarkable, not only for the sensitivity with which he describes the poetic qualities of his five chosen authors, but also for the consistent concern with which he explores the underlying spiritual factors influencing all five in various ways. He treats them as witnesses, bearing testimony to a reality greater than themselves. For Philip the authentic artist is always a messenger, pointing us towards a realm of eternal beauty and harmony.

This approach is evident in the opening chapter of *The Marble Threshing Floor*, which is devoted to Dionysios Solomos (1798-1857). Solomos was an Italianized native of the Ionian Isles, who only mastered Greek as an adult and who was captivated by Byronic notions of heroism and liberty. At first sight he does not seem a promising candidate as a spokesman for sacred tradition. But Philip thinks otherwise. He notes how Solomos, explaining his aim as a poet, uses the significant phrase 'the Great Realities';

in Solomos's eyes, the ultimate purpose of his poetry is to reveal a higher and transcendent truth. In this way he exemplifies an attitude towards art that is neither 'classic' nor 'romantic' but 'traditional'. According to this traditional understanding, Philip continues, 'the artistic process neither begins nor ends with the individual.... Art begins with a supra-individual world that cannot be known by observation or discursive reasoning but only by contemplation. This is the world of spiritual realities, of archetypes and of archetypal experience, and it is the task of the artist to embody this world in his work.' This he does through the use of myths and symbols that participate in 'the Great Realities' or 'primordial truths' on which our human life depends. The artist can act as a veridical witness to these truths only by himself undergoing 'an inner development corresponding to Platonic initiation, in other words, a kind of dying'.[11]

Through his contemplative insight into the world of archetypes, the poet comes to realize 'that the ultimate subjective ground of individual human life and the source of life in all its various and successive manifestations, are not different; that the inner immortal self and the great cosmic power are one and the same; and that what happens in the life without is at the same time what happens in the life within'.[12] What poets such as Solomos, Palamas, Sikelianos or Seferis reveal to us is 'the actual participation of the temporal in the eternal, their simultaneity not in terms of objective facts, but in terms of actual experience'. The 'supra-rational world' to which these poets direct our gaze is to be conceived 'not as just another objective world existing in another dimension, but as this present world experienced not from the point of view of our normal consciousness but from the point of view of a consciousness obscured for us by the purely rational categories by which for the most part we allow ourselves to be dominated'.[13] Such is the function of poetry, as of all art: to raise our understanding above the level of 'rational categories', and so to disclose the interpenetration between the outer and the inner, between the temporal

[11] *The Marble Threshing Floor*, pp. 19-20.
[12] Ibid., pp. 239-240.
[13] Ibid., pp. 244-245.

and the eternal.

If I have quoted at length from *The Marble Threshing Floor*, it is because here, in his first major study, Philip has already begun to use the terminology and the ideas that dominate his subsequent work. He speaks in the first place of 'initiation', and this 'initiatory' language reappears in his earliest theological book, *The Greek East and the Latin West* (1959), although it is less in evidence in his later writing. He also emphasizes – and this remains a constant *leitmotif* in his theological and ecological enquiries – that human beings possess a faculty of contemplative insight that is far superior to the discursive reason. Philip usually describes this aspect of the human person as the intellect (Greek *nous*), but he does not mean that it is 'intellectual' in the commonly accepted sense of that word. For him the intellect is not analytical but intuitive, not ratiocinative but visionary. Through this faculty of contemplation we can attain the realm of the divine archetypes, the sphere of primordial reality; through it we come to discern the correspondence between the inner world and the outer. Art and theology, properly understood, are both expressions of this contemplative faculty. As Philip states in *The Marble Threshing Floor*, 'Contemplation must precede the act of creation. By contemplation is implied the raising of the consciousness from obscuration to vision, from the outward present to the inward presence.' It is only through such contemplation that we can 'respond to the universal truths'.[14]

Philip's evaluation of the broader historical and cultural setting out of which modern Greek poetry arose is admirably conveyed in the collaborative work that he wrote with John Campbell, *Modern Greece* (1968). Despite the passing of the years this remains, in my view, the most illuminating introduction to the subject. But the more profound and more personal meaning of Greece in Philip's own life is best expressed in the brief but masterly essay which he wrote as an introduction to his anthology *The Pursuit of Greece* (1964), and which was reissued as the opening chapter of his book *The Wound of Greece. Studies in Neo-Hellenism* (1978). Here he sees

[14] Ibid., p.234.

Greece as a land in which the past scarcely ever dies, and in moving terms he evokes its 'living fate': '… the living fate of Greece, which is not a doom but a destiny, a process rather in which past and present blend and fuse, in which nature and man and something more than man participate: a process, difficult, baffling, enigmatic, with its element of magic, its element of tragedy, working itself out in a landscape of bare hills and insatiable sea, in the miraculous cruelty of the summer sun, in the long generations of the lives of the Greek people'.[15] There is nothing narrowly exclusive about Philip's love of Greece. What he values in the Greek tradition is not its ethnic particularism but its universality and its truth.

5/30/12

Sacred Tradition

The ideas that Philip adumbrated in *The Marble Threshing Floor*, within the context of modern Greek poetry, he went on to deepen in his theological writings. His approach to Orthodoxy, and indeed to any religious faith, is well summed up in two words used in the title of the present work: 'Sacred Tradition'. Let us look more closely at each of these key terms. Philip is profoundly convinced, in the first place, that human beings can only attain the truth through affiliation to a tradition. We *receive* the truth, we cannot simply make it up as we go along. By tradition Philip means, in his own words, 'the preservation and handing down of a method of contemplation'. Here, as in *The Marble Threshing Floor*, we note his emphasis upon the contemplative faculty. Contemplation, he adds, 'must precede action'. This is true at every level, alike in artistic creativity, in social *diakonia*, and in religious life.

All genuine tradition, Philip explains in the first chapter of this book, rests upon divine revelation, and this revelation is contained first of all in Scripture, in a Holy Book or Books. But Scripture is not to be approached simply in an archaeological fashion, as a written record from the distant past, but it needs to be interpreted by 'inspired spiritual masters' who are alive in our own day. Here Philip

---

[15] *The Pursuit of Greece*, p. 15.

insists upon a theme central to the experience of the Orthodox Church, as of other religious faiths: tradition is made living and contemporary through the continuing witness of charismatic guides or 'elders' (in Greek, *gerontes;* in Slavonic, *startsi),* of spiritual fathers and mothers in each succeeding generation. In the words of Martin Buber, 'The *way* cannot be learned out of a book, or from hearsay, but can only be communicated from person to person.'[16]

Tradition is also made vibrant and immediate, within Orthodox Christianity, through the celebration of the Divine Liturgy. This is 'a most crucial aspect of sacred tradition', for tradition can be transmitted to us 'only by means of a ritual, sacramental or liturgical act'. More broadly, sacred tradition has two aspects: *praxis* or ascetic observance, understanding the term 'ascetic' in the widest sense, and *gnosis* or spiritual knowledge. There can be no *gnosis* without *praxis,* no Orthodoxy without Orthopraxy. Sacred tradition is not just an ideology or a philosophical theory, but signifies the active pursuit of a spiritual Way. In this manner tradition is not static but dynamic, not individualistic but communal, not theoretical but practical, not abstract but mysterial or sacramental.

The human faculty whereby we apprehend tradition is not the discursive reason *(dianoia),* as employed in mathematical calculations or in deductive and inductive argumentation, but the intellect or noetic insight *(nous).* Already in *The Marble Threshing Floor,* as we have seen, Philip employs the reason/intellect distinction, and it is a differentiation that remains crucial throughout his later writings. We shall never appreciate Philip's point of view unless the difference between the two is firmly grasped. The reason forms abstract concepts on the basis of sense-data, and by manipulating these concepts it argues from premises to a conclusion. The intellect, on the other hand, 'is not simply a classifying faculty but is a mirror of the divine Intelligence'. It is 'supra-rational, intuitive and immediate', and it confers 'metaphysical knowledge'.[17]

Such is Philip's idea of tradition. What, in the second place,

[16] *The Tales of the Hasidim:* vol. 1, *The Early Masters* (Schocken Books, New York 1968), p. 256.

[17] On the reason/intellect distinction, see in particular *The Rape of Man and Nature,* pp. 33-35,80-86; also the glossary in the English translation of *The Philokalia,* tr. G.E.H. Palmer, Philip Sherrard and Kallistos Ware, vol. 1 (London 1979), pp. 361,363.

does he mean by the term 'sacred'? As he states at the beginning of the work which he devoted particularly to this topic, *The Sacred in Life and Art* (1990), 'The sacred is something in which the Divine is present or which is charged with divine energies.' If, then, we say that tradition, art, life, earth, nature, or anything else is 'sacred', this means that 'it is the expression or revelation of something infinitely more than itself, something which it but discloses or manifests'. Thus the sacred denotes 'the ingression of that which is wholly Other'. Strictly speaking, then, God alone is sacred. This is evident in the Divine Liturgy of the Orthodox Church, when shortly after the consecration the priest elevates the Holy Bread and exclaims, 'Holy things to those who are holy', to which the people respond, 'One is holy, One is Lord, Jesus Christ, to the glory of God the Father.'[18]

Yet, although in the ultimate sense One alone is sacred – that is to say, God Himself – it is also true that all existing things are sacred, at any rate in their inner essence, by virtue of the fact that God continually creates and indwells them. (In Chapter 10 of this book, as elsewhere in his writings, Philip insists that divine creation is not an event in the past but a continuing relationship in the present; it signifies, not God acting upon the universe from the outside, but God acting upon it from within.) Philip therefore rejects any dichotomy between the sacred and the secular. Although the creation has been distorted by evil and sin, no created thing is intrinsically 'secular' or divorced from God in its true reality. 'Nothing in life – in the created order – is, or can be, entirely profane or non-sacred.'[19] Evil is not a 'thing', an existent object, but it is a distorted attitude resulting from the misuse of their free will on the part of human or angelic beings (see Chapter 7).

Having said 'One', then, we immediately say 'All'. We are 'to perceive God in all things' (what Philip calls 'initiation into the lesser mysteries'), and we are 'to see all things in God' ('initiation into the greater mysteries'). The world of nature is 'theophanic', God's self-revelation, 'a mode of discourse' from God to human

---

[18] *The Sacred in Life and Art*, pp. 1-2.
[19] Ibid., p. 24.

creation icon ?

persons: 'All nature from beginning to end constitutes a single icon of God.' There is 'a kind of sacred order established by God in which everything, not only man and man's artefacts, but every living form of plant, bird or animal, the sun, moon and stars, the waters and the mountains, [are to be] seen as signs of things sacred... expressions of a divine cosmology, symbols linking the visible and the invisible, earth and heaven'.[20] In this connection Philip speaks of 'pantheism' in Chapter 10 of this book. The use of this particular word could be misleading, but he goes on to clarify his intention by replacing 'pantheism' with the more precise term 'panentheism'. He does not believe that the world is God but that God is everywhere present *in* the world. Although immanent, however, the Creator is also transcendent: 'This also is Thou, neither is this Thou.'[21]

This vision of the sacredness of all created things – of the world as sacrament – requires us to hold in unity the doctrines of the Trinity, the creation, and the Incarnation. Christology, cosmology and anthropology are closely interwoven; Christ the divine Logos, as creator and as second Adam, possesses a cosmic significance.[22] More specifically, this awareness of the sacred as omnipresent invites us to give full value to Christ's Transfiguration on Mount Tabor. 'Intimately allied to the very idea of the sacred,' writes Philip, 'is the word transfiguration.... The action it denotes is central to the destiny of man and of the whole created world.'[23]

Philip's sense of the intrinsic sacredness of nature pervades his poetry. He speaks with nostalgia of 'a time in which it was still simple to breathe', a time when

> in our speech we felt
> the rhythm of the soil.

[20] *The Rape of Man and Nature*, p. 64.

[21] This is a phrase used, not by Philip Sherrard, but by the Anglican writer Charles Williams (1886-1945): see *Seed of Adam and Other Plays* (London 1948), p. 12. Williams used to speak in this context of the 'inclusive-exclusive thing': see Alice Mary Hadfield, *Charles Williams: An Exploration of His Life and Work* (New York 1983), p. 113.

[22] See *Human Image: World Image*, p. 148.

[23] *The Sacred in Life and Art*, p. 85.

Even in his sombre 'Elegy for an English Winter' he underlines the sacramental character of our material environment:

> For there is an age in the life of man when the heart is
> a faithful mirror,
> when the faithful eye discerns an emblem of love in
> the blade of grass,
> when the risen sun is seal of other suns stirring wheat
> in worlds beyond this world.

Daily actions, however familiar and humble, assume a value extending far beyond themselves:

> When man eats bread prepared with his own hands, a
> poem is born.

Here Philip surely has in mind his memories of childhood on an English farm, as well as his later experience of Greek village life.

Victims though we are of our own technological arrogance, through personal love we can still recover a vision of the world as sacred:

> Yet what have we to do with this city, long since inhu-
> man,
> choked with the beauty it slaughters?
> We have entered the constellation of the heron and
> the kingfisher, and do not belong now to this age of
> brutal triviality.

The clearest poetic expression of Philip's sense of the sacred comes significantly on the last page of all in his *Selected Poems:*

> What, then, is your life but God's life too?
> ... This too, in their terms,
> is what your paintings would seem to be telling us:
> not there, not elsewhen, but now, but here, but this
> stone, this shell, this flower, this tree, this sea,
> each in possession of its own indestructible
> beauty and being, in the deathless alleluia
> of the windfall world, and if it's not in this
> instant of their eternal burgeoning, without

> before or after, that we behold in all things
> the Lord of life incessantly reborn, then
> nowhere and never will we see. For though the miracle
> is always present, it will never be alive
> and truly real for us unless in what we see
> we see the sacred message, God's unchanging eye
> gazing from his myriad changing masks into our own
> now hallowed eyes....

'Not there, not elsewhen, but now, but here': we are to apprehend the sacred, the transcendent, the eternal, in the immediate present, at *this* moment, in *this* place. As he writes in another poem:

> There is nothing
> but experience immediate and direct
> that has no place
> and no time
> that is eternal
> but not everlasting
> that cannot be named
> or defined
> or analysed
> because it has never been
> and never will be
> but is always
> now
> this instant....[24]

'The faithful eye discerns *an emblem of love* in the blade of grass', states Philip; and here he points to the one essential quality without which we shall never appreciate the sacredness of the world. Created things can acquire sacramental value for us only if we perceive them with the eye of love. The true contemplation of nature involves on our part 'the loving of every created reality'.[25] Philip's standpoint is that of St Isaac the Syrian, when he writes about the merciful heart: '... a heart on fire for the whole of creation, for humanity, for the birds, for the animals, for demons and for all

[24] *In the Sign of the Rainbow*, pp. 43, 45, 62, 63, 114, 168, 72.
[25] *The Sacred in Life and Art*, p. 21.

that exists'.[26] Love is the one and only key: 'Apart from love there is no reason for the existence of the world – "God so loved the world" – and apart from love the world has no purpose in existing.' Love is 'the ultimate irreducible touchstone; it is the seal and consummation of the sacred'.[27]

When Philip speaks in this way about love as 'the seal and consummation', he has in mind among other things the experience of sexual love between man and woman. He is convinced that the distinction between male and female, and their nuptial relationship with each other, are 'not something arbitrary or accidental, but a manifestation of an ultimate mystery hidden in the depths of divine life itself'.[28] He works out this idea in his short study *Christianity and Eros: Essays on the Theme of Sexual Love* (1976), where he shows how, through sexual love realized in its full sacramental sense, each partner 'offers himself or herself to the sacred being of the other, to the God in the other... each becomes for the other an icon'. The sexual relationship, when brought to its true personal fulfilment, 'transforms their individual existence into a single reality', establishing 'a single heart and a single soul in two bodies... a mutual awareness and recognition which is a total act of soul'. So there takes place a 'birth in beauty' which may be said to 'partake potentially of eternity'. In a 'sexualized sacramental love' the distinction commonly made between *eros* and *agape* is 'transcended and eliminated'.[29] Fortunately this book, long out of print, has now been reissued (1995); it deserves to be more widely known.

From Within and From Above: Setting the Compass
Arising out of Philip's understanding of tradition and of the sacred, we can identify two methodological principles, closely connected with each other, which are to be found in all his books,

[26] A M. Allchin (ed.) and Sebastian Brock (tr.), *The Heart of Compassion: Daily Readings with St Isaac the Syrian* (London 1989), p. 9; cf [Dana Miller (tr.)] *The Ascetical Homilies of Saint Isaac the Syrian* (Holy Transfiguration Monastery, Boston 1984), p. 344.
[27] *The Sacred in Life and Art*, p.21.
[28] Ibid., p.108.
[29] *Christianity and Eros*, pp. 2-3,47.

from his first study *The Marble Threshing Floor* to the posthumous work now before us, *Christianity: Lineaments of a Sacred Tradition.* These two principles can be encapsulated in the phrases 'From within, outwards' and 'From above, downwards'. Both principles are formulated with especial clarity in the last public lecture that Philip delivered, 'For every thing that lives is Holy', words which he took from one of his best-loved authors, William Blake. This address was given in 1994 to the Temenos Academy on 13 June and then to the Friends of the Centre on 27 June, and it appears as Chapter 9 of this book.

'From within, outwards': in Philip's words, 'It is the prevailing conceptual paradigm of our consciousness, and the reality that we attribute to it, that determine what what we think is real and what we think is unreal.... Unless we first know ourself we cannot know anything else either.' The way we see things in the outside world, that is to say, depends upon the way we think and upon the way we see ourself, and this in turn depends upon the way we are, upon 'the quality of our own being, the purity of our soul and the level of our intelligence'. Our world-image is a reflection of our self-image, and our self-image is a reflection of our self-being. As Philip expresses it elsewhere, 'The eye sees in things only what it looks for and it looks only for what it already has in mind.... As one is, so one will see the world.... In the end what the world looks like depends on the image we impose upon it.'[30] The course of life follows always the course of thought; it is never the other way round. 'As Blake well knew, the first fight to be fought is always the mental fight.'[31]

This conviction that our perception of reality depends upon our perception of ourself leads Philip to take issue with those who maintain that all human knowledge is derived from sense-perception. This cannot be the case, in his view, for the senses do not provide us with objective data, regardless of our inward state of soul. On the contrary, the way in which we perceive things through the senses is determined by the purity of our own heart or, con-

[30] *Human Image: World Image,* p. 130.
[31] *The Sacred in Life and Art,* p. 157.

versely, by its state of corruption. 'That is why Herakleitos can say that the senses are false witnesses for people with impure souls.' If our consciousness is unregenerate, then our sense-perception will not be objective but highly subjective and, indeed, delusory. Only the saint sees things as they truly are.

To know the world, then, I need to know myself. But what is my true self? Here Philip's second basic principle comes into play: 'From above, downwards.' I shall not understand who I am, and so I shall not understand what the world is, unless I realize that I am formed in the image of God – a created expression of God's infinite self-expression. If I work not from above downwards but from below upwards, as the theory of evolution does – if I see myself simply as a kind of superior ape, in whom self-consciousness has emerged as an epiphenomenon of some physical process – then I shall fatally misinterpret my own self, and so I shall have a distorted view of everything else as well. 'Know yourself' means 'Know yourself as God-sourced, God-shaped', acknowledge your divine origin, recognize that you are a sacred being. Apart from God we are unintelligible as human persons. The divine is the determining element in our humanness; losing our sense of the divine, we lose also our sense of the human. As Philip puts it, 'God is the inmost centre of our reality.... The very concept of man implies a relationship, a connection with God. Where one affirms man one also affirms God.'[32]

Generalizing this principle 'From above, downwards', Philip writes: 'In the whole visible, natural world there is nothing that does not express or represent something of a higher invisible world, the spiritual world.' Here it is at once evident how deeply and decisively Philip was influenced by the Platonic doctrine of Forms or Ideas. The things in the realm of nature, he continues, are 'essentially effects, never causes': 'each has its equivalent, or archetype, or Divine Name, on the spiritual plane, and is the external expression, the material extension of this archetype'. Causation, therefore, is not linear but vertical: 'causation and continuity are properties of the realm of archetypes or Divine Names.... All causality resides in the divine archetypes, in the incessant renewal of their

[32] *The Rape of Man and Nature,* p. 20.

epiphanies from instant to instant.' It is precisely these archetypes
that are revealed in sacred art by the poet or the iconographer.

There can, then, be no understanding of the sensible world without a knowledge of the intelligible world, no true insight into
created reality without participation in the uncreated *logoi* or inner
principles which the Logos has implanted in each existent thing.
'In no way is it possible to separate physics from metaphysics. There
can be no true science of phenomena – of visible nature – that is
not based on and rooted in a science of the spiritual realities of
which visible phenomena are the spatio-temporal manifestations
or "signatures".'[33] In this connection Philip quotes St Gregory of
Sinai: 'A right view of created things depends upon a truly spiritual knowledge of visible and invisible realities.... A true
philosopher is one who perceives in created things their spiritual
Cause, or who knows created things through knowing their
Cause.'[34] This spiritual knowledge of created things in the light of
their uncreated Source cannot be attained simply through the use
of the discursive reason (*dianoia*), but only through the intellect
(*nous*).

There is, then, no separation between divine Cause and created
effect, between archetype and icon, but an 'indissoluble interpenetration' between the two. According to Philip, in the Christian
West it was Latin Scholasticism in the twelfth and thirteenth centuries that initially undermined this unitary vision of reality by
adopting a 'bifurcated, dualistic approach'. Following Aristotle, the
Scholastics made a division between natural and supranatural
knowledge. Natural knowledge, instead of depending upon an understanding of the divine archetypes, was based solely on the
exercise of sense-perception. As a result the natural world was sundered from the world of the archetypes, from the realm of Solomos's
'Great Realities', and it became treated as a separate, autonomous
object of study. This led in turn to a progressive desacralization of

---

[33] *Human Image: World Image,* pp. 9, 131.

[34] Ibid., pp. 89-90, citing Gregory of Sinai, *On Commands and Doctrines* 25
and 127, in *The Philokalia,* vol. 4 (London 1995), pp. 217, 245. I have followed
the translation in *The Philokalia,* rather than that which Philip gives in *Human
Image: World Image.*

nature, apparent first in the modern scientific revolution of the
sixteenth, seventeenth and eighteenth centuries – dominated as
they were by mechanistic and mathematical modes of thinking –
and then in the catastrophic pollution of the environment during
the twentieth century. Rejecting the 'double truth' of Scholasticism, Philip insists passionately upon the unity of all things in
God. 'This world is the other world. Every natural form of life and
being, down to the most humble, is the life and being of God.'

If Scholasticism transgresses the principle 'From above, downwards', then so in another way does C. G. Jung, as Philip maintains
in Chapter 6 of this book. One might have expected Philip, in his
own combat against contemporary materialism, to regard Jung as
an ally. Philip does indeed recognize many positive elements in
Jung's thought: the Swiss psychologist rightly protested against
'the simplifications of scientific rationalism', and urged us to face
the realities of our own inner world; he highlighted the deep affinities between human beings and the realm of nature; and he
appreciated the value of myth, discerning in it 'the revelation of a
divine life in man'. But Jung went astray, Philip believes, in accepting the presuppositions of Darwinian evolution; in affirming, that
is to say, 'From below, upwards' rather than 'From above, downwards'. Instead of seeing human personhood as God-sourced, Jung
interpreted it in terms of the unconscious; and this he regarded as
our psychic 'prehistory', the 'earlier evolutionary stages of our conscious psyche', to use his own words. Thus, whereas in the Christian
view human consciousness has its roots in the divine, for Jung it is
rooted in the animal world; and so, when he uses the word 'archetype', he does so in a sense profoundly different from that ascribed
to it by the Christian Platonists.

Such are some of the points in Philip's *critique* of Jung. Philip is
certainly justified in emphasizing, as he does, the differences between Jung's theories and the tradition of Orthodox Christianity.
But at the same time we may wonder whether Philip has not based
his assessment of Jung upon too narrow a range of the latter's writings. More particularly, has Philip allowed sufficiently for the
concept of the Self in Jung's thought? And has he not oversimpli-

yes

fied Jung's understanding of archetypes? Surely they are not merely to be identified with the instincts, but they mediate between the instincts and the realm of the spirit.

The Parting of the Ways: Orthodoxy and Rome

Three years after the appearance of *The Marble Threshing Floor*, in his second major work *The Greek East and the Latin West. A Study in The Christian Tradition* (1959), Philip develops the insights that he had gained from his research into Greek poetry and applies them to the question of the schism between Orthodoxy and Rome. This book, in common with most of Philip's theological writings, received a mixed reception. Some thought it one-sided and tendentious, others found it deeply and unexpectedly illuminating. From the outset Philip is explicit about what he is attempting to do. Although he devotes considerable space to the cultural and political context in which the schism developed, he reacts firmly against the tendency – apparent in many books on the subject published around the middle of this century – to attribute the division between Greek and Latin Christendom primarily to non-theological factors. Invoking the principle 'From within, outwards', he argues that, when Orthodoxy and Rome parted company, this was due not just to political and economic causes but to fundamental differences in theology. Here, as always, the course of external events on the historical plane followed the course of thought; the outer depended upon the inner, not *vice-versa*. If we are to appreciate the true nature of our religious divisions, what matters in the last resort are not military campaigns or commercial rivalry, but the primary thought-patterns which each side has adopted. 'The breach between the Latins and the Greeks', writes Philip, 'arose from the fact that each side came to regard as absolute and irreconcilable certain differing representations, differing mental images of the Truth.'[35]

Needless to say, in assessing the development of the schism, allowance has to be made for such things as the Norman conquest of Sicily and South Italy during the eleventh century, the expan-

---

[35] *The Greek East and the Latin West*, p. 50.

sion of Genoese and Venetian trade in the twelfth century, and the sack of Constantinople by the Fourth Crusade in 1204. But we have to look beyond such matters and to concentrate upon the two major theological difficulties, the *Filioque* and the papal claims. Even these are symptoms rather than basic causes. We need to go deeper still. Behind the *Filioque* there lie two different ways of approaching the Trinitarian nature of God; underlying the dispute over papal jurisdiction there can be found two different interpretations of the relationship of the Church on earth to Christ and the Holy Spirit. The schism involves, not just a few particular points of doctrinal formulation or liturgical practice, but two divergent 'frameworks' embracing on each side the total field of religious belief.

Such is Philip's basic theme in *The Greek East and the Latin West*. It is typical of his approach that he refuses to dismiss the *Filioque* as an irritating technicality, but insists on its far-reaching consequences: 'In that issue are implicit two "world-views", and it is only the acceptance by western Europe of one rather than the other of those views that has made possible the conception, and setting up, some thousand years later, of such an organization as that of the United Nations.'[36] In the preface to the expanded second edition (1992), he adds in this connection a reference to the European Economic Community or the Common Market, which he likewise viewed with little enthusiasm.

The Greek East and the Latin West is a work of scholarship, but it has also a pastoral aim. As Philip states in the second edition of the book, it is intended as 'a kind of guide for those distressed and perplexed by the state of things around them and searching for some positive orientation within it'.[37] That same intention inspires all his theological writings. He never regarded himself simply as a historian of doctrine, but sought always to offer in a practical manner some means of escape from what he saw as our present state of dereliction and disintegration. His purpose was not to transmit theoretical information about the past, but to interpret Orthodox

[36] Ibid., (1st edn), p. vi.
[37] Ibid., (2nd edn), p. v.

Christianity in living terms as a spiritual Way at the present time.

Nearly twenty years after the appearance of *The Greek East and the Latin West,* Philip returned to the same theme in a shorter and less complex study, *Church, Papacy, and Schism: A Theological Enquiry* (1978). The sub-title here deserves to be noted: as Philip states clearly at the outset of the book, the schism between East and West is 'ultimately a matter of theology'.[38] That of course was also his conviction when he wrote his earlier book, but in its sequel the theological emphasis is far more definite. As Dimitri Obolensky points out in his helpful preface to the 1996 reissue of *Church, Papacy, and Schism,* the discussion of historical and cultural factors which appeared in its predecessor has now been largely omitted. At the same time the new volume marks a significant advance over the old by providing a fuller and clearer analysis of the nature of the Church.

Philip's treatment of ecclesiology in *Church, Papacy, and Schism* shares much in common with the eucharistic understanding of the Church developed by the Russian theologian Fr Nicolas Afanassieff and by his Greek counterpart (and at times corrector) John Zizioulas, now Metropolitan of Pergamon. 'Where Christ is manifest in the Eucharist', Philip writes, 'there is the Catholic Church. And as Christ is manifest in each local Church in which the Eucharist is celebrated, each local Church is itself *the* Catholic Church.'[39] At each local celebration of the Eucharist, it is the whole Christ who is present, not a part of him; in sacramental terms, then, all local Churches are on an equal footing, and by the same token each bishop as celebrant of the Eucharist is fundamentally equal to every other bishop. Levels of primacy within Church – not excluding the primacy of the Bishop of Rome – are secondary to this basic sacramental equality of the entire episcopate.

In his preface to the reissue of *Church, Papacy, and Schism,* Dimitri Obolensky adverts with good reason to the style in which it is written: 'Not the least of the book's merits are the precision of its

[38] *Church, Papacy, and Schism* (lst edn), p. x.
[39] Ibid., p. 15.

language and the elegance of its style – formal qualities which Philip valued highly.'[40] The same precision and elegance are to be found in almost everything that he wrote. If his arguments are sometimes difficult to follow, this is not because Philip has failed to make proper efforts to express himself clearly, but because he is a maximalist. He did not wish to cheapen or oversimplify his message. He respected the truth too highly for that.

A Loss of Cosmic Memory

In his later life Philip concentrated to an ever-increasing extent upon the current ecological crisis. His indictment of the scientific outlook which has brought about this crisis is forcefully expressed in his two books *The Rape of Man and Nature. An Enquiry into the Origins and Consequences of Modern Science* (1987), and *Human Image: World Image. The Death and Resurrection of Sacred Cosmology* (1992). It is interesting that the material contained in the first of these volumes was written over twelve years before the book actually appeared in print. It was by no means easy for Philip to find a publisher, for in many circles his ecological standpoint was not popular.

In his writings on the pollution of the environment, as in all his work, Philip was interested not in external symptoms but in the root cause, not in economic or technological factors but in the spiritual errors and distortions that underlie them. If modern Western society has lost an organic and life-giving relationship with the realm of nature – if we have turned the world around us into what Philip terms 'a vast, smouldering junkyard'[41] – this must be the consequence of some basic flaw or misconception in our primary thought-patterns. This misconception, so Philip believes, has to be traced back behind modern urban development, behind the Industrial Revolution, the Enlightenment and the Renaissance, to the presuppositions of Thomas Aquinas and medieval Latin Scholasticism. The fundamental mistake of Aquinas and the Scholastics, as we have already noted, was in Philip's eyes to posit a dichotomy

---

[40] Ibid., (2nd edn), p. xii.
[41] *The Greek East and the Latin West* (2nd edn), p. v.

between nature and the supranatural. The results of this fatal dichotomy, although Aquinas and the Scholastics neither intended
nor foresaw them, are all too evident in the tragedy that is now
unfolding before our eyes: we are defiling the water that we drink
and the air that we breathe, we are exterminating the fish and the
wild animals, we are turning the forests into deserts.

In his books and essays on the 'rape' of nature, as elsewhere,
Philip applies the two principles with which we are already familiar. 'From within, outwards': the so-called 'ecological crisis' is really
a crisis in ourselves. 'The crisis itself', he writes, 'is not first of all
an ecological crisis. It is not first of all a crisis concerning our environment. It is first of all a crisis concerning the way we think.
We are treating our planet in an inhuman, god-forsaken manner
because we see things in an inhuman, god-forsaken way. And we
see things in this way because that basically is how we see ourselves.... Our model of the universe – our world-picture or
world-image – is based upon the model we have of ourselves, upon
our own self-image.... This means that before we can effectively
deal with the ecological problem we have to change our
world-image, and this in turn means that we have to change our
self-image.' Unless we tackle the inner problem of our self-image,
all our plans for conservation, however well-intentioned, will be
ineffective; they will not touch the heart of the problem, for they
will be dealing 'with what in the end are symptoms, not causes'.[42]

Any change in our outward action, if it is to have lasting results,
must therefore be based on a change in our inner attitude. What is
needed is cosmic *metanoia*, an act of repentance in the literal sense
of the Greek word, which means 'change of mind'. As Philip observes concerning George Gemistos Plethon in Chapter 5 of the
present book, 'He understood, as few modern reformers seem to
understand, that no amount of reforming will by itself have in the
end the slightest effect unless it is accompanied by a corresponding change in religious orientation. "Everything in human life", he
said, "as regards it being done rightly or wrongly, depends on our
religious beliefs."' 'Clearly,' Philip continues, 'unless we first know

[42] *Human Image: World Image*, p.2.

ourself we cannot know anything else either, and in that case we are bound to act towards other things in a way that will violate and abase them.'

'From above, downwards': to know oneself, as was indicated earlier, is to know our divine origin. This too applies directly to the ecological crisis. We are misusing nature because we have forgotten that we ourselves, and likewise the created order in which we live, are the handiwork of God. 'Ultimately to know other things involves the same condition as knowing oneself: that we know the source of their existence, which is no less or other than the source of our existence.... By entering into a knowledge of our own divine origin we can also enter into a knowledge of the divine essences of other things as well, and thus we can see them and act towards them in a manner that accords with their true nature and identity. Short of that we inevitably violate and abuse both ourself and *a fortiori* the things with which we come into contact.'

Here, then, is the root cause of the current crisis. We have undergone a fall into ignorance that is leading us towards 'total loss of identity'. We are suffering from 'a loss of memory', 'a forgetfulness of who we are'. We have forgotten that we are sacred beings, formed in the divine image, and so, 'having in our own minds desanctified ourselves, we have desanctified nature, too, in our own minds'.[43] From this it becomes clear that there is only one way of solving our problems: we have to seek 'the way back to our origin', as Philip expresses it in one of his early poems.[44] We have to rediscover the divine presence within ourselves, and then we can reaffirm the divine presence in nature. 'Once we repossess a sense of our own holiness, we will recover the sense of the holiness of the world about us as well, and we will then act towards the world about us with the awe and humility that we should possess when we enter a sacred shrine, a temple of love and beauty in which we worship and adore.'[45]

Opening our eyes and perceiving anew the Divine within ourselves and at the same time within the world around us, we come

[43] Ibid., p. 3.
[44] *In the Sign of the Rainbow*, p. 40.
[45] *Human Image: World Image*, p. 9.

to realize our integral unity with the realm of nature. In the words of Kathleen Raine:

> Seas, trees and voices cry,
> 'Nature is your nature.'[46]

As Philip affirms, 'Our destiny and the destiny of nature are one and the same';[47] 'Inner worlds are outer worlds, outer worlds are inner worlds.'[48] The effect of losing our sense of the sacred is that we have alienated ourselves from nature; once it is desacralized, nature becomes simply an external 'object' which we exploit for our own selfish ends. It is urgently important that we should overcome this alienation, so that our relationship with the realm of nature, and the work that we undertake within that realm, can be 'repersonalized and rehumanized'.[49] Unity with nature, with a 'repersonalized and rehumanized' environment, means that we should learn to *love* the divine creation, to feel an 'ontological tenderness' for every existent thing;[50] for we cannot save and sanctify what we do not love. Only through love shall we once again experience the world as sacrament.

Many who sympathized in principle with Philip's vehement protest against secular materialism have yet felt that he spoils his case through overstatement. Is he not one-sided and unduly negative, his critics have asked, in his evaluation of modern science? Have not scientific techniques brought manifest benefits to humankind in, for example, the field of medicine? Indeed, does not Philip mistake his target? His strictures, so it has been objected, apply not to science itself but only 'scientism', not to scientific methodology as such but only to its misuse.

Philip felt that these criticisms missed the real point of what he was trying to say. He did not deny that in some respects modern science may have had beneficial results. He also acknowledged that the medieval Christian past should not be idealized, and that in

[46] *Stone and Flower* (London 1943), p. 7.
[47] *Human Image: World Image,* p. 9.
[48] *The Sacred in Life and Art,* p. 157.
[49] *The Rape of Man and Nature,* p. 73.
[50] *The Sacred in Life and Art,* p. 21.

any case we simply do not have the possibility of returning to it.[51] Furthermore, he looked on the human reason – our faculty of discursive argumentation and mathematical calculation – as genuinely a gift from God, to be used to the full in our pursuit of the truth.[52] (But he also insisted that, if it is to bear fruit, reason has always to be employed in proper subordination to the higher faculty of spiritual insight that the Greek Fathers term the *nous*.) While readily conceding all this, however, Philip still stood fast by his primary point. His *critique* concerns not the possible or actual misuse of modern science but its origins and basic presuppositions – above all, the presupposition that the visible world can and should be investigated on its own and in isolation, without reference to its divine foundation. It should be remembered that Philip was careful to launch his attack not against science in itself but against what he terms *modern* science. He believed that there are indeed genuinely traditional (but not archaic) forms of science that are rigorous and systematic in their observation of the visible world, while at the same time respecting its sacred character. A reverence for the sacred, so far from signifying imprecision in the collection and assessment of data, implies the diametrical opposite of this; as the Romanian dissident Petre Tutea used to insist, exactness and explanation are possible only if we allow for the dimension of transcendence.

To illustrate the difference between a 'traditional' and a 'modern' scientist, we need look no further than the splitting of the atom. No 'traditional' scientist in his 'right mind', that is, with a right understanding of God's creation, would ever seek to tear asunder what God in his wisdom has created as a unified whole. Such an attempt is 'diabolical', in the literal sense of that word, for the name *diabolos* means precisely 'the one who rends apart'. The explosion of the atom bomb can indeed be seen as a kind of transfiguration, but it is a transfiguration that is dark and demonic, at the opposite pole from the revelation of Christ's glory on Mount Tabor.

Two implications of Philip's approach to the ecological crisis

---

[51] *The Rape of Man and Nature*, p.65.
[52] Ibid., p.85.

will by now be clearly apparent. First, modern science is not value-neutral. It does not offer merely an 'objective' account of the 'facts', but it makes a series of assumptions that have far-reaching consequences on the spiritual level. The end result of these assumptions is to restrict modern scientific enquiry solely to that which can be quantified, which can be weighed and measured in mathematical terms, and thus to exclude any awareness of the 'inside' of things in which the divine presence may be experienced.

Second, in contrast to ecologists of the 'biocentric' persuasion, Philip is not afraid to assign a central place within the created order to the human person. It would be misleading to describe his viewpoint as 'anthropocentric', for he does not regard humanity as the measure of all things. His stance is not anthropocentric but theocentric: we are to see God in all things, and all things in God. At the same time, however, he believes that human beings have a unique role within the entire creation, for we humans, alone among all creatures visible and invisible, are formed in the image of God.

Many contemporary ecologists have of course reacted sharply against this Christian understanding of the human person as God's living icon. They believe that it has led to a disastrously arrogant attitude, causing us humans to appropriate to ourselves a selfish and destructive dominion over the rest of creation. Philip deplored as fervently as anyone the ugly exploitation of nature by a fallen humankind. But he was also convinced that the 'image' doctrine, rightly understood, so far from endowing us with an arbitrary tyranny over creation, signifies that in all our actions towards the world we are to reflect God's kenotic mercy and compassion. Precisely because we are made in the divine image, we are to treat every existent thing with a loving tenderness that is truly an image and likeness of the divine tenderness. We are not to twist and distort created things to suit our sinful desires, but we are to act as cosmic liturgists, priests of the creation, offering the world back to God in thanksgiving. Only through this act of offering shall we rediscover our own authentic identity as microcosm and mediator. Only through kenotic thanksgiving shall we render manifest the beauty at the heart of all things.

The Philokalia

Along with his writings on the ecological crisis, the other main task to which Philip devoted his later years, and on which he was hard at work until a few weeks before his death, was the English translation of *The Philokalia* of St Makarios of Corinth and St Nikodimos of the Holy Mountain. He collaborated on this with the late Gerald Palmer (d. 1984), the originator of the project, and with myself. Our plans for a complete English version of *The Philokalia*, based on the original Greek, were made initially in 1971. The first volume came out in 1979, followed by a second in 1981 and a third in 1984. Unfortunately Philip did not live to see the appearance of the fourth volume, published in August 1995, but he had corrected the proofs before his last illness. Also he had worked through the whole of the material to be included in the fifth and concluding volume, but its final revision will have to be undertaken by myself alone.

While the production of the English *Philokalia* has been a genuinely co-operative venture, it is important to acknowledge the extent of Philip's contribution. It was he who undertook the main revision of the preliminary translations for volumes two, three and four; at the same time I was assigned the much lighter task of preparing the introductory notes preceding the texts from each author, together with the footnotes (apart from those dealing with numerology). Philip's revision was subjected to a thorough scrutiny from the other two editors, and we made many changes in it; but, had it not been for the thousands of painstaking hours that he had already devoted to the preparation of the English version, our progress would have been much slower. The glossary that appears at the end of each volume was drafted jointly by Philip and myself, with many improvements suggested by Gerald.

It required a real sacrifice on Philip's part to complete his share in the translation of *The Philokalia*. Especially in his final months, he pushed himself to the limit of his strength as he worked on the material in volume five. Sadly this kept him from his own writing. While this is something that we must all regret, it indicates the depth of his commitment to the English *Philokalia*. Personally I

learned more than I can say from working with Philip on the translation. Often we spent hours discussing a single phrase or even a
single word. Exhausting though these sessions were, they taught
me to appreciate the value of words in a way that I had never done
before. Again and again I recognized in Philip a true
master-craftsman.

Once, when talking with Owen Barfield, C.S. Lewis referred to
philosophy as 'a subject'. 'It wasn't a *subject* to Plato', objected
Barfield, 'it was a *way*.'[53] Such was exactly Philip's perspective. He
always looked on philosophy and theology as 'a way', and this was
true pre-eminently of his attitude towards *The Philokalia*. At the
beginning of the first volume of our English translation, in the
general introduction for which Philip prepared the preliminary
draft, he calls *The Philokalia* 'an active force revealing a spiritual
path and inducing man to follow it'. The work, he insists, does not
simply communicate 'information' but calls us to 'a radical change
of will and heart'.[54] Here, once again, it is evident how Philip saw
the doctrinal and spiritual tradition of Orthodoxy not just in theoretical and historical terms but as a living reality. As its translators,
the three of us regarded *The Philokalia* not as a voice from the
distant past but as a practical guide for all who at this present
moment are journeying on the spiritual Way. As with many great
works, however, including the Bible, the true value of *The Philokalia*
will not be apparent except to those who search.

I am glad that several of our editorial sessions on the translation
of *The Philokalia* took place on Athos at the Serbian Monastery of
Chilandar. To share together, even for no more than a few weeks,
in the daily prayer of the Holy Mountain, enabled the three of us
to understand the inner spirit of *The Philokalia* in a way that we
could not otherwise have done. But it also helped me to appreciate, far better than before, what Greece and Orthodoxy meant in
Philip's own life. Athos, as we have already noted, had a special
place in his heart. During our walks day by day along the deserted

[53] A. N. Wilson, *C.S. Lewis: A Biography* (London 1990), p. 108.
[54] *The Philokalia*, vol. 1, p. 13.

Athonite paths, and in our evening dialogues on the balcony at Chilandar, I began to sense the spiritual values that mattered most to him. It was in personal conversations such as these, long and deep, that Philip's brilliance, the subtlety and variety of his thinking, could be felt to the greatest effect. As Kathleen Raine writes, 'Philip lived in a rich world of ideas worthy of ancient Athens'[55] — and, we might add, of Christian Cappadocia in the days of St Basil or of Byzantium in the days of Theodore Metochites and St Gregory Palamas.

'For every thing that lives is Holy': Blake's phrase, used by Philip as the title of his 1994 lecture, sums up his central and dominant concern. Those who only knew him from his writings, which could at times be passionate and polemical in their tone, may not always have realized how deep was his respect and reverence for each thing and person, how gentle and humble he was, how sensitive to the distress or uncertainty of others, how ready to listen and to respond. He was a highly entertaining companion, a generous and affectionate friend.

Bishop Kallistos (Ware) of Diokleia

---

[55] *Philip Sherrard,* p. 19.

Chapter One

The Meaning and Necessity of Sacred Tradition

Over the last decade it has become only too clear that our subscription to the dominantly materialistic and mechanistic philosophies which determine the course of what we call the "natural" sciences and their ramifications in the technological, industrial, political, economic, educational and practically every other sphere, has led us to build a type of society that desecrates and mutilates human and natural life in all its aspects. At the same time it has become equally clear that the values embedded in these philosophies are utterly useless in helping us to resolve any of the problems which our subscription to them has created for us. We cannot prevent the proliferation of armed conflict and mass murder while we still regard the production and sale of deadly weapons not as an inhuman form of criminality and hypocrisy, but as something in which nation states and their human labor forces can quite legitimately engage in order to support their economies. Nor can the fight against pollution and mass starvation or anything else have any chance of success, so long as the means through which it is waged involve the same "logic of production", the same free-market selling techniques and the same ruthless competitive exploitation that have produced these ecological and social catastrophes in the first place. Worse than this, we realize that to speak, as we do, of our culture, when what we mean is the indulgence of the few in which the majority takes no part and has little interest, is merely to play with words in an effort to hide the lack of any genuine creative vitality. In short, it is not going too far to say that our subscription to these philosophies has reduced us to a state of spiritual, mental and cultural degradation for which it would be hard to find a parallel in the history of mankind.

What does this signify? Or, to ask the same question in another way, if the values which have led us to produce our present state of affairs are clearly so disastrous, what values are we to put in their place? What is it that distinguishes cultures that retain a grasp on life which we appear to have lost? Is there some element present in what we acknowledge to be the great civilizations of the world which is not present, or at least not cogently present, in our own latter-day civilization, if we can still call it that?

If we are to judge from the art of these civilizations we are bound to say that there is. For whether we speak of the art of the ancient Greek world, or of the art of India, or of the Islamic world, or of our own Christian world down to the time of the Renaissance, it is of a religious art that we are speaking. It is an art, that is to say, dedicated to the expression or revelation of realities that are more than human or natural, realities that we denote by the word "spiritual". It is an art which presupposes that there is a realm of what we may call spiritual archetypes, or of eternal harmony, that constitutes the underlying structure of the natural or physical world, and that is the source of the life and activity on which this world depends.

Thus, the art of these civilizations is dedicated to revealing and to making as coherent as possible for us the nature of the spiritual realities that lie at the root of and that manifest themselves in human and other life. It is to aid man in what is his central concern, that to which everything else is subordinate: his search for communion and harmony with these realities. For when what is to be realized and experienced through such communion and harmony is regarded as the source of all vitality and significance, of all inspiration and beauty, as that which in fact alone is truly real, then not to make that the central concern of life would be to show a curious lack of judgment. And of that concern, art is a vital aspect. It is a vital part of the communion and harmony which it supports. If it stirs the feelings, it is yet meant to convey a knowledge. If it makes use of what is natural and human, it is yet the interpretation – the science – of what is supranatural and more than human.

Basically, then, what has been lost from our culture, or the element that is missing from it, is the recognition and knowledge of the realities of the spiritual realm, and hence of communion with them. That is to say, it is the religious sense and understanding of life. For although we may speak of archetypes and metaphysical principles, and may acknowledge that these are the shaping forces of the art of mankind's great civilizations, it is quite impossible for most of us to know what is meant by them except in an abstract and theoretical way. It is impossible for most of us to experience, with all the intensity which it must possess, a reality that is more than human.

The religious myths that underlie the cultures in which we recognize the presence of some quality that now eludes us are, for the people of such cultures, not mere human inventions but symbols and images that make possible a direct and constant intercourse with the universal principles of life; and if these people occupy themselves so much with such images and symbols that they not only fill their rites and their places of worship with them, but also paint them on their pottery, weave them into their clothes, sing of them in their songs, dance in obedience to them, lay their fields out after their pattern, score them on rock and tree, and even cut them into their own flesh, that is because they recognize how their very existence, as well as the existence of the culture of which, as of a living organism, each of them is a part, depends on that intercourse. And yet it is impossible to interest the vast majority of us in any of these images and symbols.

A whole language of the soul, a whole spiritual science, has been lost to us, and what this means is that to all intents and purposes we are ignorant not only of these images and symbols but also of the reality of the archetypes of which they are the expression. Such ignorance is now endemic to our education, our science, our culture, to the pseudo-knowledge of the learned, the pseudo-skepticism of the unlearned, to the whole bewildering phantasmagoria that

typifies our disinherited world. This might not be of great importance if the reality in question were merely one alternative among
many possible levels of reality, each of an equal or neutral value.
But when what is at issue is a matter of existence – our life or
death – and when what has been lost is the capacity to commune
with the sources on which that existence depends, then there is a
consequence for us which cannot be dismissed. If the values according to which we have formed the modern world are those
which have led to this state of affairs, it is surely important that
there should be some reassessment and, if it is not too late, some
fundamental change of mind.

What kind of reassessment and what kind of change of mind?
Here, as a preliminary, we must affirm a distinction in modes of
understanding and vision, and in the levels of reality to which they
relate, whose recognition is essential if we are to grasp, first, why
we have been reduced to such spiritual poverty and, second, what
the prerequisites are for escaping from it.

We can introduce this distinction by way of Herakleitos. According to Herakleitos, although we all possess a common Logos
– a common principle of divine and creative wisdom – yet most
people live as if they had a private understanding of things. In
other words, there is a knowledge or wisdom that is supra-
individual, which all people in their right mind possess; and there
is also a purely individual notion of things according to which
people live when they are not in their right mind.

This distinction is taken up and developed by Plato. He speaks
of that which is always real and has no becoming and of that which
is always becoming and is never real. The first is the world of invisible and divine ideas, that must not be thought of as static
abstractions or concepts, but as dynamic energies of which all that
is visible and changing is the external form or appearance. The
second is precisely the visible and changing world which, considered in itself, has no absolute reality, since it is but the effect, or
outward manifestation, of what is invisible and changeless. To consider the second apart from its relationship to the first is much the
same as to consider the shadow without reference to the subject

which casts it. The shadow, of course, has a certain reality; but it would be extremely foolish to pretend that it possesses this reality in its own right and independent of its subject.

To these two levels of reality, the one intelligible and the other sensible, correspond the two types of knowledge which Herakleitos indicates: the axiomatic and universal knowledge of first principles, and the ever-shifting and conjectural knowledge of contingencies. The first, having to do with "that which ever is and does not begin", is what Plato calls truth, while the second, concerned with "that which begins and perishes", is a matter of opinion. In fact, the second is not real knowledge at all; for, as Plato points out, such knowledge about things that change will itself change as the things change; and if this change of knowledge from one thing to another is always going on, at the time of change there will be no knowledge at all, and thus no one who knows and nothing to be known. Hence: "All true knowledge is concerned with what is colorless, formless, and intangible . . . not such knowledge as has a beginning and varies as it is associated with one or another of the things that we now call 'realities', but that which is really real."[1]

Christian authors in the same way speak of these different levels of reality and of the two types of knowledge that typify them. "For that truly hath a being which remains unchangeably", writes St. Augustine;[2] and again: "The intellectual cognition of eternal things is one thing, the rational cognition of temporal things is another."[3] "Eternal things" are what St. Augustine elsewhere calls "principial forms, or stable and immovable essences of things; not themselves being formed, they are eternal and always in the same state, as contained in the intelligence of God; they are not born and they do not perish, but it is by them that is formed all which can be born and perish, and all which is born and perishes."[4]

According to St. Maximos the Confessor, the multiplicity of

---

[1] *Phaedrus* 247C 6-8, D7-E2.
[2] *Confessions* VII.11.17.
[3] *De Trinitate* XII.15.25.
[4] *De 83 Diversis Quæstionibus* 46.

these causal forms – _logoi_, he calls them – is rooted in the one divine and universal Intelligence, that is to say, in the divine and universal Logos. Each created thing is defined in respect both of its essence and of its becoming by its own particular causal form, which is itself embraced by this divine Intelligence or Logos.[5] Or, as St. Dionysios the Areopagite puts it: "God confers on all things his vision, participation, and resemblance, according to the divine idea of each being."[6]

Thus, all things are in various and multiple ways immanent in the Divine. This gives the world its essential unity, its diversities and differentiations being rooted in the same divine Intelligence. In other words, there is an immense reflection of the intelligible in the sensible and of the sensible in the intelligible. The intelligible world contains the causes of, and is mirrored in, the sensible world, while each sensible thing is a symbol of, and is gnostically present in, the intelligible world. Through what is sensible we may perceive what is intelligible, provided we have cleansed our organs of perception. But any real knowledge of the sensible realities must depend entirely on our knowledge of their intelligible or spiritual essences. Indeed, it may even be said that he who only sees what is sensible does not really see anything at all.

The error, then, is to imagine that sensible things are the only reality, or can be known without reference to intelligible things; that, in fact, we can really understand the shadow without reference to the subject casting it. This is what we imagine when the light of divine knowledge is eclipsed in us and we are left with only such knowledge as we think our individual and natural minds can adduce from sensible things. Since, as Aristotle remarks, the realm of the sense is a negligible part of the whole, and that part cannot be known apart from knowledge of the whole, it follows that such knowledge as we think we derive from it when we attempt to know it without knowledge of the whole will simply be conjectural.

It is worthwhile to consider in more detail just what is involved

---

[5] *Ambigua* 7, *PG* 90, 1071C, 1091BC, 1084CD.
[6] *Divine Names* 1, *PG* 3, 588D.

in the loss of divine knowledge, since it is crucial to the thesis of this chapter. The first point to stress is the distinction in man of two faculties: the spiritual intellect and the natural reason. The spiritual intellect is that which the Christian authors referred to above call the "God-like" faculty in man, the divine spirit breathed into us in the act of our creation, the consummation of the divine image in which we are created and that which in the deepest part of ourselves we are. It is that "mysterious eye of the soul" through which St. Augustine saw "the light that never changes"; and it may be defined, as St. Bernard defines it, "as the soul's true unerring intuition, the unhesitating apprehension of truth." It differs from the reason in that it has its seat not in the head but in the heart; and it differs again from the reason in that it is not simply a classifying faculty but is the mirror of the divine Intelligence, which fills it with the knowledge in the light of which it perceives the underlying spiritual identity of visible, material things.

This knowledge, in the light of which the spiritual intellect knows external objects, embraces the creative ideas, the archetypal *logoi* or causes, of which visible things are the manifestation. What is seen in such an idea is not an abstraction, or a concept, or an analogy, drawn from an external object through the activity of the reason. It is on the contrary the spiritual energy issuing from the Divine according to which a thing receives its existence, an energy manifesting itself in visible form. The spiritual intellect thus knows all visible things through knowing their causes, through a participation in the very ideas or energies of which they are the manifestation. It is capable of a direct perception of the intelligible and inner, or real, nature of everything that is, of which the sensible form is but the outward manifestation. Its way of knowing is through spiritual experience and intuition and not through concepts and discursive reasoning. To quote St. Maximos again: "The immediate experience of a thing suppresses the concept which represents this thing. I call experience knowledge in act which takes place beyond all concept. I call intuition the participation itself in the object known, at a level above all thought."[7]

[7] *Quaestiones ad Thalassium* 60, PG 90, 624AB.

The second point which must be emphasized is that this spiritual intellect cannot be operative or awakened in us – we cannot share in its activity – unless we first of all free ourselves from alien hostile attachments and persuasions, false and self-centered ideas and habits, and submit ourselves to what surpasses us, to the source of light and of the divine ideas which only then can illuminate our mind. When the mind is cut off from this source, when it has lost its roots in the heart (and this is the condition of our "fall" and of our "fallen" state), our experience and intuition of what always is, really and unchangeably, is lost, and all that is possible are purely conjectural and hypothetical theories about things. We are left with a kind of pseudo-knowledge, not with the knowledge itself.

At the same time, we cease to know ourselves, since it is only through the intellect that we may perceive the center and substance of what we are, and with this now being darkened in us, we can have only a peripheral and accidental opinion about ourselves. In fact, before we can know anything, in the real sense, we must first of all know ourselves, for unless we know that, through the intellect's intuition of the spiritual and creative energy that makes us what we are, we can never know the energies or causes by which everything else is made. That is why the condition of any real knowledge is our purification of ourselves to the point at which our intelligence becomes again receptive to the light of the divine Intelligence, to the grace of God, the point at which the mind, satellite of the heart, is brought back to the heart, where it is truly rooted in the source of light and fully vivified by its power.

The intellect, then, reawakened in us, orients us towards the divine and the universal. When it has once again become transparent to the divine Intelligence, then we see and know ourselves and see and know everything else in the pure mirror of the intellect. We are thus able to refer ourselves and each thing to our, and its, supra-individual origin, the divine Logos Himself. When we lose this contact with and participation in the Logos, then, closed within our individual selfhood and the ego-consciousness that goes with it, we refer all things to ourselves as end, regarding ourselves as self-sufficient beings. Created free in God, we seek to be free in our own *proprium*, in our own ego. We commit a kind of apostasy, a denial of what is superior to ourselves, the sin of pride which turns rapidly to greed: the sin of Adam.

Our mind then, preferring its own opinion to the common and universal Logos, desires to use all for its own purposes and enjoyment. Realizing its power over material things, and turned towards them, our mind first engenders in itself their sensations, then, by a process of abstraction, forms images and concepts of them. A sort of mental fornication takes place, in which the mind debauches and loses itself among a welter of such concepts and images, which it divides, multiplies, contracts, enlarges, orders, disarranges *ad infinitum*.

All this is the natural and inevitable consequence of our loss of participation in the divine Intelligence. No longer able to realize our dependence on what surpasses us, we now regard ourselves as independent and self-sufficient; we want all for ourselves, and having at our disposal only the material world, we turn to that and use it, not as a means through which we can contemplate and glorify the Divinity, but as something we can exploit to satisfy all the needs and greeds of our inflated and ego-centered selves.

It is possible to trace, through those three crises of modern Europe which we still call the Renaissance, the Reformation, and the Age of Enlightenment, this movement of a mind which has broken with a reality of a spiritual or metaphysical order and has more and more asserted its own self-sufficiency. Beginning with a denial, already explicit in the works of some of the scholastic philosophers, that through direct intellectual vision we can perceive the divine source of our own existence, and hence the divine source of all created things, the first stage of this movement is the assertion that the human mind can acquire a valid type of knowledge without reference to divine knowledge. Thus, a purely relative and individual faculty usurps the position of the divinely-oriented intellect.

By the time of Descartes, this process is complete. The human mind is said to be quite capable of formulating a valid type of knowledge not only without reference to divine knowledge, but also without reference to the sensible world and its phenomena. The human mind becomes the self-sufficient arbiter of knowledge. Finally the human mind itself, as part of this downward movement, increasingly takes its cue, not from the ideas that have their source in the universal Logos, but from *dicta* invented by whatever philosopher or group of philosophers happens to hold the stage, *dicta* that become ever more mechanical and banal as the human mind disowns its divine inheritance.

6/3/12

There is no longer any question of truth in an absolute sense, but only of theories which are no more than the conceptualized fantasies of minds that have lost their links with any genuine reality, whether physical or metaphysical. In these circumstances, it is inevitable that these theories are as numerous, and change as rapidly, as the individuals who make them. With the intellect obscured, and the reason chained more and more to the service of material ends, it is not surprising that the final stage of this mental aberration is an attack on the human mind itself, not in the name of that which is superior to it, but in an appeal to the infra-conscious and subjective worlds of pseudo-mysticisms, to sensation, psychology, occultism, and much else of an equally anti-spiritual nature.

What afflicts us, then, the cause of our confusion, anxiety, guilt, despair, is first of all a disorientation of our thought, a disease of the mind. It began with a defection of the mind, and like a slow poison has spread through the whole of life. The fundamental hierarchies of our being are overturned, and those primal relationships which link us to the sources of energy and permit the full deployment of our possibilities have been destroyed. We have reduced ourselves to a fraction of what we are, and our idea of the world to a mere caricature. Full of an immense futility and a despicable cunning, we go on extending our conquest and distributing our wealth over the deserts of the material world, but we have no strength to face and grapple with those realities in communion with which alone our existence achieves significance. Superbly equipped to fight each other, we are defenseless against the terrible punishment decreed for those who refuse their Maker and Savior that tribute of love, that gesture of confidence, without which no one can live.

Such a decline into unreality and meaninglessness is inescapable once the forms and values that condition a society become dissociated from their archetypes in the spiritual realm or, rather, when the thought and actions of that society's members are no longer based on a religious sense and understanding of life and on their corresponding practices. And this is but another way of saying that such a decline is inescapable when once the thought and actions of the members of a particular society are no longer determined above all by their allegiance and adherence to the norms of a sacred tradition. When these norms cease to be effective for the majority of its members, society simply disintegrates. In other words, the integrity of a society and the communal effectiveness of a sacred tradition are inseparable.

Why is this the case? Sacred tradition in the highest sense consists in the preservation and handing down of a method of contemplation. A method of contemplation, in its turn, is what makes it possible for us to transcend our bodily, psychic and merely ratiocinative life, to go beyond our sensations, feelings and argumentative logic, in order to attain through intellectual vision a knowledge of and communion with the Divine, the source of all things. A corollary of this is that it permits us to perceive physical things as symbols of what lies beyond them. It permits us to perceive the hidden workings of reality, the spiritual essences that all things enshrine and of which they are the visible and tangible manifestations.

Surely, it might be said, this is something we can achieve for ourselves, if we feel so inclined, without the need of any tradition, with its superstructure of metaphysical or theological theory and its often elaborate ritual. We have simply to meditate, to pray even, or to take certain mind-altering drugs. We can expand our consciousness by purely natural means – means within our own natural scope – without resorting to means that claim to be supranatural and sacred.

It is true that in our ordinary human state, everyone has some concept of the nature or reality or meaning of existence. We also have some idea of our own potentialities and qualities, and of how we can best cultivate them. In addition, something in us – we call it our conscience – indicates to us whether we are acting rightly or wrongly, although to judge by the actions in which human beings are only too often engaged this capacity is frequently in abeyance, or at least ineffective. But in spite of this there are profound and crucial aspects of our nature, as well as profound and crucial potentialities within us, of which we would remain ignorant were we not told about them.

These aspects and potentialities are above all connected with our relationship to the divine and with the knowledge of what constitutes human perfection and of how we may attain it. The nature of this relationship, and hence the knowledge of what constitutes our perfection and of how we may attain it, are matters of which we cannot be aware unless God reveals them to us in a form that we are capable of grasping. Without such revelation we cannot know what human perfection consists in or what our true potentialities are, and still less can we know how to actualize them; for our human potentialities go infinitely beyond the parameters of any kind of perfection we can visualize as possessing on our own account or that can be actualized without divine intervention and guidance.

Even the absolutely crucial fact, on which hang, as it were, all the law and the prophets, that in addition to our ratiocinative faculty we possess a faculty of vision – the spiritual intellect – upon the actualization of which depends our capacity to attain a direct and experiential knowledge of the reality of things, is something of which we remain ignorant unless we are told about it; and nor can we know, unless we are told about it, how we can actualize this faculty. Revelation is the only means at our disposal through which we can grasp the full scope of such potentialities and receive guidance as to how we can cultivate them. It delineates and describes reality in modes that we can grasp.

To reject revelation is thus to reject the possibility of attaining the perfection of the human state. It is to ensure that we fail to fulfill our roles as human beings. Conversely, to the extent to which we conform to the norms provided by revelation, we will be led to actualize the potentialities of our nature. Since it is only through such actualization that we can integrate the otherwise uncoordinated and anarchic impulses and proclivities of our being, it follows that our failure to conform to the norms provided by revelation means that we live in a state of disintegration and life-crippling frustration, a state that will be reflected in the state of the society of which we are members. Without roots in the common ground of our being – in the universal Logos – we are condemned to an individualism that is as desolate as it is self-destructive.

The norms of revelation are those that constitute the norms of religion or of sacred tradition. Thus, what has just been said with respect to the norms of revelation applies equally to the norms of sacred tradition: to the extent to which we conform to the norms provided by sacred tradition, we will not only become aware of our full human potentialities but will also receive the understanding and guidance necessary for their actualization. Conversely, to the extent to which we reject sacred tradition and fail to conform to its norms we will remain in a state of disintegration, frustration and misery, a state which will be projected in our society.

It is only through the surpassing of our self-centered individualism and the ego-consciousness that goes with it that we can live in harmony not only with our own selves but with all other living things, human and natural, as well. Such a surpassing of our self-centered individualism does not entail the elimination of our individuality as such. It entails the re-uniting of our individuality with its true center and subject, its personal divine archetype, by virtue of which we constitute a person and not simply an individual.

A sacred tradition, then, will possess two main aspects. The first is what may be called the gnostic aspect, in that it pertains to the knowledge of what constitutes the fully realized and perfected human state, of the relationship with the divine that such a state presupposes, and of the corresponding relationship between God, ourselves and the natural world that we describe as cosmology. The second aspect concerns the guidance and the means whereby we can actualize the full potentialities of the human state, which at the same time requires that we actualize our proper relationship with God, other people and with every other living thing in the natural world. This aspect may be called the aspect of spiritual practice, or spiritual method, through which we can attain the state of contemplation and glorification in which the purpose of sacred tradition is consummated.

PRAXIS

6/7/12

Before there can be any question of sacred tradition in the authentic sense of the words, these two seemingly independent aspects of gnosis and method have to be in such close conjunction and interrelationship that to all intents and purposes they constitute two aspects of a single undivided reality. There cannot be a sacred tradition when all the emphasis, or the greater part of it, is placed simply on gathering information about the spiritual life, just as there cannot be a sacred tradition when all the emphasis, or the major part of it, is placed on following blindly an external discipline of ritual or ascetic or moral action. One can say that all metaphysical or theological or philosophic doctrine that does not have as its purpose, and does not culminate in, experiential spiritual illumination is vain speculation, while all searching for mystical experience not grounded in sound doctrine is likely to end in disaster and disintegration. The two aspects of gnosis and spiritual practice, wisdom and method, have to go hand in hand, and to balance each other.

Bart!

This is an important point to stress from the start. Possibly under the influence of the modern scientific mentality, according to which knowledge is something we can acquire by learning and certainly without going through any ritual ascetic purification, we have developed the habit of thinking the same applies where spiritual knowledge is concerned. That is to say, we tend to think that by studying the works of the inspired spiritual masters and interpreters we can acquire spiritual knowledge, and that all the external aspects of a spiritual tradition – its ritual and ascetic practice – are somehow secondary and may not be important at all and so can be dispensed with.

This (and the reasons will become clear later in this chapter) is not the case at all. Both are of equal importance. Knowledge unaccompanied by its corresponding ritual or ascetic practice will remain simply abstract knowledge, just as ritual or ascetic practice unaccompanied by its corresponding intellectual component, the understanding of the inner meaning, is likely to remain unproductive of spiritual growth. An anti-traditional or anti-spiritual mentality is always at work in the attitude which tends to play down the importance of the whole formal – ritual and ascetic and ceremonial – side of religion.

The aspect of gnosis or wisdom in a sacred tradition is represented by that which we call doctrine. Of course, all religions have a doctrine – in fact it is precisely because the doctrine of one religion may seem at odds with the doctrine of another religion that there have been so many religious wars and such animosity between people holding different religious beliefs. This has led many people to question the value of doctrine altogether, which is an attitude that complements that of those who question the value of religious practice. Yet doctrine, for reasons we have seen, is an essential element of every sacred tradition and cannot be displaced. As to why there are diversities of doctrine among the sacred traditions, this is a theme that will be discussed in a later chapter.

The first constitutive element of a sacred tradition is, then, doctrine. Such doctrine enshrines the knowledge imparted by God through revelation, often in the form of a Holy Book or of Holy Books, and interpreted by the inspired spiritual masters of the tradition concerned. As such it is, in accordance with the strictly etymological sense of the word, a metaphysical knowledge: it is concerned with that which is beyond or after physical or natural knowledge. This means that the doctrine of a sacred tradition is also beyond the natural sciences in all their forms. It means that it is something that lies altogether beyond the scope of the modern sciences and of the modern scientific mentality. It is not simply that the modern sciences have so far failed to investigate things that belong to the domain of metaphysical knowledge because they have not yet advanced that far, which they will do one day if only they push forward with their investigations. This is not the case at all. The domain of metaphysical knowledge consists of that which by its very nature lies outside the range of these sciences, and far exceeds in scope all that they can embrace, however far they may push forward with their methods of analysis and dissection.

In addition to this, the modern sciences are always dependent to some extent upon some form of experimentation; but metaphysical knowledge is essentially that of which no experimental or external investigation of this kind is possible: being "beyond physics" it is also beyond experiment, beyond every kind of statistical or mathematical verification or demonstration. Consequently, the scope of every separate science can be extended indefinitely without it ever reaching a point of contact with metaphysical knowledge. This is something of which certain modern scientists, who claim that quantum physics, for example, is approaching the state of Eastern metaphysics, appear to be unaware. They do not appear to realize that by definition physics can never be metaphysical – or, at least, can only become metaphysical by ceasing to be physics. Metaphysical knowledge is a supra-rational, intuitive, and immediate knowledge; the domain of metaphysical knowledge is the domain of eternal and immutable principles revealed directly by God and apprehended by human beings only when they have attained the state of contemplation or intellectual vision.

Such vision is not within the scope of the human reason. Still less does it have anything in common with intuition as it is understood by philosophers like Bergson or by writers like D.H. Lawrence, for whom intuition is a purely instinctual and subconscious faculty that lies beneath the reason and not above it, and has its source in impressions received through the body and the senses, and in feelings and images aroused in us by the experience of our physical being and our subjective emotional reactions to them. Intellectual vision is, as we have seen, a function that belongs to an organ that is superior to the reason. It belongs to a kind of transcendent intellect, which is able to apprehend directly the truths of the spiritual realm.

How can we set about realizing that which is beyond the scope of our ordinary or natural faculties? How can we raise ourselves, or be raised, above our ordinary individual state so that we can attain the experiential vision of the transcendent realities, a vision that by definition is supra-individual? How, in other words, can we awaken, and bring into operation, the organ of vision through which we can perceive these realities – awaken and bring into operation our spiritual and transcendent intellect?

The answer to this question introduces us to the second of those two aspects which, as I said, together constitute an integral and authentic sacred tradition, the aspects of gnosis and spiritual practice, wisdom and method. Because here what comes into play is a process of initiation into the contemplative state – an initiation which if pursued through to its term allows us actually to experience the spiritual realities of which the doctrine has been the gauge and the promise.

Initiation, or contemplation, has as its purpose the actualization of the spiritual intellect to the point at which, transcending its own natural powers, it comes to share in the spiritual vision of God Himself. God is God because He possesses this spiritual vision of things. To share in this vision we must ourselves be begotten by God – be born of the Spirit – and become ourselves God-like. Initiation thus leads directly to the consciousness of God, to the merging of our consciousness with that of God. When this happens we contemplate God in all things and all things in God, not through the natural vision of our intellect but because the vision of our intellect is now that with which God perceives things. Our organ of vision has become God's organ of vision.

Initiation, then, may be said to have two main stages. The first is that whereby we come to grasp our own causal principle, or to become aware of the divine image in ourselves. We come to realize that we are the epiphanic form of a divine archetype. At the same time we come to realize that each visible reality is the epiphanic form of the Divinity. We come to perceive God in all things. This stage of initiation is not achieved by way of any exterior action. It is achieved by an ever-deepening process of inner concentration on the part of the intellect operating according to its own impetus and nature, with the help of its imaginative power.

It also leads to the limits of what we might call, adopting the terminology of ancient Greek initiatory rites, the lesser mysteries. So far, there is no question of being more than a natural human individual or of being in any effective possession of a supranatural or divine state. But we will at least have broken free from time and from the apparent succession of things in time, and will be in possession of something of which previously we had no knowledge at all – something that may be called the sense of eternity. Also, and more important, when we have reached this stage, and only then, we will be in a position to embark on the second stage of initiation, the stage of the greater mysteries which are characterized by the penetration into states that are supranatural, uncreated and divine. 6/12/12

In this second stage of initiation, the intellect transcends the mode of vision it has achieved in the first stage, and from seeing God in all things it comes to see all things in God. This is something that it achieves only through the direct illumination and grace of God Himself. So far, looking towards the many or the realm of multiplicity, the intellect has come to perceive in each of all these many things a spiritual quality or dimension, seeing each as the manifestation of the Divine. Now it has to transcend the realm of multiplicity, not by rejecting what it now perceives, but as it were by culling or gleaning from each visible thing the spiritual quality it enshrines, and by realizing that these qualities all harmonize with each other and are all the flower and growth of one root. Thus the intellect is led back from the many to the One and sees all things as one in the One, from whom all multiplicity derives. And to the degree to which it comes to perceive in things that belong to the natural world that which transcends this world, it enters the supranatural realm, mirroring the transcendent One.

This transcending of the realm of multiplicity is to pass through the angelic states to the realm of pure Being, and beyond that to a state that can be described only as one of divine darkness and unknowingness, the ultimate all-embracing ground of divine potentiality, symbolized in sacred tradition by the figure of the eternal feminine. Yet even when transmuted into this uncreated and infi-

ST, MARY

nite state, beings still have a positive and individuated status. To deny individuation in the divine realm is to deny the archetypal theophanic dimension specific to every visible thing. Gnostic contemplation does not consist in proceeding from a visible form to a pure absence of form, or to a pure formlessness in the sense that implies a complete absence of individuation. Such a conclusion would be to posit a conception of the supreme metaphysical essence that is reached by denying that this essence possesses any positive qualities or any individuation whatsoever – in other words, that it is negatively conditioned. In that case the divine image of every manifest being ceases to be a theophanic symbol and becomes instead no more than a mere allegory.

Through this inner transmutation, in which the contemplative path is consummated, a human being attains precisely the experience of his own theophany, that is, his person as the person in and by whom God manifests Himself to Himself in the ultimate ground of His divinity. It is God's self-determination that constitutes this theophany, and it is this theophany that constitutes this human being's individuation. Through that individuation God reveals Himself as God, but God as He is in that person. In this state the human being is truly in possession of the plenitude of his possibilities, and is perfected.

This brings us back to the question that led us to describe the two main stages of the initiatory way: given that with our own unaided powers we cannot raise ourselves above the natural individual state, how can we traverse not only the lesser mysteries but also the greater mysteries? For to traverse these two stages of initiation does presuppose not only that we grasp the principle of human individuality, but also that we attain states of being above the purely natural state. Initiation is by definition a "second birth", a birth in the Spirit: we can no more bring about, by ourselves, our spiritual birth than we can our biological birth.

Briefly, the answer to this question is that if we aspire to initiation we can only in fact enter into the initiatory process on condition that we receive a spiritual influence that bestows on us the capacity to do so. The reception of such a spiritual influence is an absolute necessity if we are to be reborn; for such an influence, deriving as it does from a supra-individual and divine source, confers on us a potentiality to go beyond the purely natural individual state and to attain levels of being that are of a metaphysical order. Just as there can be no spontaneous combustion in the material or corporeal order, there can be no development in the spiritual order without the intervention of a more-than-human spiritual influence.

Even the aptitudes and possibilities included in the natural individual state are no more than *materia prima*, that is to say a pure potentiality, in which there is nothing developed or differentiated. For this potentiality to take form and to organize itself – to develop – an initial vibration must be communicated to it by spiritual powers. This vibration is the *Fiat Lux* – the "Let there be light" of the Book of Genesis – that illumines chaos; and from the point of view of initiation, this illumination is brought about by the transmission of the spiritual influence of which I have spoken. It is only by virtue of this influence that the possibilities inherent in the human individual are not doomed to remain simply potential but are given the capacity to develop in the various phases of the initiatory process. If this is true even where the phases of the "lesser mysteries" are concerned, it is doubly so where the traversing of the more-than-individual states of the "greater mysteries" are concerned.

We are here confronting a most crucial aspect of sacred tradition. For this spiritual influence can be transmitted to the human individual only by means of a ritual, sacramental or liturgical act, or of ritual acts. Hence the absolute necessity of rites in the process of spiritual realization. This does not mean that such ritual acts, even provided that they are scrupulously observed, are sufficient in themselves to bring about such a realization. They can do so only if they are imbued with the vital spiritual influence in question. Without such an influence permeating them, they are simply counterfeits, lacking all spiritual significance.

Rites and sacraments, therefore, are a necessary condition of the transmission of a spiritual influence, but they are not in themselves sufficient to produce this influence. They do not function, that is to say, mechanically or automatically. In order for ritual forms not to be parodies or caricatures – in order for them to serve as a genuine support or vehicle for a spiritual influence – they have to be instituted by a divine or semi-divine being and to be operated by those who have received a special consecration, a special authorization and qualification to operate them. They have to be operated, that is to say, by those who constitute a sacred or hieratic order and to whom the spiritual influence has itself been transmitted.

Such an order, together with the rites for which it is responsible, are therefore essential to an initiatory or sacred tradition; and it is this tradition, functioning in a regular and uninterrupted succession on the horizontal plane of time, that constitutes the initiatory chain and alone is capable of transmitting, through its established rites, the spiritual influence without which there can be no spiritual or metaphysical realization. This means that if we aspire to such realization we have to affiliate ourselves to an authentic sacred tradition, and in this way receive the spiritual influence which it alone is capable of transmitting; for unless we do this we will never achieve that second birth which is a condition of spiritual realization, our spiritual intellect will remain unawakened and inoperative, and we will be doomed, whatever we do, to remain a prisoner of our mortal, transitory, and self-divided individual state, with all the malaise and distress that that entails.

As for what distinguishes an authentic tradition of this kind from its spurious, pseudo-traditional counterfeits – and there are a great many of these – two of its indispensable features have already been indicated. The first is that it does not owe its origin to any purely individual initiative, and the second is that it validates the idea of a regular and uninterrupted succession both of its initiatory rites and of those authorized and qualified to operate them. Further testimonies of its authenticity are to be found in the saints and holy men which it has nurtured, and in the sacred arts and crafts which have flourished under its inspiration. Moreover – and it is here that the two aspects of tradition, immemorial spiritual knowledge and the mysteries of initiation, wisdom and method, merge into a single reality – it is also the guardian and interpreter of the sacred doctrine.

Such, then, is the meaning of sacred tradition. As we have seen, its essential features are that it presupposes on the one hand a body of sacred knowledge – an immemorial Wisdom – and on the other hand a body of sacred rites and practices through the operation of which a spiritual influence is transmitted that alone makes it possible for us to bring about in ourselves those inner transformations in our consciousness, and indeed in our whole being, that put us in effective possession of the Truth, and that alone make it possible for us to live the Truth. These two presuppositions in their turn posit a third: the existence of an organization, of however loose a structure, through which both the sacred doctrine and the sacred initiatory rites are transmitted chronologically in an authentic and uninterrupted form. One can say that unless these three features coinhere and are actively present, there is no sacred tradition in the true sense of the words.

Where there is no such tradition and active participation in it, there is not likely to be any spiritual realization, in the proper meaning of the word. For although we may think that formal attachment to the discipline of a particular sacred tradition is unnecessary because the Spirit blows where it wills and so can inspire and illumine those not attached to such a tradition just as well, or even better than, those who are so attached, it is surely presumption and spiritual pride (the least spiritual of characteristics, whose presence in a person would in any case preclude any visitation by the Spirit) to imagine that the Spirit will choose us for special and privileged attention when we have already rejected or scorned perfectly good and well-tried ways through which the Spirit has already chosen to manifest His influence.

In an age of such spiritual confusion as our own, and in an area so exposed to chicanery and charlatanism, to possess clear unambiguous criteria according to which we can distinguish the genuine from the spurious is indispensable if we are to pursue a true spiritual way. As for the need of finding such a way, in the form of an authentic sacred tradition, as a precondition for the development of potentialities in life, love and consciousness which by and large remain unrecognized, and certainly unnurtured, by the ideologies, philosophies and sciences that dominate our present-day society, this should also be clear from what has been said. The actualization of these potentialities requires that which all sacred traditions call a second birth, a birth in the spirit; and how can a being act by itself, on itself, before it has been born?

This returns us to the question with which we opened the main theme of this chapter, the meaning and necessity of a sacred tradition. For, we asked, given that the values which have formed and continue to dominate the modern world are those that have brought us to our present impasse and state of dereliction, what reassessment and change of mind are needed in order for us to recover our equilibrium and lost integrity? The initial answer to this question is fairly obvious: it is that unless we reverse the premises of the type of thought and action whose ascendancy in our consciousness has led us to produce the techno-scientific inferno in which we find ourselves, we will not escape the disaster towards which it is ineluctably propelling us. For it is quite clear that no amount of taking thought, no amount of scheming and deliberation, discussion and conference, is of the slightest use while the fundamental categories within which the mind itself operates remain unchanged.

It has to be recognized that the real question before us is not, as we often like to think, this, that, or the other thing, but only whether we choose submission to the best of what we are, to the divine in us, or whether we do not. The issue is one of freedom, but of freedom to choose between obedience to what is superior or domination by what is inferior. If we cut ourselves off from what is superior we automatically fall under the sway of what is inferior. That is the punishment.

The essential thing to grasp is that the disease which has its origins in a defection of the mind can only be cured through a change of mind, a remaking of ourselves. It can not be cured in any other terms. If the errors of thought and judgment of which we are now the victims are not corrected, nothing will be saved. And they can be corrected. The gate of salvation is never shut. The divine image in us, that which sparkles with the vitality of the Logos and is capable of releasing us from the constricting limits of this world and of restoring our lost spiritual communion, always remains. It is still conscious in us, even if we are not conscious in it. Nothing can injure or destroy the powers which it alone can realize.

However radical our defection, it cannot affect what is essential in us; it cannot touch our deepest nature; it can never be more than accidental. Our original nature remains always inviolate. What punishes us, our death even, is but parasitic; it will cease to exist as soon as we cut it from us. And it may be precisely at the point at which the disease is at its worst, and when we have really given ourselves up, that the reaction will begin, and we will seek our cure in the one direction in which it can be found.

This brings us to the more definitive answer to the question posed above, to which the initial reply is that we have to reverse the premises of thought and action, and of the values they represent, which still dominate our consciousness. For the cure to our present situation cannot consist simply in our freeing ourselves from these premises and values. It has been the thesis of this chapter that we can achieve an integrity of being, and hence a viable form of human society, only provided that we first become aware of our true potentialities as human beings, and then pursue a course of life through which we can actualize these potentialities in existential terms.

We have further maintained that the only criteria according to which we can distinguish between what we may happen to think we are and that which we are in our essence as human beings – as well as those according to which we can distinguish between truth and error, reality and illusion – are the criteria provided by revelation and enshrined in sacred tradition. In other words, there can be no cure for our present situation until our lives, public and private, are once again established on a religious basis, something which can come only when we live according to the norms of a sacred tradition.

This in its turn presupposes two other conditions. First, that we possess a sacred tradition according to whose norms we, should we choose to do so, are able to live; and second, that this tradition affirms these norms in a manner consistent with the revelation to which its task is to bear witness and implement in such a way that this revelation is an ever-present reality for each succeeding generation. This means that the tradition in question must not lose its essential initiatory character, or allow it to be overlaid and compromised by disproportionate concern with secondary and contingent matters, for should it do this it will cease to operate as the transfiguring power of every aspect of human and other life. It will, in other words, betray its essential function as well as the revelation from which it derives.

Unless there is a possibility of these two conditions being fulfilled, then there would seem to be no way in which we can even begin to re-establish our lives on a religious basis. This, it scarcely needs to be said, is not simply an academic matter. It is a matter that concerns our survival in every sense of the word, spiritual, cultural, physical. For the rot has eaten so deeply into the fibers of our world, has so weakened all the threads of the social fabric, every established bond of authority and institution, of family or state, and has so exposed the emptiness of our man-made, man-centered ideas, our illusion of human happiness and prosperity, our calculations of self-help and mutual aid, that everything to which we have been used to look for support or guidance is now, if not actually destroyed, at least so insecure that we can have no confidence in it. Whether we like it or not we have come into the desolation of reality. We are set down naked beneath the stars. Nothing stands between our poor, forked, famished human condition and the great spiritual principles we have tried for so long not to confront. We know now that we cannot escape, and that it is useless to pretend to take refuge in any less absolute predicament.

It is also a dangerous predicament, not least because it possesses its own form of exhilaration: we are set free from so much irrelevance, from so much sheer and ridiculous waste. There is the cage and the doomed vociferous folly of our life within it; and there is the sea of being and the eternal realities. It is a matter of judgment: truth or error. But the stakes are not equal, and it will go hard with us, or not at all, if what we fail to choose is the universal Logos, still as always at the source of the human mind. The chapters that follow are largely concerned with discussing some of the issues in this predicament insofar as these relate to the sacred tradition that has shaped the cultural world that used to constitute Christendom, the tradition of Christianity.

6/21/12

Chapter Two

Christianity and Christendom

C.S. Lewis, in his 1954 inaugural lecture as Regius Professor at Cambridge entitled *De Descriptione Temporum,* said that we live in what he called a post-Christian epoch. There has been, from somewhere towards the end of the seventeenth century, a gradual "un-christening" of Europe. All history – all European history, that is to say – falls into three periods: the pre-Christian, the Christian, and the post-Christian. These descriptions are intended to cover cultural rather than intellectual periods; but since the course of culture follows that of thought, implicit in these descriptions of the cultural periods of our past is a historical view of our intellectual development. We have been non-Christians (or pre-Christians), then Christians, and then post-Christians.

It is very simple. Others, like T.S. Eliot, have told us much the same thing. And yet it is confusing. It is confusing because it avoids any discrimination between Christianity and that Christian society which has been created and preserved through the Church. It is possible that, if we live in a post-Christian epoch, this is not primarily because from somewhere towards the end of the seventeenth century we have deserted our Christian society. It may be because in creating and seeking to preserve this society we have sacrificed, or neglected, the essential character of Christianity itself.

Let us see how this may have come about. The early years of Christianity are, in spite of all the research done on them, still obscure, and are likely to remain so. The New Testament is written in Greek – that is, no direct account of the words of Christ, in the language in which He is most likely to have spoken, exists. The relationship between Christianity and the Essenes is not clear. But what is clear is that however much Christianity is a culmination, or fulfillment (and in what respect it is so is often very vague, even to Christians), nonetheless Christianity stood in the line of a tradition of wisdom and knowledge whose historical appearance is long prior to the advent of Christianity. It is ridiculous to go on applying to that whole period before the historical birth of Christ the term "pagan" – which came into use somewhere about the fourth century AD – in order to describe derogatively the peasant sorcerers who preserved, generally in an entirely debased form, something of the magical arts of the ancient world. It is still more ridiculous to do this with the implication that the historical birth of Christ marks a complete break with the intellectual and religious traditions of the ancient world, as if the thought and religion of the ancient world were all so much error and falsehood and as if its faith were superficial and misguided.

This is not only to forget such monuments of intellect as Herakleitos and Plato; not only to forget the non-Christian martyrs who suffered for their faith tortures as cruel as any suffered by the Christian martyrs, and borne with the same courage and integrity. It is also to forget that it was through the writings of such as Plato and his successors that many of the Christian Fathers – St. Augustine among them – were brought to Christianity. It is to forget, too, that the language of many of the Christian Fathers (and particularly of the Greek Fathers), as well as the language of the liturgies, is the language of Neoplatonism, and that when Christians came to elaborate their theory of sacred art (represented in the icon), it was in Platonic terms that they did so.

Indeed, if one is to go back to the testimony of many of the early Christian writers themselves, one might well be led to the conclusion that Christianity is little more than the restoration or revitalization of the religious traditions of the ancient world in their highest form. According to Eusebius, for example, Christianity is the restoration of the religion of the patriarchal age, which had been debased and distorted by subsequent Judaism; and St.

Augustine himself writes: "That which today is called Christian religion existed also among the Ancients and has never ceased to exist from the origin of the human race until the time when Christ Himself assumed human form and men began to call Christian the true religion which already existed beforehand."[1]

In these early stages, too, there was much in Christian form and practice that was reminiscent of the initiations or the esoterism of the ancient mysteries like those of Eleusis, or Samothrace, or Lemnos. There was a *lex arcani*. Origen talks of faith being useful for the masses, and further says that the intelligent are more congenial to God than the unintelligent. He explicitly speaks of secret doctrines that can be taught only to the initiated. Clement of Alexandria says the same thing, and such a secret (and oral) tradition is referred to by St. Cyril of Alexandria, St. Gregory Nazianzen, Dionysios the Areopagite, and many others. Unless one is automatically prevented by prejudice, one has to recognize that in its essential form Christianity is an initiatory religion that is in many ways similar to the mystery religions of the pre-Christian world.

This means that at the heart of the Christian revelation is a vision according to which the Light of Wisdom, radiating from its source in God, "the Father of Lights", is mediated through the angelic orders to the humblest of creatures, the degree to which it is received being determined only by the limitations of each creature's capacity to receive it. As Dante writes in the opening of his *Paradiso*:

> La gloria di colui che tutto move
> per l'universo penetra, e risplende
> in una parte più, e meno altrove.[2]

No creature is excluded from participation in this glory, for it streams forth to the totality of all being, and is present to, and within, all creatureliness, however remote it may appear to be from the source, and however much it may appear to belong to the world of multiplicity. At the same time, the degree to which a creature

---

[1] *Retractationes* I. 13. 3.

[2] "The All-mover's glory penetrates through the universe, and regloweth in one region more, and less in another." (Trans. Rev. Philip H. Wicksteed.)

can assimilate this glory, and to which it can participate in it in an active and not simply a passive mode, depends upon its degree of purification, and upon the degree to which it can raise itself, or allow itself to be raised, above the level of its simple creatureliness through the penetration of the Holy Spirit.

In other words, there is a hierarchy of spiritual illumination in spite of the fact that the Truth is accessible to all. There is a spiritual knowledge which, although inherent as a potential within all human beings, remains occluded and veiled for those whose level of spiritual realization does not allow them to pass beyond the material and external aspect of things. And the perception of this spiritual knowledge depends, as we saw in the last chapter, upon the awakening of an organ of vision which makes it possible for us to perceive it, for it cannot be perceived by the natural faculties of sense and reason. The awakening of this organ of vision – a matter of divine grace – in its turn depends, not exclusively but to all intents and purposes, upon the following of the path of spiritual realization which may be compared, *mutatis mutandis*, to that of the mystery religions of the pre-Christian world.

Yet although the following of such a path – the path of gnosis and contemplation – is open to everyone, those who can attain in this life the knowledge and illumination to which it leads are relatively few. There are higher and lower degrees of sanctity, higher and lower degrees of spiritual intelligence. Moreover, guidance as to how the path is to be followed is to a large extent oral guidance, given by a spiritual master already initiated into its mysteries to those whom he considers qualified to receive it. In this respect there is an esoteric aspect of Christianity which once again is similar to that of the pre-Christian mystery religions.

At the same time Christianity is not simply a mystery religion in the pre-Christian sense. It is not an esoterism confined to an élite of initiates. Indeed, one of the aspects of Christianity that distinguishes it from the religious sects of the pre-Christian world is precisely that it breaks through the barrier between the esoteric and the exoteric, the non-manifest and the manifest, the One and the many, the inner and the outer – a breaking through that is confirmed in the rending of the veil of the temple.

Christianity reveals that such a barrier represents a distortion of things. Its central message is that God, in manifesting Himself, becomes "other" than Himself and makes Himself His own symbol without any lapse from His essential reality in the process. It is this expression of the non-manifest in the manifest, of the absolute in the contingent, of eternity in time, of the One in the many, that overcomes dualistic conceptions of the relationship between God and the world. And this surpassing of such conceptions has its counterpart in the surpassing of the barrier between the esoteric and the exoteric. There are no longer two spheres, the one reserved to an élite, the other open to the public. There is but one sphere: the light shines forth in the darkness, and the apostles are not constituted as an enclosed order to protect the Truth from profanation, but are sent out into the world to proclaim it. Christianity, without denying the implications of its own revelation, cannot be indifferent to even the most profane aspects of the social order, or the world. Its concern is not with flight from but with the transfiguration of the world.   6/23/12

This did not mean that the Church initially had any specific program for the christianizing of society. Originally Christianity possessed no legislation applicable to the social order, nothing which corresponds to the *shariyah* of Islam. It constituted a kind of society within a society, again like the pre-Christian mystery religions; and Christians had to survive in spite of society and its laws, not with their support and protection. In fact, they possessed if anything the idea that there was a very clear and categorical line of demarcation between the realm of the state and that of the Church.

Explicit in the Christian Gospel is, if not a denial, at least a severe limitation on the powers of the temporal ruler. "Render unto Caesar the things that are Caesar's and unto God the things that are God's" Christ had said (Mt. 22:21), indicating that there were whole realms of human thought and action over which the state has no competence; and He Himself had set the pattern for Christian behavior, in the face of the state's claim to provide an order within which human life could be perfected, by His triumphal entry

into Jerusalem, an entry whose climax was the Cross with its un-
mistakable repudiation of any this-worldly Messiahship: in the
hostile terrestrial city He had perfected the loyalty tested in the
wilderness and sustained with patient devotion all the way from
Galilee to Gethsemane. The state is not the Kingdom, the will of
God cannot be consummated through the authority of its rulers
and custodians: it was to this understanding that the Christians of
the first centuries after Christ's advent remained faithful. Christianity spread for three centuries not with the state, but in spite of
it, not in conquest but in catacombs.

This did not mean that Christians were resolutely and uncom-
promisingly hostile to the state. If God's purpose for man could
not be fulfilled within or by the state, this did not signify that the
state and its ministers played no part in God's providence. On the
contrary, they played a most legitimate part, one which St. Paul,
for instance, was able to recognize and proclaim in categorical terms:
"Let everyone submit to those who are in authority, for there is no
such authority that does not come from God, and those who hold
this authority have been appointed by God. Thus anyone who re-
sists authority is opposing the divine order . . ." (Rom. 13:1-2).

It was not to denying to Caesar his throne that Christians of
these early centuries devoted their energies. Far from this being
the case, they were, in things lawful and honest, readily obedient
to the civil power, even though that power might be wielded by
figures such as Nero or Domitian; and even when confronted by
the choice of insurrection or suffering they consistently chose the
second. They were in the state as followers of the new Gospel, not
against it as supporters of a new Caesar.

Yet it was precisely as followers of the new Gospel, not as citizens of the state, that they were bound by the most absolute
loyalties; and if they did not deny Caesar his throne, they were not
on that account ready to recognize Caesar's throne as that of God,
or its occupant as divine. Nor did they entertain the idea that the
state might cooperate in the realization of the Kingdom of God,
or might align its political forms and institutions with the precepts of the Gospel in such a way that the will of God might be

actualized in the rule of its authorities and custodians.

This understanding of the relationship between Church and state was radically displaced by the advent of Constantine the Great and by the introduction of what is in effect a new idea in history – the idea of the Christian state and society, or the idea of Christendom. According to this idea, God's activity among mankind is directed not solely towards the salvation of individual souls but towards the salvation of mankind as a whole, towards the working out in time of the corporate redemption of His people. Society as a whole could and should participate, by means of an internal transformation begun in and through time, in and through history, in the Kingdom of God.

This meant that the social-political organism of humanity, the forms and institutions of the state that molded its corporate and terrestrial destiny, were no longer a matter of (comparative) indifference to Christians. Indeed, they came to be regarded as the means whereby mankind must realize itself in the living body of the divine Kingdom, in the Church as the bride of God. The state was to be a worldly instrument in the hand of God for the realization of His purpose. By acting, however unconsciously, in the light of such a conception, Constantine the Great changed the whole pattern of European, and Christian, history: the state could and should be dedicated to the realization of the Kingdom of God, and he himself had been elected by God to achieve the corporate salvation of His chosen people in the new Christian society, in a theocratic Christendom. Ultimately there should be only one society, that of the universal Christian empire whose boundaries are potentially coterminous with the whole world.

This radical change in the understanding of the relationship between Church and state implicit in the Constantinian settlement did not necessarily mean that the essential initiatory character of Christianity, with all that this implies, would be eliminated. But it did mean that there was now a danger that in its concern for the salvation of society as a whole – to be realized only through bringing everyone into the universal Christian state – the Church in its terrestrial manifestation might be led to sacrifice, or at least to compromise, something of this essential initiatory character. That in so doing it would lose its authority even as a social institution is a consequence which would not become apparent until it was too late.

How might this have come about? There would seem to be two main causes, the one necessarily related to the other. The first may be described as the development of an attitude of idolatry towards dogmatic and ethical formulations. In principle, of course, there can be no common measure between the Truth as such and any of the forms, verbal or other, in which it may clothe itself in manifestation and so be known to us; and in this sense the Truth must remain forever unknown to us, and the only consistent position for us to adopt is one of complete agnosticism. On the other hand, the Truth may be made known to us through revelation – and in this respect every aspect of manifestation is a revelation of the Truth, a theophany; or we may, through the process of initiation of which we have been speaking, be led to penetrate beyond the "name and form" of any explicit manifestation and so to attain to an intuitive perception of the Truth in its eternal and unchanging state; in both instances the position of complete agnosticism is modified or displaced.

In any case it must be remembered that any formulation of the Truth is relative to the Truth itself; and though there are degrees of relativity, none can claim absolute superiority in relation to the others: in the nature of things there can be no rigid exclusivity where the formulation of the Truth is concerned. And it must also be remembered that the corollary which depends from this is that a great deal of the Truth lies beyond any formulation whatsoever, and particularly beyond any verbal formulation.

All this may be perfectly understood and the necessary allowances may be made for it when the teaching of a religious doctrine, especially in its higher aspects, is a matter largely of oral instruction between a qualified spiritual master and his disciples; Christ Himself set the example for this in reserving to the apostles alone the interpretation of certain things which He could only display in parables to the multitude – so that "seeing they might not see and hearing they might not understand" (Mt. 13:13) – and when He said that while the truth should be proclaimed from the house-tops, yet pearls must not be cast before swine.

Yet when, with the conversion of Constantine and thereafter, the Church more fully embarked on its social mission, it became increasingly difficult to maintain the distinctions and balances involved. For then the Church was compelled to fix the doctrine, or at least certain aspects of it, as well as the moral and social conclusions deriving from those aspects, in formulations which could be grasped by the multitude quite apart from whether the inner nature of these formulations could in any way be adequately understood by the majority of those to whom they were addressed.

The Church was compelled to do this for two reasons. First, it had to distinguish its own doctrine from the heresies which continually threatened to obscure it or to distort it; and second, since its concern was now with society as a whole, it had to define the faith in such a way that each member of society, irrespective of his or her spiritual development or understanding, could confess it as a readily recognized token of his or her subscription to the laws of that society. For in a Christian society, of which the Church is the sponsor, what ultimately determines membership is not race or speech or culture, but the acceptance of the tenets of the Christian faith defined in terms that are accessible, and applicable, to all.

This does not mean that the dogmatic or ethical formulations, or the creeds of the Church, are in any sense untrue, or may not be an expression of the eternal and unchanging Truth as explicit in the circumstances as words can phrase it, and of universal significance. But it does mean that the insistence on these formulations in an exclusive sense, both in relation to rival formulations of heretical doctrines and as a condition of membership of the Christian society, involves grave danger that they may come to be regarded as the only forms in which the Truth can be expressed, and as themselves embracing the Truth in a more or less exhaustive, or all-inclusive, manner. It is here that the attitude of idolatry of which we spoke may develop.

Second, the initiatory, and dominantly gnostic and contemplative, character of Christianity may be sacrificed or compromised when the guardians of the Church in its terrestrial form become so concerned with achieving a Christian society that they develop an attitude toward the Church in which its social role as a corporate body is stressed to the exclusion of practically everything else. When this happens, the qualitative concern for the perfection of the life of the individual Christian through reunion with God in the *visio beatifica Dei* gives place to the quantitative concern for making everyone a member of the Church and for reintegrating the whole congregation of the faithful with the *civitas Dei*. What then becomes important is not the knowledge that the purpose of the Church is fulfilled in every man or woman or in every congregation that God, through direct and personal contact, chooses as a vessel of divine wisdom, but rather the institutions, the laws, and the traditions through which the universal Christian society may be established.

The quantitative and collective becomes, more important than the qualitative and personal. That the faithful should lead good Christian lives in moral terms (which means in obedience to the laws and institutions of the Church) is regarded as of more concern than the initiation of the few into the mysteries of the Kingdom of God; and the well-being of the whole Church regarded as a single corporate entity is of more concern than the well-being of any one of its individual members. And as the Christian society is founded upon and held together by subscription to the tenets of the Christian faith, the maintenance of this faith in an increasingly inflexible and, one might say, in an increasingly simplified or literal form, becomes an overriding preoccupation, and any expression of the Truth which appears to deviate from this form is regarded as a threat to the stability and security of the universal order which the Church is required to implement. This is why the development of an attitude of idolatry towards dogmatic and ethical formulations, and the development of the idea of the Church as above all a social institution, go hand in hand; both are symptoms of a certain loss of consciousness endangering the essential mission of the Church on earth.

That something of this loss of consciousness did take place is demonstrated by the attaching of increasing importance to certain theories and practices affecting the form of the Church in the centuries following the conversion of Constantine and the adoption by the Church of its extended social role. For there is no doubt that these theories and practices implied an attitude which regarded the Church and its institutions and laws as divine instruments for achieving a christianized version of the universal empire of the Romans, not merely in a territorial sense but covering every aspect of social and political and private life. It was the Church's function, it came to be thought, to mold the secular world in accordance with the principles of right order as embodied in the Christian faith; and this was to be achieved by means of a more or less totalitarian ecclesiastical state.

How this attitude developed, and may be justified, given the intention, it is not altogether difficult to see. The purpose of human life, in the Christian view of things, is to be incorporated into one body, the *unum corpus* of the Pauline epistles, which is to be identified with the body of Christ Himself. This incorporation has ultimately a spiritual or mystical significance, and the society which redeemed Christians are to form is the heavenly society of the Kingdom of God. This society is the Church, the bride of Christ, or His mystical body (*corpus mysticum*), as a non-material or supra-terrestrial reality. But Christ had also given the Church a material or terrestrial extension: He had founded it upon earth. This terrestrial form of the Church is not of course unrelated to its heavenly or mystical form. On the contrary, it is a projection of this heavenly or mystical form, and only exists as a reflection of the latter. It is, so to say, the counterpart of the latter, a translation of the divine form of the Church and the heavenly society into an earthly form.

In this way it may be said that the Church has a dual character, and in this respect reflects its founder as a divine-human personality: it is both the mystical body of Christ, a spiritualized reality, and an earthly body of living men and women. And just as the purpose of the heavenly form of the Church is fulfilled through the incorporation of all Christian souls into the mystical body of

Christ, so the purpose of the earthly form of the Church is fulfilled through incorporating all living men and women into its
society. The Church, that is to say, whether regarded from the heavenly or the earthly point of view, is a corporation and, more
particularly, its terrestrial manifestation is a civil society or a single
corporate political entity of which all men and women are potentially the members. The purpose of the Church on earth is to
embrace the Christian people – and ultimately all people – in a
universal body politic united by the common bond of the Christian faith.

There are two interconnected consequences of this. The first is
that if the Church on earth is to form this universal Christian
society, it must be suitably equipped. It must possess powers, institutions, and laws which will allow it to establish the order that
conforms to the will of God. In fact, it was claimed, the Church
does possess these assets through the very act of its founding: the
Christian revelation provides among other things for the whole
organization of the universal society and for the institutions and
laws necessary for its preservation; and this whole framework of
earthly government is modeled on the pattern of the divine order
of the universe. Thus the Church does not have to acquire anything it does not already possess; it has only to assert, against often
diabolic opposition, what is already its own by divine filiation, and
what is the visible expression of God's plan for mankind.

Moreover, as Christ is the head of the heavenly society, and as
the government of the terrestrial Christian society must parallel
that of its paradigm, it follows that there must be a physical representative of Christ, His viceregent or vicar, who will preside over
the Church in its earthly form and be the head of the Christian
society. This role was originally assumed by the Christian emperor,
and in the Christian East continued to be filled, both in the Byzantine world and, subsequently, in the Russian world, by the
Christian emperor. So intermeshed did the Church and the emperor become in this respect that by the late fourteenth century
the Patriarch of Constantinople, Antonios, could write to the Grand
Prince of Russia, Vasili I, that "it is not possible for Christians to

have a Church and not to have an empire", and that the emperor of this empire must be the Emperor of Constantinople.

In the Christian West the same role was increasingly assumed by the Pope of Rome, who claimed his presidial authority, on somewhat arbitrary grounds,[3] from Christ's commission to St. Peter. The pope is Christ's representative on earth and possesses the sum total of jurisdictional powers over the Church on earth; he is the final authority as to what constitutes the Christian faith and the supreme legislator converting celestial ordinances into positive laws on whose enforcement depends the Church's capacity to fulfill its purpose on earth.

The second consequence is that if the only way to salvation for the individual is through membership of the Christian society, and further, if the Christian society is represented in the ecclesiastical state, it follows that salvation depends upon submission and obedience to the laws and institutions of the state and to those who administer them. You cannot be a good Christian, that is to say, unless you are a good citizen of the Christian society, for it is only in and through this society that it is possible to achieve the good life. Moreover, the individual citizen can have no rights and privileges apart from this society or set over against it. This notion itself derives from an almost Aristotelian conception of the relationship between the whole and the parts of which it is composed. The part has identity and reality only insofar as it partakes of the whole, and is absorbed by it, while the whole alone possesses true reality and is, moreover, far more than the sum of its parts, existing outside them and complete without them. In the same way the Church as the Christian society exists over and above all its members; and while each member can only achieve significance insofar as he or she participates in the corporate life of the Church, the reverse is by no means the case: the single individual is of no account when compared with the status and claims of the Christian society as a whole. It is in the corporate reality of this society that the good life resides, and to share in this the individual must subject himself or herself totally to its external jurisdictional and

[3] See my *Church, Papacy and Schism* (London, 1978), pp. 29-30 and 54-7.

institutional forms and its divinely-appointed functionaries.

This view of the Church as above all a social and corporational organism with its own laws and its own government, and an imperial right to control all the affairs and all the citizens of what was potentially a universal society, was in western Christendom given vigorous expression and application in the great reforms which began in the age of Pope Gregory VII in the second half of the eleventh century and continued with greater or lesser momentum through the following centuries. Briefly, the scope of these reforms was to adapt the terrestrial form of the Church into a vast *instrumentum regni* linking all men and women with the Kingdom of God. Everything had to be brought under ecclesiastical control, all men and all lesser institutions, stretching from the emperors down to the village and the manor and even the serf's cottage. There was no distinction between the spiritual and temporal powers, Church and state: all power, all authority, resided exclusively in the *sacerdotium*, and ultimately in the pope as the head of the Church, and must be delegated from there. All uniqueness of local communities, of local sacramental centers, was to be absorbed in the all-embracing inclusiveness of the universal ecclesiastical corporation, all bishops were to be reduced to one bishop, the *dominus urbis et orbis*, with his seat at Rome. 6/28/12

At the same time, since all power resided in the pope as head of the Church and all government was ultimately ecclesiastical government, authority in all matters was only to be exercised either by the pope himself or by his personal representatives, the bishops and the priests. There was, that is to say, a vast clericalization of the Church, a vast clericalization of the Christian society. Since the organization and running of this society depended upon laws and decrees deriving from a knowledge of the Christian faith and its principles, and only the *sacerdotium*, with the pope at its head, was in a position to possess this knowledge, it followed that society must be governed by the *sacerdotium*.

It was the ordained that had to rule, it was they who were God's chosen people. The unordained could only be governed; they could only occupy an entirely subordinate position, their choice lying between being good citizens (that is to say, obedient to the laws of the Christian society) and so orientated towards heaven, or bad citizens (that is to say, offending against the divinely established order) and so going to hell. And as conformity to the laws of the Christian society was the hallmark of the good citizen, and so of the good Christian, the principles of divine righteousness had to be translated into a readily accessible moral code according to which the average man could regulate the conduct of his life.

Morality, in a purely abstract sense, became enormously important, and offense against the moral law had to be punished in the same way as offenses of a secular nature, for indeed there could now be no real distinction between them: both were offenses against the law of the state, and it was service to or offense against the well-being of the state that distinguished good from evil. It was the well-being of the whole of Christian society that now defined the purpose of the individual Christian, since individual well-being could be found only in serving the community as a whole. Such service was indeed both a political obligation and a divine command. It is here, in this necessity to serve the Christian society against its external and internal enemies to the point of martyrdom or the infliction of death, that lies the justification for the Church's central engagement in such unedifying enterprises as the crusades, the Holy Inquisition, and the burning of a St. Joan of Arc, a Savonarola, or a Giordano Bruno.

This overwhelming concern on the part of the Church to produce a Christian society did not of course mean that it completely lost its initiatory character. The sacraments remained the sacraments, and the contemplative traditions of the monasteries were never extinguished. Nor is the descent of the Church into the social order and its concern for every aspect of social life something against its nature: they are, as we saw, implicit in the initial revelation of Christianity itself. But first the initiatory character of the Church – personal and local, not social and collective – was pushed into the background. The contemplative life – the direct and personal contact with and experience of the Truth in a way that might be felt to challenge both the institutionalization of the Church and the idea that the pope is the sole repository of revelation on earth – became not the norm to which all should aspire, however remotely, but the hidden exception. Bishops and priests, it might be said, came to be regarded as of greater authority and higher in the Church than non-ordained holy men or prophets; they were looked to, and claimed to be looked to, as more representative of the Church than the latter. The prophetic element and the graces of personal spiritual knowledge, when they appeared to run counter, as they often did, to the dogmatic and moral order that the Church elaborated in its concern for the stability of society as a whole, were suppressed.

Indeed, it tended to be officially forgotten that there was a path of knowledge and love, or rather of knowledge through love, leading to divine wisdom that did not necessarily coincide at all with the path of merit. Uniformity, even if it meant a certain mediocrity in the living of the inner spiritual life, was to be preferred to the disturbing, possibly disruptive, insights of the visionary or the inspired poet; obedience to the moral law even in a purely external manner was to be preferred to obedience to the inner conscience or to the claim that submission to the divine will may, and often does, conflict with the official prescriptions for good Christian conduct.

Second, the manner in which this attempt to christianize society was carried out set in motion a series of chain reactions which were to result in exactly the opposite effect to the one intended. They were to result, in fact, in that de-sacramentalization of society which is our inheritance. For the claim of the pope to be the head of the totalitarian ecclesiastical state – to be both universal priest and king – and to concentrate in himself all spiritual and temporal power on earth, cut right across the claims of all emperors and kings, and effectively excluded the lay power from any real participation whatsoever in the government of society.

It was not that the temporal power disputed the basic conception of a universal Christian society; but it insisted that in achieving it, a separation had to be made between the spiritual and temporal spheres of authority and action, and it was this that Christ Himself had indicated when He commanded that the things of Caesar should be given to Caesar and when He Himself rejected an earthly crown. The *sacerdotium* held absolute authority in all matters spiritual, but emperor or king was responsible for the temporal life of his kingdom, and provided he acted in ways that were in keeping with the principles of Christianity the *sacerdotium* had no right to intervene. As Dante among others was to point out, the temporal power derives its authority directly from God, and though the Church might "crown" this authority, this did not signify that it was only by virtue of the Church's permission that it had any status at all. When the Church did, to all intents and purposes, claim that this is precisely what it did signify, the lay rulers were forced into revolt.

They revolted on the grounds that in the sphere of secular things they were subject to none but God in relation to the corporate societies over which they ruled. But since the *sacerdotium*, represented by the pope, claimed that as these lesser corporate societies were absorbed in the larger corporation of the whole Christian society, so the local authority of temporal rulers even in secular matters was absorbed in the universal spiritual and temporal sovereignty of the pope, the revolt in practical terms was compelled to take the form of seeking to establish the independence of the local kingdoms from papal interference. The result was the creation of a number of independent national kingdoms, some of which, in seeking purely political emancipation from papal control, were forced to reject that control in spiritual matters also, so inextricably entangled had the two spheres become in papal thought and practice. In this way the papal-imperialist conception of a Christian society resulted in the fragmentation of Christendom.

Nor was this all. The vast clericalization of the Church and the reduction of lay members as a whole to a position of complete subordination in which all freedom of individual conscience was suppressed, in its turn stimulated a revolt against the priesthood which corresponded to that of the lay rulers against the pope. For if God had created man in His own image, there were, it could be argued, good grounds for asserting that every individual, however fallen his state, had something of the divine in him, and through this stood in direct relationship to his Maker and was in this respect his own priest and, it might be added, his own confessor. Doubtless this argument, pushed to extremes, must lead to a state of complete anarchy in which everyone becomes his own judge of what is right and wrong. But the attempt to deny it altogether, and the reality upon which it is based, could only result in an assertion of individual independence in a way that eventually involved an attack on all priestly interference in matters of private conscience, on all priestly control over the innate liberty of the people of God to work out their salvation in their own way.

In this respect, the Church's efforts to create a supra-individual and all-embracing ecclesiastical state may be said to have set in motion a process of which the *reductio ad absurdum* is the modern secular democratic regime, of which the so-called rights of the individual and the liberties of the subject are the ethical cornerstones. When it is further remembered that in its anxiety to form this state, the Church was led increasingly to translate the metaphysical principles of the Christian religion into coercive moral rules to which everyone must be obedient, it is not surprising that one of the absurdities in which the revolt of the individual has resulted is the attempt to construct a moral code which has no basis in religion at all, and finally even to deny that there is any morality.

For when the metaphysical principles of a religion become of less effective account than the moral rules which derive in an entirely secondary manner from them, so that religion itself for all practical purposes becomes a matter of morality – of good conduct on a dualist right or wrong basis – and not primarily a matter of spiritual knowledge and understanding, then it will not be long before the principles themselves are forgotten. When this happens, religion degenerates into being an ethical system, of no greater, if no less, authority than any other such system; and the forms of religion, their living roots in their supra-terrestrial reality now ignored, degenerate into being no more, if no less, than instruments for the maintenance and preservation of a particular social order.

When this happens, the stage is set for the emergence of a purely secular society of which modern western society is an example.

Meanwhile, a somewhat similar process had been going on in eastern Christendom, with ultimately very similar consequences. From the time of the Council of Nicaea (325), at the conclusion of which the dissenting bishops were deposed and banished by Constantine the Great, the emperors openly and frequently interfered in the internal life of the Church, suppressing, dictating, and avenging, in order to subject it to the state and to make it serve the ends of their autocratic power. The Byzantine state considered itself a Christian state, and the emperors, when they subordinated the Church to their needs, regarded themselves as the instruments of God's will in forging and maintaining the structure of a potentially universal society. Their purpose was not in the least to destroy the Church – it constituted the keystone of their imperial ideology – but as it were to tame it, to bring it to heel and finally to confuse the ideas of the Kingdom of God and the kingdom of Caesar to the extent that they became virtually interchangeable.

The organism of the Church did not so much suffer from the external force of the state as secretly go along with it, from inside, in a process of identifying the Church with the empire, of erasing the borders between Church and state, and of affirming their indissoluble unity in the way we have already noted that the Patriarch of Constantinople affirmed it towards the end of the fourteenth century. The consummation of this process was achieved in the reforms of Peter the Great of Russia (reigned 1682-1725), through which the Church was effectively reduced to being little more than the department of state – the "Department of the Orthodox Confession" – in the imperial government responsible for religious affairs. That Peter had to kill a disloyal patriarch while implementing his reforms is entirely consistent with previous imperial policy as inaugurated by Constantine the Great when he deposed and banished the dissenting bishops at the Council of Nicaea – it was simply the price the Church had to pay for its "symphony" or "union" with the state.

It is by no means accidental that the process set in motion by

Constantine the Great, sustained throughout the Byzantine period and in imperial Russia and culminating in the communist revolution in 1917, should result – as did the corresponding papal campaign in western Christendom – in the attempt to establish a universal society on a purely secular and materialist basis. Both in the Christian West and in the Christian East, the Church's cooperation in a process that demanded attributing a sacred character to the forms and institutions of the state has inevitably resulted in the secularization of these forms and institutions. Reciprocally, the secularization of these forms and institutions in its turn leads to attributing to them a kind of pseudo-sacredness; and the totalitarian secular state takes the place of the Church as the welder of a potentially universal human society.

What is the upshot of all this? It is that the un-christening or secularization of modern western society is a direct consequence of a loss of Christian consciousness, first among the official guardians of the Church and then among the congregation of the faithful; and that this loss has expressed itself in, and was further stimulated by, an attempt to transform the Church on earth into a vast corporational organization concerned above all with the creation of a universal Christian society. As a result of this attempt, carried out in the way it was carried out, the essential nature of the Church was pushed into the background. Understanding of, and concern for, the metaphysical principles of Christian doctrine became more and more confined to those of its aspects, and their moral derivatives, that could be expressed in forms, verbal or other, applicable to Christian society as a whole; and the presence of those who not only were themselves illuminated by these principles, but also were able, directly or indirectly, to influence in their light every aspect of life, was discouraged and attenuated, and even suppressed, with the consequence that the living reality of the Church on earth itself became increasingly attenuated and even suppressed.

In the face of what appears to be the Church's subordination of its essential initiatory and contemplative purpose to the pursuit of establishing a universal Christian society, it is pertinent to ask: by virtue of what is Constantine the Great acknowledged by the

Church to be a saint? By virtue of the fact that he used the sword of Caesar to compel his subjects to submit to the Christian faith? But was it not precisely this sword that the devil offered to Christ in the third temptation in the wilderness? By what contortion of values is that which is presented in the Gospel as the instrument of the devil acclaimed by the Church as the weapon of Christian righteousness?

The whole tragic issue is presented to us with unequivocal clarity by Dostoyevsky in his tale of the Grand Inquisitor. Why, the Inquisitor asks of Christ, did you reject that last gift of the devil, the sword of Caesar? And he continues: "By accepting that third counsel of the mighty spirit you would have accomplished all that man seeks on earth, that is to say, whom to worship, to whom to entrust his conscience, and how at last to unite all in a common, harmonious and incontestable ant-hill, for the need of universal unity is the third and last torment of men. Mankind as a whole has always striven to organize itself into a world state. . . . By accepting the world and Caesar's purple, you would have founded the world state and given universal peace. For who is to wield dominion over men if not those who have taken possession of their consciences and in whose hands is their bread? And so we [the Church] have taken the sword of Caesar and, having taken it, we of course rejected you and followed *him* [the devil]."[4] In so doing did not the Church commit itself to denying the Christian revelation at its heart?

The Church has failed in its imperial venture, and the world that once constituted Christendom has left the Church. The dream which the Church failed to fulfill has been taken over by such secular and materialist organizations as the European Community; but now the attempt to fulfill it is in terms that demand that the members of this potentially world-wide union betray the last vestiges of their spiritual identity and human dignity, and surrender to the first of the devil's temptations in the wilderness – to live by bread alone and not by every word that comes from the mouth of God.

[4] *The Brothers Karamazov*, Book 5.5 (trans. David Magarshack).

Yet at the same time as the world has left the Church, the Church appears to have left the world. Its "witness" in the face of the depredations whose inroads have brought us to the present de-christianization of practically every aspect of life, public and private, can only be described as lamentable. It is not the Church that has spoken up against the giant monstrosity of modern industrialism, still less against the inhuman perversion of thought, represented by the whole modern scientific movement, that it presupposes and that fosters it. It has made no pronouncement that can be said to reach anywhere near the heart of what we call the ecological crisis, for which indeed, as we shall see in a later chapter, certain of its own theologians prepared the way. The task of telling the truth in the face of these manifestations of the secular, materialistic spirit has been left over the last two centuries to people like Blake, Dostoyevsky, Yeats, and other such prophetic individuals.

Of course the Church continues to bear witness through its liturgical mysteries and through personal sanctity and prayer; and in spite of secularization and even if not directly through the Church, Christian principles continue to be operative, although on a declining scale, in such spheres as the making of moral choices, respect for human and other life, courtesy, and the search for non-material, non-worldly, and eternal values. But the spirit that aspires to transform life and the world appears to have abandoned it. The Church simply stumbles along at the heels of the world, adopting ideas and practices entirely alien to it but which in spite of it have shaped the dominant forms of our contemporary society. The truth is that the Church is profoundly in bondage to secular culture. At the same time, the failure of the Church to conquer the world and to spiritualize its culture is seen as a rejection of the Church by the world, as an unforgivable act of disobedience on the part of the world. Hence the Church has now virtually washed its hands of the world: the world and its culture can now go to the devil in their own way. That is simply a just punishment for their apostasy.

The other side of this coin is that the Church and the Eucharist have lost their meaning as an integrating and creative focus of communal life. From being a "common cause" they have become a means of individual salvation. The Christian's own religiousness has become his chief preoccupation. And in this context the concept of the Christian's responsibility for the fate of the world has inescapably lost all meaning.[5] This is not merely the tragedy of Christianity and the Church; it is the tragedy of the world itself, or at least of the area of the world that once constituted Christendom.

For life in this world – in this secularized, materialized, techno-scientific world – is a life of increasing despair and misery. Whether we like it or not, it is impossible to live a human form of life without God and without a sense of the presence of God informing all our actions as well as the social modes within which we live. It is impossible to live a human form of life in a world that lacks meaning, that lacks reality, that imprisons us within a welter of artifacts of an ugliness and banality that defy description, within types of work that from computer technology and the mass media downward not only do not require from us the use of anything that properly can be called intelligence and imagination but that demean and shatter our dignity, stifle every true creative aspiration within us, and reduce us to little more than ciphers and automatons in a *danse macabre* of ignorance and fatuity.

This is the tragic dénouement of life in a society whose dominant forms, like those of our modern society, reflect a world-view in which to all intents and purposes God plays no part. For without a living participation in the Divine and in the absolute and unconditional values that mirror its reality, a society and its culture end in denying themselves and degenerating into a counterfeit that may have the appearance of some kind of culture but which is essentially false, worthless, and inhuman.

Where the area of the world represented by what was once Christendom is concerned, the only means for recovering such participation is the sacred tradition of Christianity. We can only emerge from the terrifying blind alley in which we find ourselves and once more perceive the true light which we have denied and

[5] See my *Rape of Man and Nature* (Ipswich, 1987).

cut ourselves off from by refounding our life on a religious basis, and for us the only religion that can provide such a basis is Christianity. Christianity and the possibility for us of spiritual and cultural renewal are inseparable.

Christianity is the religion that lies at the root of every significant manifestation of our culture over the last fifteen hundred years and more. It lies at the root of our architecture – from our cathedrals and numberless country churches down to the humble cottages of our villages – of our art, our music, our painting, our poetry throughout this period, shaping and informing their beauty and meaning. It impregnates the hills and valleys of our landscape through the presences and sanctity of the saints and the holy men and women who once inhabited them – presences which we may have forgotten and do not honor but which are ready to move into our lives as soon as we turn towards them and invoke their blessing and their succor. It is the only sacred tradition we possess that is capable of providing us with the living sacramental and liturgical forms of worship essential to the full activation of any genuine spiritual life – forms wrought and consecrated by Christ Himself, however they may subsequently have been elaborated in the life of the Church.

Such forms cannot be invented by man; nor can they be replaced by those of other sacred traditions that are not part and parcel of our whole spiritual and cultural inheritance: to attempt to replace them in this way would simply result in psychological dislocation and schizophrenia. In short, without Christianity and the Church our world – the world that once constituted Chistendom – is doomed to disintegration and nemesis. Only Christianity and the Christian Church are capable of diffusing throughout the social order that spiritual influence which alone can counterbalance and overcome the otherwise uncontrollable forces of sterility and disruption.

Yet the Church will not be in a position to diffuse such an influence until it has accomplished its own internal renewal. Such a renewal has two aspects. The first consists in overcoming and freeing itself from its imperio-ecclesiastic inheritance and its corollary, that the relationship between the Church and the world is conceived in terms of suzerainty and submission. Not only must the Church renounce every idea of itself forming, or of itself being party to the formation of, a universal Christian state, as well as the idea of contributing to the formation of any kind of world state. It must also renounce the idea that it should constitute a kind of state within a state. It must renounce, that is to say, the idea that Christianity subscribes to the exercise of coercive authoritarianism, whatever form this may take.

This means that where the Church in the Christian West is concerned there must be an explicit and conscious renunciation of the kind of claim summarized and dogmatized in 1302 by Pope Boniface VIII in his famous bull, *Unam sanctam*: "Urged by faith we are bound to believe in one Holy Church, Catholic and also Apostolic...", outside which there is "neither salvation nor remission of sins", as well as of the claim implicit in this bull that the Church is potentially the universal body politic of which the pope is the head. It also means that it must explicitly and consciously renounce the type of infallibility defined by the Roman Catholic Church at the First Vatican Council (1870). This in its turn means that both in the Christian West and in the Christian East (where the Ecumenical Councils of bishops presume a similar infallibility), the Church as a whole must renounce the claim that the Christian revelation constitutes the sole and exclusive revelation 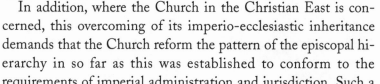 of the universal Truth.

In addition, where the Church in the Christian East is concerned, this overcoming of its imperio-ecclesiastic inheritance demands that the Church reform the pattern of the episcopal hierarchy in so far as this was established to conform to the requirements of imperial administration and jurisdiction. Such a pattern now constitutes a total anachronism, in that, for instance, bishoprics in the main urban centers of a long vanished empire that were accorded the rank of patriarchates still retain a status for which the *raison d'être* (purely a matter of state interest in the first place) can no longer in any way be justified. At the same time the panoply of grandeur and sovereignty with which the bishops were invested in imperial times and still assume is quite out of accord with the understanding that each Christian is as equally a representative of the royal priesthood as every other Christian, clerical or non-clerical.

The second aspect of the renewal, without which the Church will be powerless to play its role in the transfiguration of the world and in bringing the world into the Kingdom of God, consists in reaffirming and giving pride of place to its essential gnostic and contemplative nature. For ultimately the diffusion of a spiritual influence through the whole social order will depend not upon any kind of crusade or "Christian renewal movement" undertaken by the serried ranks of clergy and congregation, but upon the presence of those of whom it is said "Blessed is the kingdom wherein dwells one of them, for in an instant they will do more lasting good than all outward action has ever done." It will depend, that is to say, upon the presence of saints and sages, holy men and women, inspired poets and prophets, whether they are affiliated to the Christian tradition or to some other sacred tradition, whose lives are dedicated to the pursuit of spiritual vision and the glorification of God. And it is by following the path of gnosis and contemplation – the mystical path – that such people become total offerings, holocausts, of divine light and life.

This means that the Church is unlikely to foster and suscitate the presence of such people to any great extent unless it once again distinguishes its essential character from, and reaffirms it in the face of, those theories and practices that have reduced it to becoming little more than a social institution of Christian welfare oscillating between extremes of senile protection, modernism, and effete imitation; with a teaching of vague, ill-assorted and eviscerated theological notions compounded with negative moral precepts. Whether it is able to do this remains to be seen. All that can be said is that unless the Church is able to do it, and unless in its terrestrial form it becomes essentially the expression of a spiritual wisdom and illumination untrammeled by these theories and practices, then we cannot justifiably talk of possessing a human society at all, let alone one which is, in any sense of the word, Christian.

AMEN!.   8/10/12

Chapter Three

Christianity and Other Sacred Traditions

Towards the end of the last chapter I remarked that one of the conditions of any renewal within the Christian Church is that the Church renounces the claim that the Christian revelation constitutes the sole and exclusive revelation of the universal Truth. For it has to be admitted – with regret, not to say with shame – that in the past, Christians by and large have regarded all non-Christian religions and all non-Christian religious experience as so obviously suspect as to be either too dangerous to study or else not worth the trouble of being studied. Indeed, the characteristic Christian reaction to non-Christian religions has been a mixture of repugnance, fear, and aggression.

At the same time it is said that the Incarnation of the one true God in the historical figure of Jesus Christ and the consequent founding of the Church on earth represent a radical change in the whole nature of reality, and so make all previous religious doctrine spurious and outmoded, since such doctrine relates to an order of things that has now been displaced and superseded. The only doctrine that now authentically represents the new order of things is that proclaimed by the Church on the basis of the new revelation of the Truth as expressed in the Gospels. Christianity is the one true religion, and access to it is possible only through subscription to the Christian creed and membership of the Christian Church. Salvation is an exclusive prerogative of Christians, and is automatically precluded by adherence to any doctrine other than that proclaimed by the Church.

Yet today, when the age-old barriers between the major sacred traditions of the world have broken down, the question arises as to whether Christianity is so inherently exclusive as it has claimed to be. Is belief in such exclusivity incumbent upon a Christian? Can we be Christian and at the same time recognize that salvation is equally possible without formal membership of the Christian Church? And if we can be, what must be the positive theological grounds for this recognition, since clearly unless it is based on principles compatible with Christian dogma it can be no more than an expression of goodwill and may even be no more than a matter of sentimentality?

This question is not simply a practical one. It concerns more than the question of Christian mission and world peace. It is a question about the Truth itself. If the Spirit is present and operative only within the framework or the bounds of the Christian Church as a historical institution, then the way in which the spiritual life is lived is one thing; if He is present and operative in many other forms throughout the world, it is quite another. It has been well-said[1] that in practice and in content, love is one thing if Christianity is exclusive, and a very different thing if Christianity is inclusive. Obviously a dialogue conducted on whatever level can never have any serious meaning if, in the minds of those who engage in it, there continues to lurk the suspicion that the non-Christian religions are all at heart corrupt and that what they claim to be their highest perfection and their ultimate fulfillment is nothing but a form of illusion.

It might be said that few intelligent Christians retain such a suspicion today. Be that as it may, it is none the less true that a certain legalistic dogmatism that has long prevailed in the Christian world and was based largely on ignorance of other religions still persists. And, more important, there is still an absence of an understanding that can accommodate and justify a recognition of

[1] By Georges Khodr, in his article "Christianity in a Pluralistic World" (*Sobornost*, Summer 1971, pp. 166-74), to which I am indebted here. I am also indebted to William C. Chittick's essay, "A Sufi Approach to Religious Diversity", published in *Religion of the Heart*, ed. S. H. Nasr and W. Stoddart (Foundation of Traditional Studies, Washington D.C., 1991), pp. 50-90.

the spiritual authenticity of non-Christian traditions in positive theological terms.

What possibilities for such an understanding does the Christian tradition appear to offer? Here the starting point must be the Acts of the Apostles, which is indeed the first book of Christian ecclesiology. In Acts (10:35) it is stated that "in every nation the man who is god-fearing and does what is right is acceptable." Barnabas and Paul tell the people of Lystra that "In past ages God allowed all nations to go their own way"; and yet, they add, "He has not left you without some clue as to His nature" (Acts 14:16-17). There is among the Gentiles a yearning for the "unknown God" (Acts 17:23), a search for God who "is not far from each one of us, for in Him we live and move and in Him we exist" (Acts 17:27-8).

This indicates some degree of openness to the non-Christian world. But there is no sign that this world is given any positive theological status. Rather the opposite would appear to be the case, for "gods made by human hands are not gods at all", the assumption being that all gods other than the Christian God are made by human hands. Indeed, Paul is quite categorical: "a false god has no existence in the real world" (1 Cor. 8:4); and in Revelation, a very ecclesiological book, any non-Christian religion is identified as a lie (21:8) and as a deceit (22:15). It would seem therefore that the New Testament simply continues the line of the Old Testament, and that for the apostles of Christ, as for the prophets of Israel, religions other than their own are an unmitigated abomination. The famous exception to this general rule is Paul's speech to the Athenians, in which he tells them that they worship the true God without recognizing Him, for His true identity has not been revealed to them. In other words, they were Christians without knowing it.

Thus from the beginning there appear to be two different attitudes to the non-Christian world. First, there is the entirely negative attitude inherited from Judaism, in which the gods are identified with man-made images of wood or stone and viewed as demons fighting against the one true God. This attitude progressively hardened as dogmatics crystallized into an official body of doctrine and as the Church and Christianity assumed an explicit institutional identity. Evidence of this hardening is provided by the battle against heresy, which aroused in the minds of apologists of all periods a hostility to error often amounting to hatred. Moreover, the intolerance of Christians towards each other had direct repercussions on their attitude to non-Christian religions, and this only made the hatred worse. One must either save the other man or kill him.

Yet alongside this negative attitude is the more positive attitude implicit in Paul's speech to the Athenians. This attitude was given a basis in doctrine by many Christian theologians. As one might expect, it was related to the understanding of the divine Logos and His incarnation in human form. For Justin Martyr, for instance, a seed of the Logos – the *logos spermatikos* – is implanted in the whole human race and throughout creation before Christ's birth in the flesh,[2] so that those who lived according to the Logos, like Socrates and Herakleitos among the Greeks, and Abraham and Elijah and many others among the "barbarians", were Christians before Christ.[3]

Clement of Alexandria sees the whole of mankind as a unity and as beloved of God. Basing himself on Hebrews (1:11), he affirms that it was not only to Israel but to the whole of mankind that "God spoke in former times in fragmentary and varied fashion". Mankind as a whole is subject to a process of education, a pedagogy. The whole world "has had as its teacher Him who filled the universe with His energy in creation, salvation, beneficence, lawgiving, prophecy, teaching and indeed all other instruction".[4] Within this divine economy, philosophy has a special role: it is not merely a stepping-stone to a specifically Christian philosophy. It is even "given to the Greeks as their Testament".[5] Greek and by implication all other non-Christian philosophies are fragments of a single whole which is the Logos. And this "living according to

[2] *Apologies*, II, 8.
[3] Ibid. I, 46.
[4] *Protrepticus* XI.
[5] *Stromateis* V:8.3.

the Logos" that is a capacity inherent in all peoples, Christian and non-Christian, is not simply to be equated with living rationally, nor is the Logos implanted in creation merely equivalent to the "rational law" of the medieval Scholastics; for "the Logos of God... ordered our world and, above all, this microcosm man, through the Holy Spirit".[6]

Faced with the question of whether what Christ's mission signifies is a reaffirmation of an understanding of things that had always been known, and by some fully known, but had been forgotten or distorted, or a radical change in the nature of reality itself, and hence in the nature of what is to be known, Origen chooses the first alternative. There is, he writes, "a coming of Christ before his corporeal coming, and this is his spiritual coming for those men who had attained a certain level of perfection, for whom the whole plenitude of the times was already present, as for example the patriarchs, Moses and the prophets who saw the glory of Christ."[7] The prophets, he adds, "have received the grace of the plenitude of Christ..." and "led by the Spirit they have attained, after having been introduced to the figures (*typoi*), to the vision itself of the truth".[8] For St. Maximos the Confessor, before His advent in the flesh the Logos of God dwelt among the patriarchs and prophets in a spiritual manner, prefiguring the mysteries of His advent.[9]

A similar attitude is to be found in certain western theologians. A figure as venerable as St. Augustine affirmed that since the dawn of human history men were to be found within Israel and outside Israel who had partaken of the mystery of salvation, and that what was known to them was in fact the Christian religion, without it having been revealed to them that this was the case. And St. Irenaeus sums up this line of patristic thought when he says "there is only one God who from beginning to end, through various economies, comes to the help of mankind".[10]

[6] *Protrepticus* I:5.
[7] *Commentary in John*, I, 7.
[8] Ibid. VI, 3.
[9] *PG* 90, II37BC.
[10] *Adversus haereses*, III, 12.13.

Complementing and underpinning this doctrine that prior to His advent in the flesh the Logos is present in man and in all creation, and may be apprehended by all men irrespective of time and place, is an understanding of the universality of the Incarnation itself. This understanding affirms that through the Incarnation the divine Logos incorporates Himself not in the body of a single human being alone but in the totality of human nature, in mankind as a whole, in creation as a whole. Thus St. Cyril of Jerusalem writes: "Not in vain does John assert that the Logos came and dwelt among us, for in this way he teaches us the great mystery that we are all in Christ and that the common personality of man is brought back to life by His assumption of it. The new Adam is so called because he acquires for all human nature all that pertains to happiness and glory, just as the old Adam acquired what pertains to its corruption and shame. Through the medium of one the Logos came to dwell in all, so that the only Son of God being established in power, His dignity should be shed upon the whole human race by the holiness of the Spirit; and thus should be verified in each one of us that saying of Scriptures: 'I said you are Gods and sons of the most High' . . . The Logos dwells in us, in that one temple He took through us, so that we should possess all things in Him and He should bring us all back to the Father in one Body."[11] Or as the Pseudo-Chrysostom puts it, "By the sacrifice of Christ the first man was saved, that man who is in all of us."[12] This means that all human nature – in fact, all created being – participates in divine life, whether single individuals are aware of it or not. Each single human being, through energizing in his individual life that original Adamic nature in each of us which has been fully restored or resurrected or transfigured in and through the incarnation of the Logos, can realize his own participation in the life and character of ultimate Reality itself.

Unfortunately this understanding, rooted in a doctrine of the universal Logos inherent in the creation that He has brought into existence, succumbed to an ecclesiology which identified the

[11] *PG* 73, 161-4.
[12] *PG* 59, 725, 723.

Church on earth more or less exclusively with a corporate collective institution operating within history and with a definite outlook on history. In short, ecclesiology was historicized. The Church took on an increasingly sociological form, identified with Christendom. Christendom – the Christian society or the Church – was the dwelling-place of peace, light, and knowledge. The non-Christian world was the dwelling-place of war, darkness, demons. The area outside the Church, outside the historical, institutional, sociologically defined community of the Church, had either to be christianized – saved by being incorporated into Christendom – or it would perish. Non-Christians, heretics, and schismatics had to be brought into or returned to the Church by all means available – by missionary activity, by proselytism, or by cultural colonialism when persecution and war and military occupation became impracticable or unacceptable – for only in this way might the reality of "one flock and one shepherd" be achieved.

The established institutional Church becomes the center of the world. The history of the Christian Church, as a sociological entity, becomes history itself. What occurs in the experience of the Christian world fashions history. The rest of the world is a-historical until it accepts and adopts Christian experience and Christian modes. This experience and these modes are in fact destined to dominate the world. Non-Christian religions – religions such as Hinduism, Buddhism, and Islam – are regarded as by definition inferior and even diabolical. Consequently those who adhere to these religions can be saved only by becoming historicized and by adopting the superior hierarchical form of Christianity. The rest of the world must come into the time-continuum of the Church through a salvation achieved by the universal extension of the Christian way of life founded on the authority of the Christian tradition.

This attitude stems from a linear view of history bound up with a monolithic ecclesiology which sees Christianity as a series or succession of salvation events destined to culminate in the appearance of Christ as the end of the history of the Old Covenant and as the end of human history. It is a view which tacitly ignores the idea of an ever-present eternity that transcends history. Similarly it ignores the idea of the Church in which Christ the Logos is seen, not merely chronologically but ontologically, as the immanent principle of the mystery in which the divine is disclosed at every point of time and in every creature, so that every human being and every created thing is a theophany and stands in an immediate, trans-historical relationship to the divine archetype of which he or it is the manifestation. Concomitantly, it also tacitly ignores the idea of the universality of the Incarnation: that the divine event signified by the Incarnation is not simply the incorporation of the Logos in the body of a single historical human being but also, and more importantly, an incorporation of the divine in the human as such, so there cannot be an individual human being of whom the Logos is not the ultimate subject, however unactualized He may be in any particular case.

Finally, this view of history and the type of theology that lies behind it are basically anti-contemplative. For the mentality nourished on this theology, contemplation is little more than a form of escape from the "real" world, a retreat from history and from time that is selfish and ultimately barren. What is important for this mentality is the idea that the Logos of God has broken through the structures of a collapsing world to establish a new eon, a new age. Contemplation, with its abstraction, its turning inwards towards the self in the expectation of a pure and gnostic light, is therefore regarded as but a refinement of the old and unregenerate eon, before God entered into history, and thus as having little to do with the Christian Kingdom of God. We are not called to purity of heart or to the gifts of wisdom and understanding. We are not invited to that virginity and simplicity of spirit which even now apprehends the light of the Transfiguration. We are simply asked to wait for the Second Coming of the Kyrios and for the definitive establishment of the Kingdom. Our contemplation should take no other form than the song of praise and the pure and spotless sacrifice which we continue to offer in memory of the Lord "until He comes".

This description, if taken in an absolute sense, would of course

be an exaggeration; but it none the less remains true that the major thrust of post-medieval Christianity has largely displaced the
contemplative vision of things expressed by people like St. Symeon
the New Theologian or Meister Eckhart and the tradition to which
they belong. This makes dialogue with other religions, especially
with the dominantly contemplative Asiatic religions, virtually impossible. In fact, if Christians are to integrate other religions,
positively and creatively, with their own doctrinal perspective they
have to go beyond and discard this concept of linear "salvation
history" which represents the final flowering of that negative attitude of exclusivity which Christianity has inherited from Judaism
and which, as we saw, is already explicit in the Acts of the Apostles.

This attitude must be replaced by a theology that affirms the
positive attitude implicit in the writings of Justin Martyr, Clement of Alexandria, Origen, the Cappadocians, St. Maximos the
Confessor, and many others. The economy of the divine Logos
cannot be reduced to His manifestation in the figure of the historical Jesus: the idea of God-manhood possesses a significance
that is intrinsic to human nature as such, quite apart from its manifestation in a historical figure who exemplifies it. Correspondingly
the Church cannot be reduced to a visible institutional and sociological form. The Church, in Origen's words, is the cosmos of the
cosmos. It is the innermost reality of humanity and of creation
itself, even if this is not recognized. It is the *locus* within which the
Christic mystery is continually unfolded. It is also the *locus* of the
Pentecostal event – of the manifestation of the Holy Spirit who in
person reveals to creation the interior presence of the Logos.

It is the task of Christians and above all of Christian theologians to recognize and affirm this presence and this mystery not
only within the boundaries of the historical Church, but also in
those other testimonies to this presence and this mystery that are
to be found in other religions. It matters little whether the religion
in question has a historical character or not. It is superfluous to
ask whether it regards itself as compatible with the Christian Gospel. The Logos in His *kenosis*, His self-emptying, is hidden
everywhere, and the types of His reality, whether in the forms of

persons or teachings, will not be the same outside the Christian world as they are within it. Yet these types are equally authentic: any deep reading of another religion is a reading of the Logos, of Christ. It is the Logos who is received in the spiritual illumination of a Brahmin, a Buddhist, or a Moslem. Indeed, if the tree is known by its fruits, only spiritual blindness can prevent us from recognizing that those who live and yearn for the Divine in all nations already receive the peace the Lord gives to all whom He loves (Lk. 2:14).

Yet given that Christians themselves are willing to recognize the implications of the doctrine of the universal Logos, and that sacred traditions other than their own are divinely-instituted ways of spiritual realization, this still does not resolve the problem of accounting for the divergencies between these various traditions. How are we to account for the appearance of conflict and disagreement between their doctrinal forms? We could say that there are many different Gods, and that each God has an individual and distinct form in which He expresses Himself. But this, quite apart from the other problems it raises, still does not get us much further forward, for we are then faced with the question of determining which of these Gods is the Supreme God, for clearly, if things are to have any coherence at all, there cannot be more than one God who is supreme. If on the other hand, we start with the idea that there is one Supreme God or Reality, one absolute and all-embracing Truth (and this in one form or another is the common confession of all the great traditions), how is it that this Truth reveals itself in forms that appear to be so incompatible?

One answer to this question is that these divergencies or apparent incompatibilities in the external forms in which the Supreme God reveals Himself do not correspond to any inherent oppositions in His own nature, but to the difference in aptitudes, capacities, and temperaments of the various groups of humanity to which each particular form is addressed. Truth is one; but in expressing Itself in a way which is accessible to the human intelligence, It has to take account not only of the limitations of the human state as such, but also of the various, though relative, divisions within mankind that are themselves expressive of various facets of the divine plenitude. Put in its broadest terms, one might say that the differences between the various traditions are due to the differences in the cultural *milieux* for which each is providentially intended and to which each has therefore to be adapted.

What is involved in this proposition? Behind the changing appearances of the phenomenal world – of the world as it appears to us through the organs of our senses – is an underlying metaphysical order, a series of changeless and universal principles from which all derives and on which all depends. Our life, in any true sense of the word, in its turn depends not only on the recognition, but also on the realization of these principles. But because of the inherent limitations of the human state, we cannot recognize and realize them directly, in their naked essence. We can only be gradually, and stage by stage, initiated into them. This is where the various traditional forms come in: they are the indispensable aids and supports whereby we can be led into the full recognition and realization of the metaphysical principles on which our proper life depends.

At different times and different places, the Supreme, either through direct revelation of a Messenger or Avatar, or through the inspired activity of sages and prophets, has condescended to clothe the naked essence of these principles in exterior forms, doctrinal and ritual, in which they can be grasped by us and through which we can gradually be led into a plenary awareness of their preformal reality. These forms may be many – in a sense there may be as many ways to God as there are individual human beings – but beneath this multiformity may always be discerned, by those who have eyes to see, the essential unity of the unchanging, non-manifest, and timeless principles themselves.

This of course is not in itself a new idea. One need go no further than the western Gnostics to find it applied to an extreme and often, it would seem, ludicrous degree. Basing themselves on the notion of the essential unity of the Truth underlying the various forms of religious myth and symbol, they felt justified in interpreting these latter in the light of the former. Thus Zeus, Dionysos, Orpheus, Epimenides, the mysteries of Eleusis, the laments for Attis, all had their equivalents in the Christian cult. Adonis, Endymion, Attis were all images of the soul, and myths about them could all be interpreted on this supposition. Support for such interpretations might be found in a passage from the Bible (torn violently out of context) and in Assyrian, Phrygian, and Egyptian mysteries. Oceanos is a symbol like the Jordan; the cup found in Benjamin's sack of wheat is the mystic cup celebrated by Anacreon; and so on. One Gnostic sect had in its meeting-place crowned images of Pythagoras, Plato, Aristotle, and Christ. It is the fashion nowadays to pour scorn on such Gnostic assimilations of, and speculations from, one religious form to another, and indeed the tendency was to make a kind of amalgam out of all the religions. But it should be remembered that at their base was an assumption similar to the one of which we have been speaking: that "all truth is one"; that it is this Truth which underlies the diversity of its formal expressions; and that he who is initiated into a realization of the preformal nature of the eternal principles of this Truth is thereby qualified to discern the essential unity which these formal expressions represent. It is with these presuppositions too that those who today accept the "traditionalist" or "syncretist" position seek to resolve the appearance of diversity, and often of conflict and disagreement, between the traditional forms that, in spite of everything, still function in the modern world.

This way of looking at things may help those who are affiliated to a particular religious tradition to admit that their tradition does not possess a monopoly of the universal Truth, and that traditions other than their own may very well be revelations of the same Truth given quite a different form because of the differences in aptitudes, capacities and temperament of the various groups of humanity to which each particular form is addressed. There is the Truth as it is "laid up in heaven" in its preformal and purely metaphysical state; and there is this Truth as it is when translated into the various doctrines and symbolic languages of the human race, each of which by definition possesses its own color and limitations, although this does not in any way prevent it from being an authentic language through which one can approach a knowledge of the Truth in its universal and unarticulated stage. After all, this is not so very different from what happens on the purely human plane when we translate, for instance, an abstract philosophical idea from one language to another.

Yet although in this way the door may be closed to the claim of the unique exclusivity of any one particular tradition, it is still left open to what is virtually a disguised form of this same claim to exclusivity, and that is the claim that one particular tradition is a superior, and perhaps even infinitely superior, revelation of universal Truth, and in this respect is, if not exclusive, at least so preeminent that to all intents and purposes it is unique. For while it is one thing to say that all traditional forms ultimately express the same universal Truth, it is quite another to say that they all express it to the same degree. Thus in spite of the first proposition, one is still left with the question of determining whether or not one particular tradition represents it more fully than the others.

This question, it is true, need never become acute until and unless there is some conflict or disagreement between the traditions themselves; and even then, once again in theory, this is only possible where there has been some faulty interpretation, so that it may be resolved the moment one has situated it correctly. But when it comes to the point, it does seem to be impossible to avoid making, implicitly or explicitly, a qualitative judgment about the relative completeness or incompleteness of the various traditions, and attributing to the principles of one tradition a certain superiority or priority.

In effect, to resolve an apparent conflict or disagreement between traditions one requires initial principles in the light of which it can be resolved. These principles one may say are "laid up in heaven", and this is a justified attitude as long as one is content to leave the apparent conflict or disagreement to be resolved "in heaven". But as soon as one seeks to resolve it through humanly intelligible interpretation, then one must bring one's principles down from heaven and recognize them in a humanly intelligible form – in, that is, the doctrinal form of one of the traditions which, because of its superior nature, is capable of resolving the conflict or disagreement with which one is presented.

Thus the Gnostics, to return to them, although they claimed to interpret in the light of universal principles, actually recognized these as most fully enshrined in a form of Greek religious speculation allied to the Christian religion, and this became for them the tradition according to whose criteria they interpreted and resolved the appearance of conflict and disagreement between the various religious forms. Or the Neoplatonist Proklos, although he claimed to speak in the name of "the truth which is as old as the universe", actually recognized this truth as most adequately revealed in the inspired writings of Plato and in the Chaldaean Oracles uttered through their servant Julianos, the theurgist "whom it is unlawful to disbelieve" (though even so, according to the later Neoplatonist Psellos, the perfect coincidence of the inner content of these two forms of revelation was due to the fact that Julianos had been in consultation with Plato's ghost); and this for Proklos became the tradition. Or in our own time, those who seek a primordial and universal tradition behind the particular religious forms tend to see its principles contained in essence in one particular form – in, for instance, Neoplatonism, or the Vedanta, or in some form which is a fusion of several forms.

It is worth examining more closely quite how this shift from the idea that there is what we have called a paradigmatic body of Truth or of universal principles "laid up in heaven" to the idea that this is most fully expressed in one particular formal tradition, comes about, for it is the crux of the difficulty with which we are dealing. The assumption, we said, is that behind all traditional religions lies the same metaphysical Truth or, conversely, that each tradition embodies in diverse ways the same unchanging and eternal principles. The Truth itself is therefore what is truly universal, while the various traditions at best amount to a translation of this Truth into a humanly intelligible mode. Thus the traditions themselves are not universal or, rather, are only universal to the degree to which they participate in the Truth itself. Theoretically then there is this paradigmatic body of total and disembodied Truth, and there are the various traditions over which it stands and within which it is partially enshrined.

Yet when, we said, any conflict or disagreement between the traditions arises, one is faced with the question of deciding where the Truth is most fully represented: which tradition, that is, most fully represents the disembodied and universal principles. To answer this question implies that one is already in possession of the knowledge according to which it can be answered: clearly to discern to what degree a particular tradition is universal already presupposes that one has the knowledge which makes it possible for one to do this, this knowledge necessarily being no less than the highest humanly possible. It is precisely here that what one might call a *petitio principii* is involved and that the shift in question takes place.

As we have seen, the degree of knowledge one possesses will be that represented in the tradition from which one has obtained it: otherwise one would not be in possession of it. To say then that this is the highest degree of knowledge, the fullest expression of the Truth possible (which one must say if one is to carry out the act of discernment with which we are concerned), and consequently that the tradition through which one has obtained it is a universal tradition in the full meaning of the words, is simply to argue in a circle. It is to use as one's criteria of what constitutes the highest degree of knowledge, and hence of where this is fully represented, precisely those principles enshrined in the tradition from which one has obtained them in the first place.

One may then go on to recognize that these same principles are also represented fully in other traditions, or even in a superlative way in one other particular tradition, so that it is this latter and not one's own tradition that one regards as the most purely universal in character. But this does not alter the fact that the assumption that the degree of understanding and knowledge one has obtained through a particular tradition is the highest there is, is an arbitrary assumption or an act of faith; and that had one obtained one's knowledge and understanding from a tradition whose basic principles do not, at least on the level of human intelligibility, harmonize with those of one's own tradition, one might, and probably would, have been led to quite a different assessment of what constitutes the highest understanding and knowledge and hence in which tradition they are most fully expressed.

Does this mean that the proposition with which this discussion opened – that each of the great religious traditions is a valid expression of the Truth – must be rejected, and that Christians are quite justified in claiming, if not that their tradition is the sole authentic revelation of the Truth, at least that in so far as the doctrine of other traditions diverges from that of the Christians it is simply false and misguided, possibly even the work of the devil? This does not follow at all, and certainly there can be no justification for the claim in question, since such a claim cannot be made without violating some of the most profound insights that lie at the heart of the Christian tradition itself. To conclude this chapter I will try to show in what sense this is the case.

Here the first thing to be borne in mind is that the form or tradition through which an individual or group of individuals worships and is brought into communion with God depends upon a two-way relationship: it involves both God and man equally. In the Christian tradition, the basis of the understanding of this relationship is the affirmation that God creates man in His own image. Human beings are images of God and as such they share in all God's qualities. In our original state – our original ontological state, that is to say – this image is not simply potential; it is actual, or in the process of actualization: we actively and consciously participate in God's deifying energies and through such participation we may fully actualize all the divine qualities inherent in us by virtue of the fact that we are created in the image of God. The full actualization of these divine qualities is what is meant by our perfection: we become perfect as our Father in heaven is perfect and thus achieve our deification.

This is the situation when we are in our original or natural state, the state symbolized for us by the figures of Adam and Eve in paradise, when the channels of communication between God and ourselves are unblocked, and the reciprocal flow of life and love from the divine to the human and from the human to the divine is unimpeded. When in this state, to achieve deification – to actualize the qualities of God in ourselves in such a way that they become our own qualities – does not require that we receive spiritual guidance through any indirect means: we receive it directly from God, for our consciousness is open and transparent to the divine consciousness.

As a consequence of what in Christian terminology is described as the fall – and we shall see more fully in a later chapter what this represents – the channels of direct communication between God and human beings are, if not blocked, at least so impeded that the human consciousness is no longer transparent to the divine consciousness. Instead, it becomes subject to the illusions, distortions, fantasies and so on that typify the ego-dominated human state. We are, as it were, sundered from God – sundered from that which is real – and so can no longer commune with the source of our own being or, correspondingly, with the source of the being of anything else. Our mind becomes tied up in knots of our own making, those that Blake calls the "mind-forged manacles".

In this situation we cannot rely on our own counsel as to how we can actualize the potentialities of the divine image within us; for not only is this image now occluded, hidden, veiled by the ignorance and confusion of our fallen state, but in addition such actualization demands that we give up what we now think we are – the false identity we now attribute to ourselves – and this we cannot do without guidance as to what constitutes our true reality and on how we are to recover it. Without such guidance we cannot become perfect. Without divine intervention we cannot attain beatitude or immortality, or escape from our wretchedness.

This intervention and guidance are provided in the divine revelation that lies at the root of every sacred tradition. Generally speaking, such revelation takes the form of a Holy Book or scriptures, and of teachings of prophets, saints, and holy men and women based on the scriptures though verified in the light of personal spiritual experience and divine inspiration. It is by means of the guidance provided in this way that we are able to follow a spiritual path through which we may eventually recover the fullness of our divine image, and to do this with the assurance that we are not merely being seduced and deluded by the false lights of our confused and distorted ego-consciousness.

It is at this point, however, that we confront the question of the limitations which necessarily and inescapably characterize every such divine revelation. These limitations are imposed from both poles of the two-way relationship between God and man. They are imposed from above, from the side of God, and they are imposed from below, from the side of man. They are imposed from the side of God in the sense that it is impossible for all God's knowledge or all His wisdom to be *in actu* and fully expressed in one single form of revelation, or even for that matter in multiple forms of revelation. God in His non-manifest nature transcends all forms, whether intelligible, imaginable or sensible. In this sense He is beyond all determination and limitation. But if He is to reveal Himself to human beings in their fallen state He has to determine Himself, and hence to limit Himself, in a specific intelligible, imaginable or sensible form; for unless He does so we cannot possess the concrete and determined inner vision of God which alone makes it possible for us to worship Him. And since God is infinite, there is nothing to prevent Him from choosing to reveal Himself in an infinite number of limited forms, all of which He Himself, in His non-manifest nature, infinitely transcends, and all of which, both singly and collectively, fail to exhaust the plenitude of His knowledge and wisdom: however many the forms in which He reveals Himself, aspects of His full reality will always remain undisclosed.

This does not mean that every form we take to be a revelation of God is necessarily a revelation of God; nor does it mean that certain forms in which He reveals Himself do not enshrine His reality more fully than others. But it does mean that no single form of revelation can justifiably claim to be the only, still less the total, form of revelation through which human beings can attain a concrete and personal vision of God and so achieve salvation; for to make such a claim is to do violence to the nature of God Himself.

What I have just said also points to the limitation imposed on every form of revelation from below, from the side of man. God is the source of revelation, and from the side of God the form of a particular revelation will be determined by the aspects of His infinite Truth that God chooses to express through it. But man, in the individual and collective sense, is the *locus* or medium of this revelation; and a corollary of the affirmation that man is created in the image of God is that each single individual, let alone the cultural and linguistic group of human beings to which he belongs, will express this image, and therefore the divine qualities that constitute it, in a unique way.

At the same time, the degree to which a particular human being actualizes, or fails to actualize, these qualities will determine the mode in which that person exists and knows – will determine his or her mode of consciousness. This in its turn is another way of saying that the mode in which each human being exists and knows, or the mode of his or her consciousness, depends upon his or her experience of God. Everything is a particular mode of God's self-disclosure. A tree is a divine reality that expresses itself in the form of a tree.   PLATO

Yet the degree to which I can consciously experience the unique divine reality, of which I am the self-disclosure, will depend on the degree to which I have actualized, or failed to actualize, its presence within me, for it is such actualization, or failure to actualize, that determines the mode of consciousness through which I am able to experience things, God and His image within me being among them. It is the limitations of my mode of consciousness that limits my experience of God and consequently my experience of myself.

This means that I have to realize, first, that God is not limited to the mode in which He is epiphanized in me or to the form in which I am capable of perceiving Him; and, second, that the mode in which God is epiphanized in me and the form in which I am capable of perceiving Him will be different from those in which He is epiphanized in and can be perceived by other human beings. Not to recognize this, and not to act in the spirit of such a recognition, is for me to commit, actively or passively, an act of tyranny.

In the light of what has just been said we can now see more clearly why God's revelation of Himself, or His self-disclosure, is inevitably limited from below, from the side of man, both in the individual and, *a fortiori*, in the collective sense. Divine revelation cannot but accommodate itself to the mode of existence and knowledge – the mode of consciousness – of the being or beings to whom it is addressed, for the simple reason that unless it is so accommodated it cannot be experienced or received. There is absolutely no point in God revealing His Truth to me in a way that I am incapable of experiencing or receiving it. At the same time, the Holy Spirit does not force people, and He cannot inspire people beyond their capacity to receive inspiration. Correspondingly, the most lucid revelation is concealed from us when we have become incapable or unworthy of perceiving it.

If I and the section of humanity to which I belong are incapable of receiving and experiencing the Truth except in a form that is perceptible to the senses, then the Truth must put on the "robe", or the appearance, of the dark world into which it has to descend in order to communicate itself to us. It has to clothe itself in sensible images, of one form or another. In making such a descent, or in putting on such a robe, the pure light of the Truth is in its turn occluded, hidden, and veiled by the darkness of our ignorance, ineptitude and sin. Had the eyes of our heart not been blinded in this manner God could simply have projected spiritual, non-sensible forms of His wisdom into our sanctified intellect, open and transparent to the divine consciousness as it is in the pre-fallen Adamic state. Then the injunction, "Be fruitful and multiply", would be understood to signify that we should propagate these intelligible or spiritual forms (of beauty, of love) throughout the world.

In eating of the forbidden Tree, Adam was forced to perpetrate the violence that consists in *naturalizing* things of the spirit instead of spiritualizing – or perceiving the spiritual dimensions of – created, sensible realities. Correspondingly, it is our state of blindness, ignorance and ineptitude that, in the case of the Christian revelation, forces God, in order to disclose Himself, and the reality of things created and uncreated, to take on a visible, "historical" human form. In this sense, both the Incarnation and the Crucifixion are the consequences of our ignominy. This is nothing for

Christians to be proud or self-congratulatory about. Had the Judeo-Hellenistic world, the type of consciousness that typifies it, been capable of receiving that revelation in a more subtle or more spiritual form, then it would have been communicated in such a form.

Correspondingly, the fact that the revelations of other sacred traditions are not centered in and do not depend upon an incarnation equivalent to that of Christ does not mean that what they claim to be the wisdom enshrined in their doctrine is spurious or false, or is in any way inferior to the wisdom enshrined in Christian doctrine. It may simply mean that the consciousness of the *milieux*, human and cultural, to which these revelations are given is of such a type or quality that God does not have to manifest Himself in a visible, historical human form in order to communicate a true knowledge and understanding of things. Or, to put this in another way, it could be said that had God manifested Himself in such a form to these other *milieux*, He would not have been crucified.

When Christians attack or vilify a faith other than their own on the grounds that its doctrinal or other forms, viewed in the most literal and exoteric manner, conflict with their own, they are simply usurping the role played by the Jews in the Gospels, who crucified Christ because it appeared to them that certain of His utterances and actions, again viewed in the most literal and exoteric manner, cut directly across the tenets of their own faith. That the Jews themselves acted in this way because they had become blinded to the inner significance of central aspects of their own faith, and that it was the awareness of this significance that Christ wished to restore to the lapsed human consciousness, is testified to by the account of Christ's meeting with Nicodemos (Jn. 3:1-11): at this meeting Nicodemos confesses his ignorance of the whole doctrine of spiritual rebirth, of which, as a "master of Israel", he should have been fully cognizant.

As I said before, none of this means that all religious traditions that claim to be based on a true revelation of God are in fact based on such a revelation; nor does it mean that even when religious traditions are rooted in true revelation, one of them may not express God's wisdom and knowledge more fully than the others. What it does mean, though, is that the fact that a particular religious community embraces a form of belief and worship rooted in divine revelation, and entirely valid for human salvation, does not in the least justify that community in maintaining that its form of revelation, and the tradition rooted in it, are the only such form and tradition through which salvation may be obtained.

Our primary loyalty and faith must of course be directed towards our own tradition and to deepening experience of that – though even here we must remember that the significance that our tradition has for us, and the degree and firmness of the assent we give to it, may well depend not so much on its own inherent "objective" qualities and possibilities as on the strength of our acceptance of it, or faith in it, in the first place, and that this may be conditioned by many factors, cultural, ethnic, political and so on, that have little to do with the tradition in the spiritual sense. If we are at all concerned with the inner nature of other traditions, we must seek to understand them as fully as we can in the light not of our own prejudices, but of their own criteria, bearing in mind always that no one can be aware of the living dimensions and potentialities of a particular sacred tradition without first experiencing them through active participation in that tradition's forms of belief and liturgical practice. Above all, we are in no position to pronounce on the spiritual value of other sacred traditions, or on the relationship of Christianity to these other traditions, unless we have first freed ourselves from the hostility, bigotry and arrogance which make a true understanding of anything impossible. Until we are free from such passions, and have replaced them with love and sympathy, we can do nothing but reveal our own ignorance and pettiness.

Liberation from this ignorance and pettiness is not possible without an act of repentance, a *metanoia*, which banishes all confessional bias and all feelings of cultural and historical superiority. It is not possible without the kind of humility which, while not avoiding compassionate admonition and even criticism, is yet able to accept, even in the form of positive unbelief, a courageous rejection of the lies which Christians themselves have for too long been unwilling or unable to reject.

Finally, it will not be possible to achieve this liberation until the contemplative tradition of Christianity once again occupies a central position in the Christian consciousness. This means that we have to disabuse ourselves of the notion that Christian contemplation is solely a matter of withdrawal and recollection, or that it is simply a folding inward upon a mysterious inner presence in "prayer of stillness", "prayer of union" or "spiritual marriage". This is a foreshortened idea of its significance. We have to recover the full liturgical and patristic dimension of Christian contemplation. We must realize that Christian *theoria* is in fact first of all a response to God's manifestation of Himself in His Logos. It is at the same time a contemplative understanding of the whole of creation in the light of the Transfiguration.

Christian contemplation, in common with that of Hinduism, Buddhism, and Islam, is centered not upon some vague inner apprehension of the mystery of man's own spiritual essence. It is centered upon God's self-emptying, the *kenosis*, which must have its counterpart in man's self-emptying, the emptying of all purely human knowledge and even of man's whole ego-consciousness. We have to lose our soul in order to find it, or in order to be in a position to encounter directly the light and power of God. It is precisely here, at the heart of the Christian way, where we encounter the Christian expression of the dialectic of fullness and emptiness, all or nothing, void and infinity, that we can make a creative response to and engage in a creative encounter with the profound realizations that lie at the heart of other sacred traditions. Outside this ground, or short of it, we will always be in a state of non-comprehension, confusion or conflict. Whether we shall celebrate the reconciliation that we have spurned for so long before the passing away of the present form of this world is something we cannot know. But we can at least make ourselves aware of what we have to do before such a reconciliation can come about.

Chapter Four

Christianity and the Metaphysics of Logic

Of the many factors which can contribute to radical divergencies in the formulation of metaphysical doctrine, one of the most crucial – and one of the least recognized – is the role accorded to logic. This is not to say that some doctrines are logical in structure, while others are illogical – that, for instance, Vedantic doctrine is logical, while Christian doctrine is illogical. It is not so simple as that. Christian doctrine, given its premises, is just as logical as Vedantic doctrine, and even just as logical as a profane thought-structure like that of modern science, whose devotees are only too insistent that this is not the case, either where Christian or any other specifically religious doctrine is concerned. What is at issue is not whether, given its premises, a particular metaphysical doctrine is logical or not. It is the role accorded to logic in determining the very premises – the primordial data – of the doctrine itself.

I could have chosen to explain what I mean by this through contrasting the Christian approach to the issue with the approach, say, of Proklos in his *The Elements of Theology*. Instead I have chosen to do so through contrasting the Christian approach with that of the great twentieth century metaphysician, René Guénon (1886-1951). If during the last century or so there has been even some slight revival of awareness in the western world of what is meant by metaphysics and metaphysical tradition, the credit for it must go above all to Guénon. At a time when the confusion into which modern western thought had fallen was such that it threatened to obliterate the few remaining traces of genuine spiritual knowledge from the minds and hearts of his contemporaries, Guénon, virtually single-handed, took it upon himself to reaffirm the values and principles which, he recognized, constitute the only sound basis for the living of a human life with dignity and purpose or for the formation of a civilization worthy of the name. He himself would not have expected to stem the tide towards even further lapse into ignorance and disintegration, let alone to turn it, for that would have been contrary to his understanding of the cyclic phase through which the world is now passing. The most he hoped for was to reawaken a consciousness of these values and principles among a few; and indeed there cannot be many now in possession of such a consciousness who are not indebted in one way or another to his work.

Achievements of such magnitude are accompanied by corresponding hazards and pitfalls; and it serves no purpose whatsoever to claim, in misplaced adulation, immunity from human error and prejudice for those who accomplish them. Certainly Guénon was not free from either. In part this was due to temperament, training and experience; in part to ignorance of the full nature of the subject with which he was dealing, as was the case with his reluctance, on insufficient grounds, to recognize in Buddhism a fully-fledged metaphysical tradition until further evidence was brought to his notice which impelled him to acknowledge that it was.[1] More recently some of the views that Guénon put forward in his book, *Le Roi du Monde*, have been criticized for their obvious misrepresentation of the facts, a misrepresentation appealing more to a sense for the occult than to a sense for the sacred.[2] On an earlier occasion some of his conclusions *vis-à-vis* the Christian tradition have been questioned;[3] and there may be other articles of which I am not aware that question or criticize certain of his ideas.

[1] See Marco Pallis, "A Fateful Meeting of Minds", in *Studies in Comparative Religion*, Summer-Autumn 1978, pp. 176-88.

[2] See Whitall N. Perry, review of English translation of *Le Roi du Monde*, in *Studies in Comparative Religion*, Summer-Autumn 1983, pp. 244-7. See also Marco Pallis, "Ossendowski's sources", in *Studies in Comparative Religion*, Winter-Spring 1983, pp. 30-41.

[3] See Marco Pallis, "Le Voile du Temple", in *Études Traditionnelles*, July-August, September-October 1964, pp. 155-76; November-December 1964, pp. 263-7; March-April 1965, pp. 55-66.

My own concern in this present chapter is not to correct or criticize the errors of judgment or interpretation that Guénon may have made after too hasty appraisal of insufficient data or anything of a similar kind. It is specifically and solely directed to clarifying the issue of which I have spoken – that of the role of logic in determining the underlying premises or primordial data of metaphysical doctrine.

The fundamental idea of metaphysical doctrine as expounded by Guénon is the idea of the Infinite which is also universal Possibility. This idea may be described therefore as the key idea, that which constitutes for Guénon what one may call the primordial datum of genuine metaphysical exegesis and which distinguishes such exegesis from thought-structures that, however much they may pose as metaphysical, are really only constructs of a philosophical kind. As Guénon himself writes: "It is to be noted that philosophers, in order to construct their systems, always presume, consciously or unconsciously, to impose some limitation on universal Possibility, something which is contradictory but which is none the less demanded by the construction of a system as such. It would indeed be interesting to write the history of the various modern philosophical theories, which possess to the highest degree a systematic character, from the point of view of the limitations they presume to impose on universal Possibility."[4] The implication of this remark is of course that from the metaphysical point of view universal Possibility – the Infinite – is by definition free from all and every limitation.

If, however, one looks closely at the idea of universal Possibility as it is presented by Guénon, one may begin to question whether he does not in fact himself impose, "consciously or unconsciously", a certain limitation on it. On probing deeper, it begins to become clear that this limitation – if limitation it is – is itself implicit in a conception of a relationship between logic and the Absolute which for Guénon assumes the status of an axiom. Going still further, one realizes that aspects of Guénon's metaphysics are themselves

[4] See René Guénon, *Le Symbolisme de la Croix* (Paris, 1950), p. 20, note 2. My translation.

less conclusions drawn from data received by way of revelation or initiation, than the direct consequences of the application to the metaphysical order of the exegetical principle predicated by the axiom to which I have referred.

In order to clarify what is involved in these statements, I must first give a brief account of the idea of universal Possibility as Guénon himself presents it. To this end it will be sufficient to consult one of his major works, *Les États multiples de l'Être*.[5] As already noted, the idea of universal Possibility is interchangeable with the idea of the Infinite. Guénon's conception of the Infinite has its origin in the proposition that "all determination is necessarily a limitation".[6] As it can be demonstrated that all limitation – or making finite – is and must involve a denial of the Infinite (*omnis definitio est negatio* is the familiar Spinozian formulation of this argument), it follows that any determination is also a denial of the Infinite. Hence the idea of the Infinite can be expressed only in negative terms. The Infinite is that which is beyond all and every determination. It is absolute indetermination, totally impersonal and unqualified. A corollary of this is that the Infinite coincides with universal Possibility, for if there were any single possibility absent from the Infinite its infinitude would be limited and hence denied by this possibility of which it was deprived. Consequently all possibilities must subsist in the Infinite. In other words, the Infinite is also universal Possibility – the All-Possible. Hence it is the idea of the Infinite which may also be designated as universal Possibility that constitutes for Guénon the supreme metaphysical principle, the Absolute that in its turn constitutes the primordial datum of his doctrinal exegesis.

The idea of possibility, however, implies its opposite, the idea of impossibility. Impossibility, Guénon explains, is pure nothingness,

---

[5] Quotations (in my translation) from this work are taken from the 1947 Paris edition, and all the page numbers given in the footnotes that follow refer to this edition. An English translation, by Jocelin Godwin, has been published under the title *The Multiple States of Being* by Larson Publications (New York, 1984).

[6] René Guénon, *Les États*, p. 17.

absolute negativity.[7] It is at this point that one is faced with the question: how does one recognize or determine an impossibility or (to put the same thing the other way round) how does one recognize and determine what is possible? As Guénon's answer to this question not only indicates the kind of limitation he appears to impose on universal Possibility but also introduces what will be a main concern of this chapter – namely, the exploration of the way in which Guénon's presentation of metaphysical doctrine is affected by his particular attitude to logic and by a particular conception of the relationship between the logical order and the metaphysical order – it is important to take especial note of it. For Guénon, an impossibility is an absurdity in the logical sense of the word. The absurd, in the logical sense of the word, is what implies a logical contradiction. Conversely, it is the absence of internal contradiction which *logically as well as ontologically* (my italics) defines a possibility.[8]

In what sense this conclusion implies the imposing of a limitation on universal Possibility will be indicated at a later stage of this chapter. What is important for the moment is to clarify the attitude to logic and to the relationship between the logical and the metaphysical orders which it presupposes, and to show what consequences this has with respect to the way in which Guénon is led to envisage metaphysical doctrine.

We have already seen that Guénon typifies the Infinite in terms that are consistent with – and that in fact depend upon – the laws of logic. According to the laws of logic, every determination must exclude all those aspects of reality not subsumed within the limits of the determination in question. A wall cannot be a tree or a cow or anything else not subsumed in the determination denoted by the word "wall". This is to say that, according to the laws of logic, every determination implies to a greater or lesser degree a limitation when compared with the sum total of reality embraced by the Infinite. It is also to say that in the ultimate logical analysis the Infinite must be beyond all determination, since any determination, as we

[7] Ibid. p. 40.
[8] Ibid. p. 17 and note 1, p. 17.

saw, implies some limitation and therefore the exclusion of some aspect or aspects of the sum total of reality from the Infinite, which would be a contradiction in terms. Hence, in terms which are consistent with the laws of logic, the highest principle in the metaphysical order – that which embraces all possible reality and is infinite in its nature – must be beyond all determination. It must be totally undetermined, impersonal and unqualified. *but God cannot be limited to not be able to be determined*

It is by means of a demonstration of this kind that Guénon arrives at the idea of the Infinite or All-Possible that, as the supreme principle in the metaphysical order, is beyond even Being itself. It is also by means of a demonstration of this kind that he establishes the law that any metaphysical principle which can be logically distinguished from the undetermined Infinite, and so must represent some determination of the sum total of reality embraced by the Infinite, must on that account possess less reality than the Infinite, because by definition it will exclude some aspect or aspects of the sum total of reality subsumed in the Infinite. The greater its degree of determination the more it will exclude of the sum total of reality subsumed in the Infinite and so, correspondingly, the less will be its own degree of reality.

Thus, for instance, Being, which represents the primal determination of the Infinite and so is sequent to the Infinite, will possess on that account a lesser degree of absolute reality than that possessed by the Infinite; and the same applies, in a gradually increasing fashion, to all those determinations which in their turn issue or emanate from Being and from what stands below Being. In this way the metaphysical order is construed as a hierarchy of gradations – the multiple states of being – each real on its own level but each possessing a degree of reality that depends on its relative proximity to the pre-ontological Infinite. Only the Infinite is absolutely real; anything sequent to the Infinite, and logically distinguished from the Infinite by the degree of determination that applies to it, will be only relatively real.

In fact, Guénon goes even further, for with respect to the Infinite any determination is, he states, "rigorously nothing" and can have

no relationship with the Infinite.[9] This is but another way of saying that any reality which may be attributed to a determination
belongs to it not in so far as it is a determination, but only in so far
as it is implicit in the order of infinite possibilities. The reality, even in
a relative sense, of a determination is not of the determination as
such – for this is "rigorously nothing" – but of the *ensemble* of possibilities of determination in so far as these *do not manifest themselves
but only imply manifestation in their nature* (my italics).[10] Ultimately
only what is a possibility is real, and this only in so far as it remains
a possibility and is not actualized.[11] Manifestation and multiplicity are essentially unreal and illusory.[12]

All this follows logically and necessarily from the two basic
propositions, first that all determination is necessarily a limitation; and second, that there is nothing in the metaphysical order
of a nature that can only be expressed in terms that violate the
principle of non-contradiction in the logical sense. In other words,
there is nothing in the metaphysical order that cannot be expressed
in terms that conform to the laws of logic because, for Guénon,
anything that cannot be so expressed is an impossibility and so can
have no place in the metaphysical order, or anywhere else for that
matter. This is not to say or imply that the metaphysical order is
not supra-logical, or that the order of logic coincides with the
metaphysical order. But it is to presuppose that the order of logic
on its own level mirrors the structure of the metaphysical order, so
that the laws of logic not only derive from, but also analogically
may be applied to, the metaphysical order.[13] This is to say that
when metaphysical Reality is reflected on the logical plane of the
human mind, the concepts it forms of itself will be – or at least in
principle should be – logically consistent and non-contradictory
because ultimately nothing in the metaphysical order violates the

[9] Ibid. p. 19 and note 2.
[10] Ibid. p. 123.
[11] Ibid. p. 127.
[12] Ibid. pp. 83, 107, 122.
[13] Or, as Guénon puts it elsewhere, "metaphysic cannot contradict reason,
but it stands above reason". See his *Introduction to the Study of Hindu Doctrines*
(London, 1945) p. 116.

principle of logical consistency and non-contradiction. There is a strict correlation or adequation between the metaphysical order and the order of logic. It is for this reason that Guénon has no hesitation in applying the laws of logic to his typification of the metaphysical realm and can affirm so positively that "logically as well as ontologically" everything in that realm must conform to the principle of non-contradiction in the logical sense of the word.

What is here being said, as well as something of its significance, may become more clear if Guénon's formulation of metaphysical doctrine is contrasted with that of a tradition such as the Orthodox Christian tradition, where the strict correlation between the order of logic and the metaphysical order is not presupposed in the same way. For the doctrinal masters of this tradition, the supreme principle of the metaphysical order is not the undetermined and impersonal Infinite, as it is for Guénon. The supreme principle is the Trinity. They recognize that the ultimate nature of the Trinity – that which they designate as the Essence – is unknowable and as such is beyond both determination and non-determination; but they do not on that account recognize in it a metaphysical principle that is superior to the Trinity. On the contrary, they affirm that the Essence, although beyond determination and non-determination, is not an impersonal or non-personalized principle, for the Essence subsists only in so far as it is "enhypostasized" in the three Persons of the Trinity. They refuse to accept the idea of an undetermined and impersonal Essence – or Infinite – that transcends the Trinity, just as concomitantly they refuse to accept the idea that the Trinity represents certain determinations of the Essence in the sense that each Person of the Trinity expresses the Essence in but a relative mode and on that account is to some extent less real or less absolute and infinite than the Essence. For them each Person of the Trinity, although distinct from the other Persons, is as real and as absolute as each of the other Persons, and the reality and absoluteness and infinitude possessed by each Person are those of Reality itself, and the Absolute and Infinite Itself, in the fullest sense of the words.

The Father, being infinite, truly could choose to be determinate – ergo Jesus
See p. 99!

This does not mean of course that they recognize three Absolutes, each with an independent Essence which happens to be the same as that possessed by the others. There is only one Absolute. But on the one hand this single Absolute is not to be conceived as constituted by the Essence in a way that involves envisaging the Essence as a principle subsisting in its own right apart from its enhypostasization in the three Persons; and on the other It is not to be conceived as constituted by any one of the three Persons in a way that involves envisaging any one Person of the Trinity as so standing apart from the other two that this Person can be regarded as an independent principle with respect to which the other two Persons are but relative. Among the Persons of the Trinity there is absolute unity and absolute diversity; and just as there is no non-hypostasized Essence, so there are no non-essentialized Persons: there is only a concomitance of one Essence and three Persons, with no priority or subordination in either direction. Thus to envisage a simple Essence that is not enhypostasized, or a Person that is not essentialized, is to do violence to the full richness and complexity of the Absolute Itself.[14]

The corollary of this is that however far one penetrates into the metaphysical realm – beyond all manifestation both formal and informal, beyond Being and into the unsoundable depths of the pre-ontological *Ungrund* itself – one will never surpass the Personhood of the Absolute, for the simple reason that there is nothing in the metaphysical realm that transcends such Personhood. The perspective on to which even the most exalted idea of the metaphysical order opens out is always a personal one.

It will be evident from this way of typifying the Absolute that for the doctrinal masters in question the Absolute not only transcends the logical order (as it does also for Guénon) but cannot be typified (short of crucially misrepresenting it) in terms other than those which violate the laws of logical consistency and non-contradiction. For, logically speaking, to recognize distinctions in the Absolute without accepting that such distinctions must imply, with

[14] For a fuller account of the doctrine of the Trinity that is here in question, see my *Church, Papacy and Schism* (London, 1978) pp. 96-110.

respect to what is distinguished, a certain relativity – even if only a relative absoluteness – is to put oneself into the position of affirming what Guénon calls an absurdity. In other words, the idea of the Trinity as presented by the doctrinal masters of the Orthodox Christian tradition cuts directly across the correlation between the order of logic and the metaphysical order which for Guénon underpins all metaphysical doctrine worthy of the name. The statement that any determination necessarily involves a limitation is a truth of the logical order. But because for Guénon there is a strict correlation between the order of logic and the metaphysical order, a truth of the logical order may be applied analogically to the metaphysical order. Hence, to posit a determination in the metaphysical order will also be to posit a relative degree of limitation in what is determined when compared with the undetermined and unqualified nature of infinite and absolute Reality itself.

In the particular context with which we are here concerned, what this signifies is that since each Person in the Trinity represents a determination *in divinis*, each Person, according to Guénon's criteria, cannot be the Absolute in His own right, because in the nature of things any determination involves a limitation and so cannot be the Absolute in the full sense of the word. Each Person in the Trinity must therefore be something less absolute and consequently less real than the Absolute Itself, for absoluteness in this ultimate sense can be the prerogative only of a totally undetermined principle. Hence, if this supreme and undetermined principle of the metaphysical order is designated by the term Essence, then for Guénon the Essence must transcend all personal enhypostasization, and subsist in Its own right as an independent principle, while each Person of the Trinity must express the Essence in but a relative mode.

From this point of view, therefore, the affirmation that the supreme principle of the metaphysical order is both trinitarian and personal merely betrays a failure to grasp the unqualified and impersonal nature of what is actually the supreme principle of this order, and indicates that one is identifying the Absolute with what is in fact a certain relativization, however minimal, of the

Absolute Itself, for this latter rigorously transcends all and every distinction. Given Guénon's conception of the relationship between logic and the Absolute, it is absolutely impossible to recognize or admit as adequate to its purpose a doctrinal idea such as that of the Trinity which implies or posits that the Absolute, in the ultimate sense of the word, can be typified only in terms which from the logical point of view are contradictory. It is because of this that Guénon himself was led to distinguish between what he called true metaphysics and what he called theology and to deny to the latter a genuine metaphysical status.

Is it, however, as simple as this? The doctrine of the Trinity expresses the unity and diversity of the three Persons in the Absolute. It expresses the mystery of an Absolute that is simultaneously One and Three, a Monad and a Triad. But the idea itself that there are three Persons in the Absolute, each of whom concretizes the Absolute in His own right and hence transcends any and every form of relativity, is not for Christians a matter of theological speculation. For them the Trinity is the primordial reality of divine life itself, a metaphysical fact disclosed through divine revelation which thus constitutes for them the primordial datum of doctrinal exegesis. As such it is the principle to which the human mind must accommodate itself on condition that it does some kind of justice to the nature of ultimate Truth.

In other words, for Christians the idea of the Trinity plays the same role in relation to the formulation of doctrine as is played for Guénon by the idea of the Infinite and All-Possible: it provides the starting-point from which doctrinal exegesis begins. That therefore it is an antinomic and paradoxical idea in the sense that from the logical point of view it does not conform to the law of non-contradiction, is not something arbitrary or due to a lack of logical subtlety and refinement on the part of Christian exegetes. *It is imposed on them by the way in which the Absolute has been typified for them by divine revelation.* That is to say, the Absolute has revealed Itself to be essentially paradoxical in character. Consequently, to attempt to resolve this paradox, either by affirming one proposition of the paradox at the expense of the other, or by formulating a "superior" idea in which both propositions appear to be absorbed in a manner that irons out any internal contradiction, is *ipso facto* to represent the Absolute in a less adequate way. In the Christian perspective the translogical and paradoxical idea of the Trinity is the most primordial idea of all. It constitutes the concept-limit, the *ne plus ultra*, of human thought, and there is not and there cannot be any other idea that represents the Absolute more adequately.

For Guénon, on the other hand, this cannot be the case because, in the way we have seen, he accepts as axiomatic the proposition that the most adequate idea of the Absolute accessible to the human mind will be and must be one that is consistent with the laws of logic. This means in effect that the human intelligence, in formulating its idea of the Absolute, does not have to accommodate itself to a metaphysical datum typified by divine revelation, accepting this as the starting-point which determines the form of doctrinal exegesis. On the contrary, any such datum must now be subjected, where its typification is concerned, to the criteria of logic, and it is to these criteria that the human intelligence must accommodate itself in formulating the idea of the Absolute. It is true that this demand that the human intelligence, in typifying the Absolute, must accommodate itself to the criteria of logic is not an arbitrary demand, for it is assumed that there is a correlation between the order of logic and the metaphysical order that justifies it and indeed makes it obligatory. But the consequence is that it is now inevitable that the concept-limit, the *ne plus ultra*, of human thought where the idea of the Absolute is concerned will be, not an idea that is translogical and paradoxical, but one which is attained by means of a purely logical demonstration. One might say that in this perspective the ultimate arbiter of the form which doctrinal expression must take is not a datum typified by divine revelation, but a datum typified by the norms of logical discrimination and demonstration.

We are now in a position to summarize the contrast whose contours, so to say, we have been delineating. In the Christian perspective, the ultimate arbiter of the form which doctrinal exegesis must take is the primordial datum typified by divine revelation, and it is to this that the human intelligence must accommodate itself, even if in so doing it has to violate the laws of logic. In the Guénonian perspective, on the other hand, the ultimate arbiter of the form which doctrinal exegesis must take is not a datum typified by divine revelation, but a datum typified by the norms of logical discrimination and demonstration, and it is to this that the human intelligence must accommodate itself.

Thus if the primordial datum typified by divine revelation – in this case the Christian revelation – is such that it compels its doctrinal exegetes to express it in terms that are logically contradictory, this in the Guénonian perspective can only be evidence that the primordial datum of this revelation corresponds not to the highest level of metaphysical reality but simply to some subordinate level – not to the absolute Absolute but to some relativization of the Absolute. To correspond to the absolute Absolute, the primordial datum of a particular revelation would have to be patent to typification in terms that conform to the laws of logic. Once again, the ultimate arbiter of whether the primordial datum of a particular revelation corresponds to the absolute Absolute or simply to a relativization of the Absolute, and hence to a relative Absolute, are the norms of logical discrimination and demonstration. And this must be so, because in the Guénonian perspective there can ultimately be no contradiction between the idea of the absolute Absolute and the supreme logical demonstration of which the human intelligence is capable. In the nature of things, the highest logical demonstration of which the human intelligence is capable must correspond to the absolute Absolute.

It will be evident from the manner in which this contrast has defined itself that the proposition concerning the relationship between logic and the Absolute which Guénon assumes as axiomatic does not have the same authority for the doctrinal masters of the Orthodox Christian tradition. Clearly these latter cannot accept that there is this correlation or concordance between the metaphysical order and the order of logic which is authoritative for Guénon, for if they did so they would reach similar conclusions, since these conclusions, given the proposition in question, are quite obvious even to the most average kind of intelligence. Moreover, the precepts of Aristotelian logic which these conclusions also presuppose, and on which Guénon leans so heavily, were the commonplaces of the philosophical training they all received. Hence if they reject, as they do, both the proposition and the conclusions in question, it is in full knowledge of what they are doing. Why, then, do they reject them? Is it simply because the primordial datum of their revelation, which they accept without question, cannot be accommodated to them? Certainly, given the primordial datum of their revelation as the starting-point, they deploy their faculty of logical discrimination and demonstration as fully as Guénon deploys his. But they deploy it only in a deductive manner. They do not, that is to say, deploy it upwards, in order to typify the Absolute Itself, because they regard such a procedure as overstepping the limits to which the laws of logic apply.

For the masters of the Orthodox Christian tradition the Absolute is not a logical principle or a principle susceptible to the laws of logic. It does not fall within the competence of dialectic to define It. Its essence is not to be construed by means of syllogisms or demonstrated or proved in accordance with some criterion other than Itself. It is Itself Its own demonstration, Its own proof, and the evidence It gives of Itself can be known only through direct revelation or prophetic inspiration. Consequently they would not agree that what is logically necessary is on that account ontologically real, or that what is possible must by definition be free from internal contradiction as this is determined by the norms of logic.

Beyond this, however, and in a more positive sense, these masters would regard logic as a function of the *ratio*; and as the *ratio* is a relative and finite faculty that can operate only with reference to a given starting-point, they do not consider that the criteria of logic are competent to establish what this starting-point itself must or must not be when what is in question is the highest principle of the absolute and infinite order. To think otherwise would be to put oneself in the absurd position of saying that the *ratio*, which by definition can operate only from a given starting-point, is competent to establish the starting-point from which alone it is capable of operating, for this of course is tantamount to saying that it can operate without a given starting-point, and this, precisely, is what it cannot do. Were it able to do this, then the *ratio*, relative and finite as it is, would be master not only of its own conclusions but also, in the present context, of the Absolute Itself. Hence, as we said, they do not regard themselves as entitled to deploy the criteria of logic in order to demonstrate, even in strictly negative terms, what the Absolute Itself must or must not be.   8/21/12

This being the case, why or on what grounds is this same proposition so authoritative for Guénon that to deploy the criteria of logic in order to demonstrate, albeit in negative terms, what the Absolute must or must not be, as well as to demonstrate what all that is sequent to the Absolute must or must not be, is not simply legitimate but even obligatory? Neither in *Les États multiples de l'Être* nor, so far as I am aware, in any of his other works, does Guénon himself give any explanation which establishes its validity as an unconditional law of metaphysical exegesis. In *Les États multiples* he simply announces it as a kind of *ipse dixit* when describing how one distinguishes a possibility from an impossibility. All one can say is that, unless it is quite arbitrary, it must presuppose, as we have noted, that the structure of the metaphysical order, supra-logical in itself, is reflected in the order of logic, so that it is by deploying the laws of logical demonstration that the principles of the metaphysical order can best be typified. In other words, it is quite legitimate to apply the criteria of logic to the metaphysical order, and to typify this order – say what it must or must not be – accordingly, because in so doing one is simply operating in a manner that has its justification in the metaphysical order itself. But this is a purely circular form of argument, and still leaves unanswered the question of who or what validates the proposition on which it depends, namely, that there is this inherent and necessary correlation or adequation between the metaphysical order and the order of logic.

Unless, therefore, acceptance of the proposition in question is either arbitrary or an unspecified act of faith, it still remains to evince objective grounds for accepting it. For it is by no means a self-evident proposition, nor is it one of which logic itself can demonstrate the authoritative nature. Indeed, there is no possible way in which this can be demonstrated without appealing to principles or criteria of demonstration that have themselves been established on the basis of precisely this same proposition, and that of course is to demonstrate nothing: it is merely to repeat the circular argument in another form. Consequently, all one can do is to assume that it is valid and then go on to apply the laws of logic to the formulation of metaphysical doctrine as though it actually were valid. But the authoritativeness of the proposition itself is beyond either proof or disproof; and one certainly has no entitlement to assert that only doctrine formulated on the assumption that it is authoritative may claim to be metaphysical.

Moreover, the application of this proposition to the presentation of metaphysical doctrine does in fact appear to reveal an incapacity to validate what it affirms. If one starts, as Guénon does, with the idea of an Absolute, reached through deploying the criteria of logic, that is totally undetermined, immutable, impersonal and so on, one is faced with the question of giving some adequate account of how or why the Absolute, in which the sum total of reality is subsumed, "passes over" into manifestation, or into the appearance of manifestation; of how or why what is determined arises from the Indeterminate, the world of change from the Immutable, the personal from the Impersonal. In Guénon's account of this process, the principle of manifestation is said to be pure Being. As the principle of manifestation, Being itself transcends the manifest order and belongs to the non-manifest order. At the same time, it is said to be the first determination of this order, and it is this fact which makes it possible for it to determine the whole hierarchy of the multiple states of being that proceed from it.

This, however, still leaves unanswered the question of by what or how Being itself is determined. The non-manifest order, Guénon writes, is made up of Being and Non-Being. Being includes all the possibilities of manifestation, formal and informal, in so far as these are to be manifested; while Non-Being includes all possibilities of non-manifestation, including that of Being itself and those of manifestation in so far as they remain pure possibilities.[15] Is this to say that Non-Being is the principle of Being in the sense that Non-Being determines Being? This cannot be said, for what is complete and infinite in its non-determination cannot determine itself without in some measure becoming less and other than itself, thus contradicting its own nature, which is an impossibility. Hence, Non-Being includes no principle or possibility of self-determination: not determined by anything (for Non-Being is "non-dual" and where there is no duality, nothing can be determined by anything), it is at the same time powerless to determine anything (for in the realm of Absolute Non-Being there is nothing to determine and nothing that can be determined).

This means that one is confronted with a dilemma. There must be a first determination, for unless there is a first determination there cannot be any subsequent determinations, so the whole theory of the multiple states of being would lack all ontological foundation. But on the other hand, in the Absolute Itself there is, according to Guénon, no principle that can determine the first determination. It is the need to resolve the contradiction inherent in this dilemma that impels Guénon to make what one might describe as a metaphysical quantum leap in order to resolve it, and to assert: "Being is not determined, but it determines itself".[16]

First Cause

This statement is worth noting. The first part, taken in itself, is tantamount to saying that a determination is not determined, which is surely a contradiction in terms; while its qualification in the second part again has the appearance of being what Guénon calls an absurdity, for it violates the law of non-contradiction, conformity with which characterizes for Guénon something that is possible. For in what sense can a determination be said to determine itself or to be its own principle? No determination can possess the principle of its own being – that is, of its own determination –

[15] René Guénon, *Les États*, pp. 31-2.
[16] Ibid. pp. 132.

in itself, for this would mean that there is some principle that stands apart from or opposed to the Infinite, and this is to contradict the whole idea of the Absolute as Guénon has expressed it. Yet, as we saw, the Absolute cannot Itself be the principle of determination without also contradicting Its own nature. Hence if Being does determine itself, through a kind of spontaneous combustion, there is a possibility of an impossibility: a possibility that a determination which does not possess the principle of its own determination in itself and is therefore, with respect to the Absolute, nothing and without any being or existence,[17] is nevertheless the principle of its own determination and does determine itself.

One can see why it is necessary to posit this inherently contradictory determination of Being, for without doing so it is impossible to account for the passage from the undetermined Absolute to the first determination, pure Being, and so to build up the whole sequent theory of the structure of the universe. But this does not make it any the less a kind of *deus ex machina* without which there can be no resolution of the dilemma in question; nor does it make it any the less a violation of the law of non-contradiction and so render it an absurdity as Guénon defines the term. It would appear that the attempt to present the supreme metaphysical principle in terms that are logically consistent necessarily introduces a logical inconsistency in accounting for any determination that is sequent to this principle, and so in accounting for any manifestation (or appearance of manifestation) of whatever kind.

Something similar occurs when Guénon attempts "to prove freedom metaphysically".[18] Because, as we have observed at the beginning of this chapter, Guénon's idea of the Absolute is one that can be expressed only in negative terms, it follows that freedom in the highest sense must be defined as an absence of constraint rather than as a power of self-determination. It is indeed impossible, given Guénon's premises, for freedom to be described in anything but negative terms. As we have also noted, for Guénon the Absolute is not only totally undetermined, but also cannot

17 Ibid. p. 19.
18 Ibid. p. 127.

determine Itself or anything else; for if It could determine Itself or anything else It would have to determine itself and other things, because otherwise it would violate Guénon's axiom that a possibility must realize itself simply because it is a possibility; and this would mean not only that the Absolute is under constraint and so deprived of freedom, but also that It would have to become less than the Absolute, which is an impossibility. Hence the Absolute, *quâ* Absolute, possesses no principle or possibility of self-determination or determination, with the consequence that freedom, in the supreme sense, can be described, not as a power of self-determination, but only as an absence of constraint.

The subsequent argument "to prove freedom" in the realm of being or manifestation falls into the same difficulties as the argument for the determination of Being. Being, the first determination, is metaphysical unity. What is one is manifestly exempt from all constraint. Hence Being possesses freedom, again in the negative sense, as a lack of constraint. Thus, while Non-Being is exempt from constraint and therefore free because it is "non-dual" (as we have noted, where there is no duality nothing can be determined by anything), Being is exempt from constraint and therefore free because it is one.

This argument, which begs certain questions in its own right, again would appear to involve a contradiction. For Being is a determination – it is, by definition, the first determination. A determination, as Guénon's axiom has it, is a limitation; and, Guénon further states,[19] a constraint is a limitation. How then can Being, by definition a limitation and hence under constraint, be exempt from constraint? Once again, the attempt to achieve logical consistency at all cost appears to result in the introduction, in however subtle a guise, of a patent contradiction.

Indeed, as might be expected from the difficulties encountered in explaining the determination of Being, there is what one might describe as a hiatus at the heart of Guénon's metaphysics; and nowhere is this more apparent than in the way in which, because of his initial typification of the Absolute (imposed on him by his

[19] Ibid. p. 127.

predication of the necessary relationship between logic and the Absolute), he is compelled to envisage the world of manifestation, the world of phenomena. In fact, given the initial typification of the Absolute, one might say that the really unaccountable thing is the existence of this world, or the appearance of its existence. It would be simple – given the typification in question – to explain the non-existence of this world; but – again given the premise – it is virtually impossible to explain its existence, or the appearance of its existence. As a consequence, existence (or the appearance of existence) can be accounted for only by saying that it lacks all genuine reality, which is tantamount to saying that existence is really non-existent.

How such a conclusion is imposed is obvious once one takes into account the starting-point of Guénon's argument. If, as he affirms, the universal possibilities in their non-manifest state are completely and totally real in themselves, in their own self-enclosed exclusiveness, in such a way that they absorb or subsume the sum total of reality in themselves, it follows that any departure from the state of non-manifestation is also a departure from the Real, a falling away into non-reality. If it were otherwise, it could not be said, as it is said, that a possibility possesses the totality of the Real in its non-manifest state: if its state of manifestation *quâ* state of manifestation possessed any reality at all, the conclusion would have to be that a possibility does not possess in itself, in its non-manifest state (in which it cannot be differentiated from the Absolute Itself), the totality of the Real, and such a conclusion contradicts the initial contention that a non-manifest possibility is totally and exclusively real in itself.

Indeed, as we have already noted, with respect to its non-manifest and undetermined state, the manifest and determined state of a universal possibility is "rigorously nothing". Hence, one is forced into the position of saying that existence, or the appearance of existence, is basically non-existent. This is why the attempt to account for the world of manifestation is, so to speak, defeated from the start, for there is not and cannot be any plausible or even possible account of what is not: manifestation *quâ* manifestation is a kind of illusion or evil dream. Any doctrine which places the sum total of reality outside and above not only phenomenal existence but also Being itself is bound to reduce Being and, *a fortiori*, phenomenal existence to a kind of insignificant shadow. Moreover, it leads to an extreme form of pantheism: not that of the divinization of existence but that of affirming its ultimate nullity and unreality. Creation – even the idea of creation – can ultimately have no positive or significant value; and the creature *quâ* creature can have no concrete eternal destiny.

This conclusion follows from Guénon's initial conception of the nature of the non-manifest and universal possibilities. In effect, these constitute a kind of Godhead without God, in the sense that they have no author. To put this another way: if one may be permitted to talk about God in the context of this doctrine, then it is not God who determines these non-manifest and universal possibilities (for by definition they are essentially undetermined and undeterminable). On the contrary, it is they that "determine" the ideal content of God's pre-ontological nature. In fact, they constitute this nature itself, in the sense that no distinction can be made between the two: God as the Absolute is universal Possibility, the All-Possible. This means that there can be no idea of God, as the Absolute, as the free determining principle of his own possibilities, and hence there can be no doctrine of creation in the Christian sense, for such a doctrine presupposes that God, as the Absolute, is not to be identified solely with his pre-ontological nature. To substitute for the idea of God who determines his own possibilities the notion of a Godhead, or *Ungrund,* of universal possibilities that not only have no author but in themselves constitute the Absolute, is to typify the Absolute as an essentially self-enclosed, self-sufficient, and totally perfect circle, impersonal, undetermined and pre-ontological, with no possible real and living relationships *ad extra.* It is because of this that one can say that what characterizes a metaphysical doctrine such as that expounded by Guénon is its radical devaluation of creation – or of manifestation – to such a point that it is reduced to being little more than a purely negative dimension. From the more specifically Christian point of view, one can say more succinctly that what characterizes it is its anti-incarnational and anti-sacramental nature.

In saying this, it by no means follows that such a type of metaphysical doctrine is basically untrue: that is quite another matter and not one that I attempt to assess here. What I have attempted to illustrate is solely how Guénon's formulation of metaphysical doctrine has been affected by his acceptance of a particular proposition concerning the relationship between the order of logic and the metaphysical order, how this has led him to typify even the supreme principle of the metaphysical order in terms that conform to the order of logic, and how this in its turn has affected his presentation of other aspects of metaphysical doctrine. For him, as we have remarked several times, this relationship is a necessary one inherent in the nature of things, and hence he regards the proposition that affirms it as axiomatic. But in default of objective grounds on which its status as a hermeneutic principle of absolute and universal validity can be made evident, it appears to be little more than an assumption the possible truth of which eludes both proof and disproof. What is more important, however, is that its application in practice appears to defeat its own purpose and to result in the error of which Guénon accuses the philosophers, namely, that of imposing a kind of limitation on universal Possibility itself.

We have already seen how the observance of the proposition in question appears to have been infringed in cases such as Guénon's account of the determination of Being and his attempt to "prove freedom metaphysically". But to show how it also results in imposing a limitation on universal Possibility itself, we have to go back to Guénon's initial typification of the supreme metaphysical principle, the Absolute that constitutes the primordial datum of his exegesis. On the basis of the truth of the logical order that all determination is necessarily a limitation, Guénon arrives at the idea of this Absolute – the Infinite, or universal Possibility – that can be expressed only in negative terms – terms such as "undetermined", "impersonal", "unqualified" and so on. But by a kind of double-edgedness which may be inherent in logic itself, to apply even negative terms to the Absolute in an attempt to preserve It from determination and hence from limitation is in fact to do the very thing one is trying not to do. For to say that the Absolute is undetermined, impersonal and so on, is at once to affirm something about It and hence to limit It – to limit It, that is, by excluding everything of a determined, personal or qualified nature from It. Indeed, even to say that the Absolute can be typified only in negative terms is likewise both to affirm something about It and hence to limit It – to limit It by excluding from It the possibility of being typified in positive terms. It would thus appear that, paradoxically and ironically, Guénon's adherence to the premise that the supreme metaphysical principle must be typified in terms consistent with the laws of logic – a premise that itself presupposes the acceptance of the proposition that there is a strict correlation between the order of logic and the metaphysical order – results in imposing on universal Possibility the kind of limitation which it is his specific intention not to impose.

Is there any way of avoiding such a predicament, or similar predicaments? Perhaps none, unless one is to adopt an apophatic attitude or negative approach to the Absolute more radical than the one adopted by Guénon. For Guénon's *via negativa* in the event does not leave the Absolute with the indetermination that is intended, but imposes on It a limitation that vitally affects his whole presentation of metaphysical doctrine. This is because the idea of the Absolute which Guénon proposes is reached in the manner exemplified on pages 17-18 of the book in question by means of a purely logical demonstration and hence by means of a kind of apodictic apophatism. A more radical apophatism – one which would not be self-defeating – would take its start in a kind of holy *agnosia* that refuses to apply any concept whatsoever, whether couched in positive or negative terms, to the ultimate nature or Essence of the Absolute.

According to this more radical form of apophatism, then, the Essence of the Absolute cannot be typified as either determined or free from determination, either Being or Non-Being, either personal or impersonal: It is beyond every affirmation just as It is beyond every negation. To say this, however, is not to say that nothing can be affirmed or denied about the Absolute Itself and hence that there is no possibility of formulating any doctrine at all. This would be the case only on the condition that the Absolute – the sum total of Reality – is identified exclusively with the Essence. This in effect is what Guénon does: he identifies Absolute and Essence, the terms are interchangeable for him, and each constitutes the supreme principle, the primordial datum of his exegesis – the idea of which he reaches by applying to it what one might call a single negativity, with the result that he concludes that the supreme principle can only be described in negative terms. But the apophatism which refuses to apply any concept whatsoever, whether couched in positive or negative terms, to the Essence does not identify the Absolute with the Essence or regard the Essence as in some sense constituting the supreme aspect of the Absolute. This apophatism, therefore, involves not a single but a double negativity: if the Absolute is free from determination, It is also *not* free from determination; if It is Non-Being, It is also *not* Non-Being; if It is impersonal, It is also *not* impersonal; if It is non-manifest, It is also *not* non-manifest; if It is not in time, It is also *not* not in time; and so on. Each negative is true only on condition of being itself denied, while the truth itself lies in the simultaneity of this double negation. This means that the Absolute Itself is both free from determination and determined, both personal and impersonal, both Being and Non-Being, and so on, with no ontological or other superiority being attributable to either of the two terms of each typification. And this is the case even if neither of the terms of each typification can be applied to the Essence itself of the Absolute, for – to repeat – the Absolute is not to be identified exclusively with the Essence. One might express this more succinctly by saying that the Absolute Itself transcends Its own Essence.

In other words, what the refusal to identify the Absolute solely with the Essence demands is the recognition that the Absolute Itself, in Its all-embracing reality, Its unknowability and knowability, Its Non-Being and Its Being, Its indetermination and determination, is such that the most adequate idea of It accessible to the human intelligence is one that can be expressed only in a form that is antinomic and paradoxical. Consequently it is an idea that does not conform to the demands of the proposition to which Guénon himself adhered with such unquestioning assent.

8/23/12

Finally, therefore, one is brought back to the issue which has been implicit throughout this chapter. By definition, one's presentation of metaphysical doctrine must begin from a given starting-point. This starting-point will be identified with the metaphysical principle that one accepts as the Absolute, and it will thus be this Absolute which constitutes for one the primordial datum or starting-point of exegesis.

However, this Absolute which constitutes for one the primordial datum of exegesis will not be the Absolute as such, in what one might call Its untypified quiddity. It will be an Absolute typified for one in a certain manner. That is to say, It will be typified as this or that, or as not this or that: determined or undetermined, personal or impersonal, Being or Non-Being, One or Three, or both of the two terms of each of these typifications simultaneously. In other words, it will not be the Absolute as such, but one's idea of the Absolute that constitutes the primordial datum of the exegesis.

This idea of the Absolute that constitutes the primordial datum of one's exegesis may be established for one by divine revelation. In default of that, however, the only alternative is to accept as one's primordial datum an idea of the Absolute established for one in accordance with some other criterion. But in the latter case it is not divine revelation, but this other criterion which establishes the primordial datum of one's exegesis; and that in effect is to make this other criterion the supreme determining principle of the exegesis itself. It is therefore of crucial importance to know what this criterion is, and why one gives one's assent to it, because in the ultimate analysis it is this criterion, and not one's idea of the Absolute, still less the Absolute as such, which determines the form that one's presentation of metaphysical doctrine will take.

* * *

Guénon himself claimed that his understanding of metaphysical doctrine is derived from the Vedanta viewed in the extreme non-dual perspective given to it by Shankārachārya; and some of the difficulties which, from the Christian point of view, it raises appear to have their equivalent in this metaphysical perspective of the Vedanta. For according to this perspective, as for Guénon, metaphysical doctrine has its starting-point in an idea of the Absolute, or the Infinite, that is totally unqualified and wholly free from any determination or particularization. To affirm anything of the Absolute is in some sense to limit and determine it, and so to make It less than the Absolute; any distinction or qualification that is made is transcended by the absolute non-determination of the "one truly non-dual" (the *ekam ena advaitam*) of the Upanishads. Pushing to an extreme its discrimination between the permanent and the impermanent, the immutable and mutable, Being and becoming, and with a *via negativa*, or apophatism, that ultimately refuses any idea of determination or differentiation in the Absolute because it regards it as necessarily implying limitations and imperfections, Vedantic thought tends to become "fixed" in the idea of the pure isolation (*kaivalya*) of the non-communicable, non-participable Absolute (*nirgunabrahma*).

It is here that the question of manifestation or of the appearance of things is posed in this extreme non-dual perspective. What is it that actually becomes, or appears to become, in manifestation? In the extreme form of the *advaita* the answer is that ultimately nothing becomes; the world does not exist, or is but the appearance of *māyā* (neither being nor non-being, neither mixture of being and non-being, nor unmixed). In a sense, there is no question at all of manifestation, for *māyā* is the category itself of the question, and it can only be posed so long as the individual who frames it is involved in *māyā*. Thus as soon as the individual has overcome the distinct consciousness of his individual self (itself an illusion) and is free from the evanescent and deficient category of *māyā*, both question and questioner disappear and are immersed in the Absolute, the true Self, the nothing-but-Self. The Absolute has never been and can never be other than It is; It thinks neither the world nor the self; It does not even think Itself, but in Itself excludes all "otherness", all "outside Itself". It is non-dual.

This idea of the isolation and purity of the Absolute has however another aspect, that of Its omnipresence. It is only from an inferior and individual point of view that one can oppose the Absolute to *māyā* or to the contingent. In reality these distinctions do not exist and are rigorously transcended by the Absolute. The reality of everything is the Absolute; for if there were any reality less or other than the Absolute, the Absolute would not be All: there would be something external to It by which It would be, not infinite, but limited. Hence, the reality of everything is the Absolute: It is perfectly and exhaustively immanent in all things, for not only can there not be anything other than Itself, but also It can have no content but Itself, for It gives Itself to Itself entirely and infinitely in Its infinite generosity. All the reality that manifestation possesses resides in its non-manifest principle and in so far as it is not different from its principle: all appearance of the effect as such, or of its difference from its principial cause, is illusory. The reality of manifestation is the same as that of its principle and there is no other reality. In this sense the doctrine is pantheistic: the All and the Absolute are one. Though in the well-known Upanishad image it is said that there are two birds on the same tree, in reality there is only one bird, for the distinction of the one from the other is but an illusory matter.

All this being so, one is nevertheless still faced with the original question, the question of the *jîvâtman* who has not yet recognized that "the flux and the absolute are the same" or – which is the same thing – his identity, essential and existential, with the infinite Self, the Brahma: whence comes this illusion of particular being and this appearance of the world? What are their mutual relationships with the Self, with the Absolute? What is their ultimate sense? Here Vedantic metaphysics, issuing from the sphere of Non-Being and Non-Duality, decomposes into two different notions which together constitute the horns of what appears to be an irreducible dilemma: one is the notion of the illusory transformation (of the Absolute into Its determinations: *vivarta-vâda*), and the other is that of the real transformation (*parinamavāda*).

The idea of the illusory transformation of the Absolute – all that is, is really the Absolute, and only because of individual ignorance does it appear other than the Absolute – preserves the total purity, simplicity, immutability, and permanence of the Absolute, but leaves unaccounted for the fact, fictitious or real, of error. The Absolute cannot err; from what cause, then, cosmic or supra-cosmic, proceeds this ignorance according to which I err in thinking myself other than the Absolute? If the idea of my separate identity is an illusion from which I must escape through spiritual realization, why does it come to be at all? And if its coming to be is only an appearance and has no ultimate reality, so that in a sense it has never really come into being, why does this appearance come to be? Here it is no answer to say that I err because of what is fated and determined by past or mediate causes, whether I am responsible for them or not, for this still leaves unanswered why I bound myself, or was bound, to think I am a particular being in the first place, and why this causal chain of ignorance of which I am now a victim was set in motion at all. Who or what, that is to say, determined this original false choice of identity? Who or what determined originally that I should think of myself? And why was it so determined?

If, in order to answer these and similar questions, the notion of the illusory transformation of the Absolute is replaced by that of Its real transformation, it is then possible to give some account of how and why the world, the self, and their identity and separateness, have arisen. But in this case the purity, non-particularization and immutability of the Absolute are sacrificed, and a whole host of fresh dilemmas are presented. It is difficult to avoid the conclusion that according to the Vedanta there can be no understanding of the relationships between the Absolute and manifestation that does not involve either an "acosmism" reducing the world and particular beings to the unaccountable appearance of *māyā* and the ignorance that goes with it, or the disruption of the absolute simplicity, immutability and transcendence of the Divine Essence.

What is striking about this doctrine from the Christian point of view is its apparent refusal to attribute any positive value or significance to creation as such. It might from this point of view be described as a pre- or anti-Incarnational thought-structure, in the sense that it does not, and cannot, embrace the reality which is revealed in the Incarnation of the Absolute in the person of the Theanthropos, Christ. There appears to be, in spite of such notions as the real transformation of the Absolute into the contingent, a total *hiatus* between the Absolute and the manifest sensible world, so much so that one might say that the really unaccountable thing is the existence of the world, or the appearance of its existence. As we remarked in connection with Guénonian metaphysics above, while it would be simple, given the premises of the doctrine, to explain the non-existence of the world, it is virtually impossible, given these same premises, to explain its existence, or the appearance of its existence. Consequently, the existence (or the appearance of the existence) of the world can only be accounted for by saying that it lacks all genuine reality, which is tantamount to saying that the existent is really non-existent, or is a kind of "evil" and negative category of thought.

For if the Absolute in Its non-manifest state is completely and totally real in Itself, in Its own self-enclosed exclusiveness, in such a way that It absorbs or exhausts the pleroma of Reality in Itself, it follows that any departure from this state of self-sufficient non-manifestation is also a departure from Reality, a falling away into non-existence. If the condition of manifestation as manifestation possesses any reality at all, the conclusion is that the Absolute does not possess the totality of the Real in Itself in Its non-manifest state. Hence one is forced into the position, logically, of saying that existence, or the appearance of existence, is, as such, basically an illusion. This is why the attempts to account for the world of manifestation have about them something of a *deus ex machina*, for really there cannot be any plausible or even possible account of what basically is an illusion. Any doctrine which places the Absolute as total Reality outside and above not only phenomenal "existence" but also Being itself, is bound to reduce both Being and, *a fortiori*, existence to a kind of insignificant shadow.

Moreover, as we also remarked, it leads to an extreme form of pantheism: not that of a divinization of existence, but that of affirming its ultimate nullity and unreality. The creature *quâ* creature can have no concrete and eternal destiny. In fact the creature *quâ* creature represents a state of bondage, mental or physical, in unreality, total deliverance from which is only possible on condition that it ceases to exist as a creature in any and every way whatsoever. There is, in other words, no place for the creature in the Absolute. As has been stated above, the Absolute is an essentially self-enclosed, self-sufficient, and totally perfect circle, impersonal and free of all distinction, with no possible real and living relationships *ad extra*, with any *alia a se*; and it is because of this that one may say that what appears to typify this doctrine, like that of Guénon, is its refusal to recognize any positive and eternal significance in creation as such, its anti-Incarnational character; and it is this which is reflected in its de-incarnational view of spiritual realization.

Quite clearly, the Christian doctrine of an Absolute that is triune and personal, and its idea that what is created and relative may have an eternal destiny within the Absolute Itself, without on that account ceasing to be created and relative, conflicts with this extreme non-dual form of metaphysical doctrine. From the point of view of this form of doctrine it amounts almost to an idolatry, or at least to a placing of the Absolute on a lower plane than that on which this form of doctrine places It, and one that can therefore be included within the superior perspective of this form of doctrine. In effect, from the point of view of such radical non-duality, and also, as we saw above, from the point of view of Guénonian metaphysics, to qualify the Absolute in any way – by saying It is triune and personal, for instance – is in some way to define It. Any definition, or making finite, in its turn can only single out and emphasize some particular aspect of the Absolute at the expense of some other aspect, and this is to make It less all-embracing, less all-inclusive, than It is before any character is added to It; it is to reduce It in some sense to being but a relative Absolute. All determination therefore is necessarily a limitation involving a certain denial of the infinite nature of the Absolute, and hence the Christian qualification of the Absolute as triune and personal can only refer, not to the Absolute Itself, but to some limited determination of the Absolute, rigorously and absolutely transcended by the Absolute Itself and as nothing in regard to It. The absolute Absolute is and must be totally indefinable, totally unqualified, totally non-determined, not admitting particularization or participation of any kind.

The argument again appears to be one of logic; and if Christians are to maintain that their view of an Absolute that is triune and personal does not represent a more limited point of view than that of such radical non-duality, then they must also claim that they do not share the same conception of the relationship between logic and metaphysic which appears to lie behind it. For what this extreme form of non-duality, like Neoplatonic doctrine or Guénonian metaphysics, appears to presuppose is that if it can be demonstrated in purely logical terms that a certain metaphysical principle is superior – more all-inclusive, less limited and determined – than another, then this first principle must on that account stand higher in the metaphysical order than the second. In this way it is possible to demonstrate the superiority of the non-dual idea of the Absolute over the Christian idea, for in logical terms any qualification whatsoever of the Absolute must imply a degree of limitation and hence of imperfection, so that only an Absolute that is totally unqualified can be totally infinite and perfect.

That is why Christians, if they are to claim that their idea of the Absolute represents the Truth more fully than the idea of the Absolute according to non-dual metaphysics, must also claim that this way of arguing from logical demonstration to metaphysical conclusion begs a question in the relationship between logic and metaphysics over which they are likely to hold views very different from those that appear to be implicit in such non-dual doctrine; and that their idea of an Absolute both triune and personal, in spite of its qualified and therefore more limited appearance from a logical point of view, none the less reflects more adequately the nature of the Absolute Itself than does the non-dual idea. Similarly, they must say that their ideas about the positive and eternal significance of the creature, although they imply an entirely paradoxical and contradictory understanding of the relationships between the Absolute and the relative, nevertheless reflect the truth of things more adequately than non-dual doctrines of manifestation. As we said, for the Christian it must be, not the logical demonstration, but the logical contradiction, or paradox, that marks the concept-limit, the *ne plus ultra* of human thought.

* * *

To sum up, in a somewhat elliptical manner, the findings of this chapter: of the two views that have been contrasted, the first envisages what one might call an extreme form of non-duality; while the second is that of the Christian tradition, especially in its Orthodox form.

From the point of view of extreme non-duality, the Absolute is in all respects supra-individual, supra-personal, supra-formal and divine. Hence metaphysical truth, which is identical with the Absolute, is also supra-individual, supra-personal, supra-formal and divine.

Yet since the Absolute is Reality itself, to the extent that nothing can be said to possess reality except the Absolute, all differentiation and individuation, everything that possesses form and is personal, and hence can be distinguished from the Absolute, represents a falling away, an alienation, from the Real. It represents something that is ultimately unreal and illusory.

All differentiation and individuation necessarily involve a limitation; and since that which is limited cannot be identified with the Absolute, which by definition is limitless, it must be other than the Absolute.

But the Absolute possesses the totality of the Real. Hence anything that can be distinguished, or that distinguishes itself, from the Absolute, and is, or regards itself, as on that account other than the Absolute, must be in bondage to the unreal and the illusory.

This means that there is not, and cannot be, any principle of differentiation or individuation in the Absolute; for, if there were, it would have to operate and so to produce what is differentiated and individuated.

Yet since that which is differentiated and individuated is on that account other than the Absolute, and as such must be unreal and illusory, to say that the Absolute possesses a principle of differentiation and individuation which is bound to operate is tantamount to saying that the Absolute is bound to produce what is unreal and illusory, which is absurd.

Hence the unity of man with the Absolute, the identity of known and knower, which is a prerequisite of any metaphysical knowledge, cannot be a bi-unity, a state of two-in-oneness, *unus-ambo*, involving the individual person and the Absolute. It cannot be a unity which does not demand that all distinction between the one and the other is transcended.

On the contrary, the unity of man with the Absolute, the identity of known and knower, can be attained only through the individual person transcending his individuated personhood and through identifying himself wholly with the supra-formal, supra-individual, supra-personal Absolute.

This view thus involves a total denial of the ultimate value and reality of the personal. It demands as a condition of metaphysical knowledge a total impersonalism – the annulment and alienation of the person.

It also involves a denial of the apophatic principle, according to which whatever degree of metaphysical knowledge a person possesses there are always degrees beyond that degree, divine gnosis being infinite.

Yet how can human thought express itself in relation to the supra-formal truth *except* in apophatic terms?

The principle of non-duality is regarded as expressed in the formula, *tat tvam asi*: "that (the Absolute) you (the Self or ego) also are".

But how is the Self named in this formula still a Self when it is equated with the supra-individual and supra-personal Absolute?

Or in what sense can the "I" who is able to say "I am" be identical with the Absolute?

Is it the real man, or the illusory ego, who declares "I am that"?

Is it enough to say "I am that" for the ego to cease from being illusory?

And if there is an essential identity of the individuated Self and the supra-personal Absolute, how does it come about that the Self falls into the delusion of thinking that it is not the supra-personal Absolute but possesses an individuated existence?

Is the individual Self responsible for having the illusion that it possesses an individual existence?

And if there is no principle of differentiation or individuation in the Absolute, how does it come about that a Self that is equated with the Absolute differentiates itself from the Absolute and thinks of itself as an individual personal existence?

A principle of differentiation, even if its action does no more than produce the illusion of being differentiated, cannot subsist in a vacuum. Either it is inherent in the Absolute; or it is a principle that exists outside the Absolute, as a principle distinct from the Absolute. But in this latter case the Absolute is not then the Absolute, since there is an active principle that operates independently of It, and hence an irreducible dualism lies at the base of things.[20]

At this point it may be asked: why this refusal to recognize a principle of differentiation and individuation in the Absolute?

Why this refusal to recognize that the Absolute exists in a multiplicity of individual existences that are distinct from It? Why is it regarded as a basic form of ignorance to say that reality is multiple?

What is the metaphysic that denies to the Absolute a principle of differentiation and individuation?

And if there is a principle of differentiation and individuation in the Absolute, how can it express itself – *i.e.*, how can the Absolute fulfill Its own nature – except by positing the *reality* of individual existents that are not equated with It?

Individuation in itself is not an illusion: it is the coming into existence of the Absolute Itself – a coming into existence in forms that are spiritual and personal individualities, imperishable and

---

[20] Dualism, which involves two entirely non-reciprocal and non-mutually-interpenetrating realities, is not to be confused with duality.

inalienable.

In fact, from this point of view – which is the Christian point of view – it could be said that the secret of the Absolute lies in the multiple forms in which It is manifest, just as the secret of these forms lies in the Absolute.

It is not my individuation, or my personal existence, that is an illusion. It is my failure to affirm, in active terms, my individual, personal and spiritual existence in God that produces the illusion; for then I attribute to myself a kind of independent, autonomous existence in which I am my own God, and it is this conception of myself that is illusory, and which for Christians is expressive of man's fallen state.

Thus, in the Christian view, man is by definition a form in which the Absolute manifests a virtuality of Its own nature; and his supreme cognitive faculty – the intellect – although deiform and capable, when purified, of direct, experiential metaphysical knowledge of God, is not to be identified with the Absolute (though it is not on that account non-Absolute), or to be regarded as undifferentiated from the Absolute, or as supra-personal and supra-formal.

This means that whatever the transformations through which a human being may pass – and they are limitless – and however profound his union with the Absolute, he will never lose his personal, spiritual and distinctive identity, for this identity is integral with his eternal destiny.

He is thus obliged to recognize that he can never exhaust the plenitude of divine gnosis, and that his stance *vis-à-vis* this gnosis must always be an apophatic stance.

Further, he is obliged to recognize that, however profound his union with the Absolute, not only will this unity always be a bi-unity, a two-in-oneness, *unus-ambo*, but also he will never exhaust the capacity for still deeper union.

This in its turn means that he can never possess *in actu* more metaphysical knowledge than the state of his union with the Absolute permits him to possess.

Lastly, he is obliged to recognize that whatever the degree of divinization, or theosis, he attains, he can never transcend the spiritual and personal form through which the Absolute manifests, and so gives concrete existence to, an inalienable and imperishable virtuality of Its own Being.

This in its turn is equivalent to saying that his knowledge and experience of metaphysical truth can never exceed his knowledge and experience of his own being, of his own self.

And a consequence of this is that, whatever the state of being and hence degree of metaphysical knowledge he has attained, this knowledge will always correspond to, and thus be colored by, his state of being, the state of his own personal identity.

Any attempt to transcend this identity with the aim of acquiring absolute metaphysical knowledge must, then, in the Christian perspective, represent no less than an attempt to transcend the hierarchical modes of the universal harmony. And: " Ἥλιος οὐχ ὑπερβήσεται μέτρα· εἰ δὲ μή, Ἐρινύες μιν Δίκης ἐπίκουροι ἐξευρήσουσιν." ("The sun will not overstep its limits; for should it do so, the Furies, ministers of Justice, will track it down".)[21]

The contrast in these two views is of course reflected in and underpinned by their respective understanding of the Absolute. The principle of non-duality is underpinned by an understanding of the Absolute which equates It with an Essence that is not only unitary but also totally undifferentiated: no distinctions whatsoever are to be recognized in it.

The Christian view is underpinned by an understanding that the Absolute is both, and simultaneously, unitary and triadic: that is to say, there are distinctions of Persons in the Absolute and these distinctions, although real and indissoluble, do not on that account disrupt Its unitariness.

Hence the Christian Absolute, which admits differentiation, is, from the point of view of the Absolute that underpins the principle of non-duality, not the absolute Absolute: the Persons of the Trinity, in this view, can only be limitations of the Absolute, and cannot therefore be equated with the Absolute, which in Itself must transcend all limitation and consequently all personalism.

This is in opposition to the Christian understanding, according

---

[21] Herakleitos, Diels-kranz 94.

to which it is incorrect to envisage an Absolute that is non-personal, or a Person that is non-Absolute.[22]

One can perhaps state this contrast in more simple terms and say that of these two views in question the first gives high priority to logical consistency, and hence tends to be cataphatic, while the second is more antinomic in its approach, and hence tends to be apophatic in character.

Thus, in the first view logical consistency is pushed to the point of affirming that, since the Absolute is essentially non-differentiated, anything that is differentiated is other and less real than the Absolute, and hence is relative, or at least only relatively Absolute; and what is relative cannot be the Absolute as such.

In the second view, on the other hand, antinomy is pushed to the point of affirming not only that what is differentiated need not be other and less real than the Absolute, and hence relative, but also that it is quite possible for the relative to be the Absolute, and the Absolute the relative, without this signifying that the relativity of the relative or the absolutism of the Absolute is on this account in any way compromised.

Or one can say that of these two views the first involves a metaphysic in which primacy of origin in the Absolute is given to a non-differentiated Essence, whereas the second involves a metaphysic in which such primacy is given to the act of being, which entails differentiation: it is the act of being which itself determines the Essence, whereas according to the metaphysic valid for the first view the act of being is seen as a non-essential, and even unreal and illusory, accident superadded to or superimposed on the Absolute.

It should be added that the notion, implicit in the concept of non-duality, that it is possible for us to realize in this present life our essential identity with the supra-personal Absolute, and thus

[22] This understanding is to some extent modified in the theological tradition that stems from St. Augustine and passes through St. Anselm and St. Bonaventure down to the Scholastics; for in this tradition there is a tendency to assert the primacy of a non-personal essence in the Trinity over the concrete reality of the Persons, thus obscuring the full integrity and coherence of Christian trinitarian doctrine.

to attain a state in this present life in which not only is our knowledge universal and infallible, but also we ourselves are impervious
to vicissitude and error, is not one that is valid in the Christian
view of things; for in this view everyone, whatever the degree of
perfection he or she has attained, is still exposed in this present life
to both these contingencies. To think otherwise is, in this view, to
ignore the mystery of human freedom, inalienable whatever the
state of grace we may have been granted.

Chapter Five

Christianity and the Challenge of Georgios Gemistos Plethon and Friedrich Nietzsche

In the middle of the fourteenth century Georgios Gemistos Plethon was born at Constantinople. Little is known of the career of this man, and of this, nothing is very remarkable. It appears that he lived for many years at Mistra in the Peloponnesos, where he settled when he was quite young and where he became a judge. He was a representative of the Orthodox Church at the Council held at Florence in 1439 on the question of the unity of the Eastern and Western Churches (it was then that he added "Plethon" to his name); and it was at Florence also that he gained the admiration of Cosimo de' Medici. He died in 1450; and fifteen years after his death a Venetian general, Sigismondo Pandolfo Malatesta, transferred his remains from Mistra to the church of St. Francesco at Rimini and enclosed them in a marble tomb on which, in Latin, a suitable inscription was written. Yet it has been said with reference to Gemistos that "the Renaissance can point to many a career which is greater, but to none which is so strangely symbolical".[1]

What is there to justify this statement? There is first of all his relationship to western scholasticism. From the time when Boethius made his translation of Porphyry's *Isagoge*, if not from an earlier date, western scholastic philosophers moved steadily along that path which was to culminate in the works of St. Thomas Aquinas. Broadly speaking, scholastic philosophy was an attempt to provide

[1] E. M. Forster, "Gemistus Pletho" in *Abinger Harvest* (London, 1942) p .186.

Christianity with a self-conscious and systematic organ of thought and of formal logic based on the teachings of Aristotle. It was an attempt, in fact, to reconcile Christian theology with Aristotelian philosophy. But in the end so intimate became this reconciliation that any attack on the philosophy of Aristotle was felt to amount to an attack on Christian doctrine itself. This created something of a dilemma. Aristotle had not been a Christian. He had been a "heathen". His writings were not divine revelation, nor were they sacrosanct. The Church could not pretend that his teaching – that of a heathen – had the same authority as the teaching of Holy Scripture. It could not prohibit attacks on Aristotle or prevent discrimination between his teaching and the mystery of the Christian faith. But when he was attacked with his own dialectical weapons or when it was pointed out that his doctrines had little or nothing to do with Christianity, so deeply was the corpus of scholastic theology involved with his concepts that it would only have been possible for the Church to condemn him through condemning that theology as well.

Moreover, the status of Aristotle in the Latin West was deeply affected by other factors. First, his writings were known only through translations, first of all from the Arabic, later from the Greek. Second, and more important, there was a lack of knowledge of any other ancient author whose works could be set alongside or contrasted with those of Aristotle. The implications of the fact that Aristotle dominated almost exclusively the theological and intellectual development of the later Middle Ages in Western Europe at least down to the middle of the fifteenth century are enormous. Had the works of any other major author of antiquity – Plotinus for instance – been available, this development might have been very different.

Western Europe was not, however, all Europe. In fact, from an intellectual point of view, during the medieval centuries the mainstream of European history was represented, not by the Latin West, but by Byzantium; and when the works of Aquinas began to be translated into Greek, they were immediately subject to the scrutiny of men for whom not only was Aristotle well-known – as he

never was in the West – from his original works and from the
works of his commentators, but for whom also Aristotle was far
from being the sole and masterful authority, even among the "heathen" philosophers. The theologians of Byzantium were as familiar
with Plato and the Neoplatonists as they were with Aristotle. Although the ancient philosophical schools in Athens had been closed
in 529 by Justinian, by the sixth century Platonism had been incorporated into the Eastern Christian tradition through the works
of Alexandrians like Clement and Origen, of Cappadocians like
St. Gregory of Nyssa, and of Dionysios the Areopagite; and subsequent Byzantine theologians, even if they used Aristotelianism
as a method, remained faithful to the earlier tradition. This is not
altered by the fact that such important figures as St. John of Damascus in the eighth century or St. Photios in the ninth century
might be counted as Aristotelians. From St. Maximos the Confessor, who embraced and developed the writings of the Areopagite,
through St. Symeon the New Theologian, down to Nicholas
Cabasilas and St. Gregory Palamas, the theology of Byzantium
was mystical and contemplative in character, a theology "which
does not demonstrate the truth, but exposes it nakedly, in symbols,
so that the soul, changed by holiness and light, penetrates without
the reason into it".[2]

Moreover, alongside and often challenging this theology was a
more purely philosophical tradition of Platonism, represented by
such figures as Michael Psellos, John Italos and Georgios Gemistos;
and it was Georgios Gemistos who, while at the Council of Florence in 1439, first pointed out to the Latin West in his tract entitled
Concerning the difference between Plato and Aristotle that Aristotle,
as compared with Plato, not only did not agree with Christianity
in the way that was thought, but in some of his doctrines might
even be said to lay himself open to the charge of atheism.[3] Thus
Gemistos was the first who in an authoritative way attacked the

---

[2] Dionysios: *Epist.* IX, 1. P.G.3, 1105 CD.

[3] See J. W. Taylor: *Georgius Gemistus Pletho's Criticism of Plato and Aristotle*,
(University of Chicago, 1921), p. 7. For an English translation of this tract, see
C.M. Woodhouse, *George Gemistos Plethon: The Last of the Hellenes* (Oxford, 1986)
pp. 191-214. (Ed.)

hegemony of Aristotle in western thought. If it is further considered that it was due to Gemistos's direct influence that the Platonic Academy was opened at Florence; that he supported Marsilio Ficino, translator of the *Corpus Hermeticum*, as its first president; and that the teaching and spirit of the Academy marked a breach in the scholastic-bound, Aristotelian cosmos, then something of the symbolic significance of Gemistos's career may be understood.

There is, however, another aspect to this career. Foreseeing the imminence of the fall of the Byzantine empire, Gemistos yet hoped that it might be possible to preserve in the Peloponnesos – the cradle, as he saw it, of Hellenism – a small but vital area in which this Hellenism could survive in a physical sense and prepare for its future. It was to this end that he outlined a series of reforms which involved a total change in the social and economic structure of the Peloponnesos; it was to this end also that he advised the building of a wall across the Isthmus of Corinth to hold back the advancing Turk; and it was finally to this end that he sought a complete regeneration and recreation of the religious life of his people.

Here perhaps we reach what is most important in Gemistos's significance. He understood, as few modern reformers seem to understand, that no amount of reforming will by itself have in the end the slightest effect unless it is accompanied by a corresponding change in religious orientation. "Everything in human life", he said, "as regards it being done rightly or wrongly, depends on our religious beliefs."[4] Yet in this question of religious beliefs, Plethon did not aim at reform within the existing structure of Christianity. He looked to a reform through the reshaping of the religious traditions of the ancient world. During his stay at Florence in 1438-9, he is reported to have expressed his belief that both Christianity and the Moslem faith would soon be superseded by a religion not greatly differing from that of the ancient Greeks.

Yet it would be a mistake to see Gemistos as one of those academic dilettantes who, having no real religious capacity, seeks to

[4] Alexandre's edition of Plethon's *Laws*, with French trans. by Pellissier, Paris 1858: *Traité des Lois*, p. 130. See also Tozer, "A Byzantine Reformer", in J.H.S. VII, 1886, p. 353 ff.

substitute for it a vacuous worship of gods and goddesses that he
somehow believes had something to do with ancient Greece.
Gemistos's reshaping of ancient tradition represented an attempt
to reaffirm certain principles which he felt had been displaced or
overlaid by Christianity. He regarded himself as the heir to the
great teachers of the ancient world, to Zoroaster, Pythagoras, Plato,
and the Neoplatonists, to mention but a few of them. These were
the masters in a tradition of which he was a humble representative. Plethon was one of the first – if not the first – of those figures
at the close of the Middle Ages who sought to base a religious
renaissance on what was fundamentally a Platonic and Neoplatonic
tradition. To grasp the significance of this endeavor, as well as of
certain aspects of the thought of later writers like Goethe, Blake, or
Nietzsche to modify, enrich or eliminate Christianity, they must be
set within the wider historical perspective of the traditions concerned.

* * *

Gemistos himself regarded Plato as his direct spiritual master,
and it was in recognition of this that he assumed the surname of
"Plethon", which he held to be a purer form of Plato's own name;
and indeed Plato is a key figure in this whole enquiry.[5] But if Plato
is a key figure, he is not altogether a straightforward one. His philosophy is complex and contradictory. For our purposes it is enough
to indicate but two contradictory aspects. On the one hand, there
is Plato the dualist, whose dualism is of an extreme nature. There
is an absolute opposition between the world of Ideas, which is
real, and the sensible world, which is basically unreal. There is an
absolute opposition between the soul and the body. The world of
Ideas, the supreme Good, is entirely removed from the sensible
world; it has no contact with it and no regard for it. The purpose
of human life is the catharsis, an asceticism whereby the soul is
slowly delivered from the prison-house of the body and takes its
place once more in the disincarnate, never-to-be-incarnate intelli-

---

[5] The following section takes up themes discussed more fully in the author's
Human Image, World Image (Ispwich 1992), Chapter 1. (Ed.)

gible world. Here, in this side of Plato's thought, is a complete gulf between the world of the senses, ultimately negative in value, and the transcendent world, in which alone reality is to be found.

There is, however, another aspect of Plato which, from the point of view of that tradition from which Gemistos claimed descent, is more important. According to this aspect, the absolute Platonic dualism is, if not eliminated, at least attenuated. For here the visible world itself is said to be penetrated by the Good, and there is a direct intermingling of the transcendent world of Ideas and the world of the senses. This second aspect of Plato – this attempt to express the omnipresence of reality, the penetration of the visible by the invisible, of the sensible world by the intelligible – is something which develops as Plato matures. At the time when he wrote *The Republic*, he attributed no positive significance to the sensible world because this world, being in disorder (ἐν ἀταξία), was without value; it was in fact evil. But in his later dialogues, above all in the *Timaeus* and the *Laws*, as the question of actually realizing the good city on earth became for him more and more pressing, so he was increasingly compelled to grapple for a vision which would embrace the sensible world, this disorder, and would integrate it to the intelligible world, to the total "divine" order of the cosmos. He was compelled to face the problem of reconciling the motionless world of Ideas with the changing world of the senses, and of finding some positive relationship between the one and the other. He had to escape from the old Parmenidean dualism of Being and Non-Being, of Truth and Opinion, by which he had hitherto been dominated, and to approach more closely the dynamic vision of a Herakleitos, who found in movement itself the secret of stability.

The solution for which he sought is first indicated in the *Phaedrus*,[6] where the soul is said to be the origin of movement (ἀρχή κινήσεως), and not something static as it had previously been regarded. This new approach is developed in the *Timaeus*. The soul, the origin of movement, is self-moving, yet moves after the pattern of the motionless, intelligible world. It is an intermediary between the static eternal world of Ideas and the sensible

[6] *Phaedrus* 245 d7.

world. Human morality must be founded on the order of the cosmos. The human soul is linked to the soul of the World. There is in the *Timaeus* a sort of trinity of Intellect, Soul (from which come life and movement), and Body of the World. There is what one might call a process of incarnation, embryonic as yet, but capable of great development. The changing sensible world takes its place in the world of Being; it is rooted in the divine world. The trinity of Intellect, Soul and Body forms "the sum total of Being" (the παντελῶς ὄν of the *Sophist*). The Demiurge that fashions the sensible world is not so much a rival and distinct power as a mythical double of the Soul of the World. The world is eternal, a divine Cosmos, an order always in movement that is subordinate to the Soul of the World, which is also eternal. The world is in a sense the living body of the divine, a revelation of the divine. Plato is here approaching a vision of the organic wholeness of things denied in his earlier dialogues.

The *Timaeus* expresses the idea of a cosmic God which was so to dominate the Hellenistic world. But this God is an objective and impersonal God. He is not a personal and subjective God. The importance of this becomes apparent when the place of man in the cosmos and his relation to the divine is considered. For the Plato of the *Timaeus*, man is not an isolated pole linked with another isolated pole which is God. The relationship of man and God is not a personal relationship, complete in itself, a mutual reciprocity between one pole and the other. Nor is this relationship any more personal for the Hellenistic sages. The God of the Hellenistic sages is essentially a God of the cosmos. Man is a part of the cosmos. Divorced from the cosmos, man has no existence. This is in keeping with the dominant trend of the philosophy of the city-states.

For the fifth and fourth centuries BC, man was first of all a member of the city, the *polis*. It was only within the larger unit of the city that he achieved his proper status. It was membership of the city that distinguished him from the animals; or at least membership of a city was proof of that element of reason in him which distinguished him from the animals. He called himself a political animal, a *zoon politikon*. It is only from this point of view that one can understand the dread and the severity of banishment from the city. To be banished from the city was to be deprived of human status; it was to be prevented from communion in all that gave human life value. Outside the city there was no fully human life.

At the end of the fourth century, after the breakdown of the city-state, man's existence as a citizen did not fundamentally change, but now, instead of being a member of a local city, he became a member of a cosmic city. But apart from the cosmic city he still had no real existence. He was still but a part of a more important whole, and his destiny could only be achieved by subordinating himself to the whole. The whole was a Living Being, a God, who was far superior to man. The world, the cosmic city, possessed a soul. It was obedient to the order of God. Man was good or bad in so far as he submitted himself to and identified himself with the divine order of the cosmos. The order of the cosmos was something external to and independent of him. God Himself was self-sufficient without man. What was important for God was not the single person but the whole. In the time of the city-state, what had been important was not the prosperity of the single person but the prosperity of the city. Now what was important was the cosmic order. This the single person could in no essential way disturb. His part was to learn the divine plan with what was most impersonal and objective in him – his reason – to obey it, to adjust himself to it, to become one with the cosmic order. But whether he did or did not was a matter of indifference to the order itself. The order itself simply was; man had not made it and it was outside him. It was eternal and complete. Even if there was no man, the cosmos would still be what it was, realized, complete, beautiful and everlasting.

Stoicism carried some of these tendencies to their limit. All that is in the world is linked. The Fire or Breath penetrates everything. It is what holds together and unifies the elements that compose each thing. One thing differs from another only by the degree to which it is penetrated by the Fire, the Logos. There is more Logos in some things than in others. There is more Logos in man than in a stone. But these differences are differences of degree, not of quality. All in the universe is joined together by the presence in everything of Fire-Breath. All lives, moves, and has its being within the universal spirit. The world is a whole. The history of the world is an unbroken chain in which not only the present but the whole world, human and cosmic, past and future, is involved.

Yet this process is still essentially objective and impersonal. Its logical outcome was an enormous sense of fatality. Such a sense was sometimes overcome by identifying Fate with Providence: what is, is for the best. Where the gnostics are concerned, it was overcome by separating the God of Fate from a totally disembodied, extraterrestrial, pure God, removed as far as possible from all contact with or regard for the world; in other words, it was overcome by resorting to a dualism even more extreme than that of Plato in the *Phaedo* and the *Republic*.

It is in the collection of writings known as the *Corpus Hermeticum* that the two sides of Plato, of which we have spoken, meet. They do not meet to be reconciled. The *Corpus Hermeticum* is not a new synthesis. The dualism of intelligible and sensible, of soul and body, is proclaimed as strongly as ever. "There are two sorts of things, the corporeal and the incorporeal; that which is mortal is of the one sort, and that which is divine is of another sort."[7] Or again: "The cosmos is one mass of evil."[8] The value of the sensible world and its participation in the divine is denied: "For all things that come into being are full of perturbations, seeing that the very process of coming into being involves perturbation. But wherever there is perturbation, there the Good cannot be."[9] Concrete reality is illusion. What is real is "that which is not sullied by matter . . . nor limited by boundaries, that which has no color and no shape, that which is without integument, and is luminous, that which is apprehended by itself alone, that which is changeless and unalterable."[10]

[7] *Corpus Hermeticum* Lib. IV.6. All quotations are from: *Corpus Hermeticum. Hermetica of Trismegistus*, ed. and trans. by Walter Scott, (Oxford, 1924).
[8] Ibid., Lib. VI.4
[9] Ibid., Lib. VI.2.
[10] Ibid., Lib. XIII.6

The body is an obstacle to knowledge of God; it must be discarded, denied, rejected: "But first you must tear off this garment which you wear – this cloak of darkness, this web of ignorance, this prop of evil, this bond of corruption, this living death, this conscious corpse, this tomb you carry about with you, this robber in the house, this enemy who hates the things you seek after, and grudges you the things which you desire."[11] In other words, the authors of some of the *Hermetica* subscribe on the one side to a complete sense-denying ethic; they exalt the transcendental at the expense of the earthly; they attack the primal instincts of man, and bid man free himself from them; they endorse and emphasize the negative and evil character of the world, of matter, and of man in so far as he is part of the world and of matter; they would have man sacrifice what is natural and earthly in himself to the impersonal, objective and transcendental Good, to the intelligible world.

On the other hand there are passages in the *Corpus Hermeticum* which affirm the participation of the sensible world in the divine world in a way far more positive than the *Timaeus* affirms it. Life is not a nightmare only, the world is not a barren nothing, the kingdom of shadows: "God is the source of all that is; He is the source of mind, and of nature, and of matter. To show forth his wisdom has He made all things; for He is the source of all."[12] The world is God's revelation of Himself; it is "in God that nature has her being".[13] The sensible, changing world is also part of an invisible, unmoving reality: "God, who is unmoved, moves in all that moves, and Him who is hidden is made manifest through His works."[14] God is ever making "all things, in heaven, in air, on earth, and in the deep, in every part of the cosmos, in all that is and in all that is not. For in all this there is nothing that He is not. He is both the things that are, and the things that are not."[15]

God – reality – is both one and many. He is a unity-in-difference, and incorporeal corporality: "He is hidden, yet most manifest.

[11] Ibid., Lib. VII.2.
[12] Ibid., Lib. III.1.
[13] Ibid., Lib. III.1.
[14] Ibid., Lib. V.5.
[15] Ibid., Lib. V.9.

He is apprehensible by thought alone, yet we can see Him with our eyes. He is bodiless, yet has many bodies, or rather, is embodied in all bodies. There is nothing that He is not; for all things that exist are even He. For this reason all names are names of Him, because all things come from Him, their one Father; and for this reason He has no name, because He is the Father of all."[16] It is an echo of the Psalmist's: "If I ascend into heaven, Thou art there: if I make my bed in hell, behold, Thou art there. If I take the wings of the morning, and dwell in the uttermost part of the sea, even there shall Thy hand lead me" (Ps. 139:8-10a).

It would seem from such passages that the dualism is overcome, but not in any way which is explicable in terms of reason, for such an attempt to explain results necessarily in the dualism from which one seeks to escape. The understanding of reality which is expressed in the *Hermetica* in such passages as these and which seems to transcend the dualism of the Parmenidean-Platonic legacy requires a mode of apprehension which is beyond that of the reason; it requires the subordination of reason to a form of intellectual or noetic perception which the *Hermetica* indicates in saying that God can be seen "with the heart alone".[17] It is the same form of perception as that indicated by Plotinus when he writes that in the vision of God, that which sees is not reason, but something greater and prior to reason, something presupposed by reason, as is the object of vision.

It is in a passage which speaks of man's erotic energies that the authors of the *Hermetica* reveal how far at times they can pass beyond the dualist point of view, beyond the objectivity and impersonality of the Greek and Hellenistic philosophical tradition, and reach an understanding of reality which escapes from dominantly rational categories. The erotic energies are those which are most readily attacked in a sense-denying, dualistic morality. Their irrational character is a scandal and stumbling-block to those who conceive "heaven" to be a state of pure rational order and

---

[16] Ibid., Lib. V.10.
[17] Ibid., Lib. VII.2.

harmony; hence they are regarded as "evil" and as something to be repressed and extinguished by a long process of ascetic discipline. The image of Eros "crucified" on the cross of reason stands above most so-called morality. The *Hermetica* in the following passage goes beyond such morality; it links the erotic energies to the highest processes of life, seeing them as manifestations of divine energy itself: "And in that conjunction of the two sexes, or, to speak more truly, that fusion of them into one, which may be rightly named Eros, or Aphrodite, or both at once, there is a deeper meaning than man can comprehend. It is a truth to be accepted as sure and evident above all other truths, that by God, the Master of all generative power, has been devised and bestowed upon all creatures this sacrament of eternal reproduction, with all the affection, all the joy and gladness, all the yearning and heavenly love that are inherent in its being. And there were need that I should tell of the compelling force with which this sacrament binds man and woman together, were it not that each of us, if he directs his thought upon himself, can learn it from his inmost feeling."[18]

It would be a mistake to emphasize too greatly this break of the *Corpus Hermeticum* with the more rational side of Greek and Hellenistic philosophy. It need only be pointed out that such a break is implicit in certain passages of the *Corpus*. Reality cannot be grasped by the reason alone; another mode of apprehension is needed, a more intuitive and contemplative mode. But in general the *Corpus* continues the objective, impersonal tradition which descends from Plato and whose course we have briefly glanced at. Thus on the one hand the *Corpus* reasserts the dualism of the Plato of the *Phaedrus*, *Symposium*, and the *Republic*. But on the other hand it also expresses that vision of the organic wholeness of life, of the intermingling of sensible and intelligible, visible and invisible, which is suggested in Plato's *Timaeus* and in some aspects of Stoicism. God does not exclude the world of the senses; reality is present in the forms of nature itself: it is not opposed to creation. Both form and matter, the ever-active consciousness and the passive non-consciousness, are aspects of a single reality, which is everywhere, in

---

[18] Ibid., Asclep. III.21.

everything: "Everywhere God will come to meet you, everywhere he will appear to you, at places and times at which you look not for it, in your waking hours and in your sleep, when you are journeying by water and by land, in the night-time and in the day-time, when you are speaking and when you are silent; for there is nothing which is not God. And do you say 'God is invisible'? Speak not so. Who is more manifest than God? For this very purpose he has made all things, that through all things you may see him. This is God's goodness, that he manifests himself through all things. Nothing is invisible, not even an incorporeal thing; mind is seen in its thinking, and God in his working."[19]

The great break with the impersonality and objectivity of Greek and Hellenistic philosophy, with its emphasis on the impersonal cosmic order and its worship of a God whom it identified with the intelligible principle of this order, comes of course with Christianity. The accent is transferred from the objective to the subjective, from the impersonal to the personal, onto the internal struggle and stress of the human soul. How much of the Christian mystery was prefigured in the mystery religions of the ancient world need not at this point concern us.[20] What is important is that with Christianity, the single individual, the human person, was brought face to face as an isolated pole with an equally living person, another equally isolated pole – God. Christianity gave to the human individual the sense that within him, a single being, quite apart from any city or any cosmic order, the deepest mysteries of life are to be found; the supernatural dwells within. He no longer has to sacrifice himself to any larger, more important but more impersonal whole in order to achieve his destiny. He is, potentially, himself the whole. His task is to penetrate into his own inner depths where he can meet and unite with that Other who is both the source and the most real aspect of his own personality. In the Christian mystery, as it is developed by the great masters of the Christian contemplative tradition, the last traces of that impersonal and "objective" form of classical intellectualism which are still present in

[19] Ibid., Lib. XI.22.
[20] See above, Ch. 3 *passim*

the thought of Plotinus are eliminated, and the whole drama of human life is focused on an inner, intimate, intensely personal exchange between the human individual and God, between the human creature and the uncreated light. It is a drama which takes place within the depths of the isolated and withdrawn human soul.

Yet at the same time as they placed reality in the unexplored depths of individual experience, restored the subjective and personal side to man's life and so rescued him from his sense of helplessness and insignificance before the vast impersonal processes of the cosmos, many Christian thinkers also allowed themselves to be inveigled by a form of dualism, similar in many ways to that of one aspect of Platonism, which led to a vast depreciation of the world as it is presented through the senses. The cosmos was "demystified", robbed of its association with the divine. The elements of the cosmos – water, earth, air, fire – were seen as controlled by spirits hostile to God. The transcendent was exalted at the expense of the immanent, the invisible at the expense of the visible. It is true that, at least so far as Greek Patristic theology is concerned, creation in its original state is said to be good and to represent a series of divine theophanies; and even in its fallen state it presents forms whose contemplation may lead the mind back to an awareness of divine beauty. But particularly in the theology that stems from St. Augustine, only too often the sensible world in itself is regarded as no more than a "lump of perdition", handed over to the forces of evil. Hence Christian asceticism based on such an attitude demanded a rejection of this world, its abandonment in favor of a supra-sensible world. In the sphere of the senses and of the passions and instincts, the devil is active. The purpose of the devil is to prevent the soul's union with God. Consequently, the first step towards such a union is the mortification of the senses and the passions, and the severance of whatever ties link man as a sensible creature to the universe.

* * *

It was against this aspect of Christianity that Gemistos Plethon initiated a reaction. In the event, it is difficult to do more than guess at the substance of his reaction: the work in which his central ideas were gathered, the *Laws*, was burnt shortly after the fall of Constantinople in 1453 by the Patriarch Gennadios, long the opponent of Plethon, and only fragments of it survive. But it is clear that he regarded as inadequate a religion which, like Christianity, seemed to be largely negative in its attitude towards the world of the senses and which, in order to account for the destructive and irrational forces of life, had associated them with a host of demons that had no share in the divine world. For Plethon, Christianity, in embracing or appearing to embrace a dualism which radically separated the world of the senses from its transcendental origin and by focusing attention almost exclusively on the historical redemption of man, had broken the great tradition of the ancient world. It had broken the myth of this tradition which had linked the visible cosmos to its invisible archetypes. It had conceived a divinity that excluded the sense of the sacredness of the natural order, a monotheism that excluded polytheism. Plethon sought to regenerate an awareness of the living realities upon which the cosmos depended. So far as one can gather, he attacked the belief in evil demons as conceived by the Christians, and sought to link every aspect of life with the divine through a whole chain of being stretching from the highest to the lowest forms of existence. In other words, he sought to refer the whole of creation to the divine and to bridge the gulf which, he thought, Christianity had opened between the two.

Gemistos Plethon was not, of course, the only person to react against this apparent dualism in mediaeval Christian thought. Rather he stood at the head of a long and distinguished line of speculative thinkers who included among their number not only his immediate successors like Ficino, Pico della Mirandola, Giordano Bruno and the Cambridge Platonists, but also writers like Goethe and Blake. It was, however, with Nietzsche that the full force of this reaction developed. But Nietzsche's attack was directed not simply against the Christian form of dualism. He saw the historical origins of this dualism not in Christianity, but in aspects of the philosophical tradition of the ancient Greek world itself, in fact in precisely that dualistic side of Platonic thought which we have indicated in an earlier part of this chapter. According to Nietzsche, it was this dualism which, before it had taken its Christian form, had already crippled the creative life of ancient Greece: "The apparition of Greek philosophers since the time of Socrates is a symptom of decadence; the anti-Hellenic instincts become paramount."[21] These philosophers represent a revolt of the reason against the instincts. They establish an absolute morality set over against life. They teach the immortality of the soul, a doctrine of the Beyond, and a denial of the senses. They turn their back on the world and thus prepare the way for Christianity.

Nietzsche, therefore, sees the great period of ancient Greece not in the fifth century BC, where it had been the fashion to place it, but in the sixth century BC, and even earlier. Then, he declared, reason and instinct, soul and body, had been at one, a single expression of life. This was the period in which the symbol of Dionysos reigned. It was the period of the affirmation of life: "In the Dionysian symbol the utmost limit of affirmation is reached"; in it there is "a formula of *highest affirmation*, born of fullness and overfullness, a yea-saying without reserve to suffering's self, to guilt's self, to all that is questionable and strange in existence itself."[22] There was no flight from life, there was no attempt to pretend that life is anything other than what it is, there was no escape into the beautiful but unreal dream-world of the Olympian gods. On the contrary, there was a yea-saying to life as it is, godless, stricken, without purpose, tragic: "The saying of Yes to life, including even its most strange and terrible problems, the will to life rejoicing over its own inexhaustibleness in the sacrifice of its highest types – that is what I call Dionysian."[23] It was this unity of life and its acceptance as a whole, for itself, with no question of a Beyond or of any purpose other than that which is fulfilled in its affirmation in spite of all contradictions and illogicalities – it was this that the later philosophers destroyed when they elevated the reason to a position of

[21] Nietzsche, *Will to Power 1*, aph. 427. All quotations from Nietzsche are taken from the English translation of his works edited by O. Levy.

[22] Nietzsche, *The Birth of Tragedy*, Appendix.

[23] Nietzsche, *Twilight of the Idols*, pp. 119-20.

supremacy over the instincts and elaborated a morality derived from that reason which in itself can never escape from the dualist attitude.

Nietzsche went on to affirm that this dualism of the ancient Greek philosophers, with the moral attitude that accompanied it, had been taken over by Christianity; and it was from this point of view that he opened his violent attack on the Christian tradition. He considered this attack his great achievement: "That which defines me, that which makes me stand apart from the whole of the rest of humanity, is the fact that I *unmasked* Christian morality."[24] Christian morality had also committed the great crime; it had also said "no" to life. It had taught a contempt for all the principal instincts of life; it had taught a contempt for the body and the sensual passions. It was a morality of self-renunciation, which "betrays the will to nonentity", denying the very roots of life. It had torn man up from the earth, uprooted him in the fullest sense. Its whole spirit was one of hostility to life. It was the creation of decadents, of men who hated life and who denied life, who having no vitality of their own could not bear the manifestations of vitality in other people and who, in desire for revenge, set up a code of values and moralities which shackled the ascending forces of life and energy and prevented man's creative growth. "Morality is the idiosyncracy of decadents, actuated by a desire to *avenge themselves with success upon life.*"[25] It was a vampirism, sucking the blood of life. It was the creation of the weak, fear-smitten herd, to ensure that no one should rise above a common level of mediocrity: "Everything that elevates the individual above the herd, and is a source of fear to the neighbor, is henceforth called *evil*; the tolerant, unassuming, self-adapting disposition, the *mediocrity* of desires, attain to moral distinction and honor."[26]

It was a criticism that the English Blake had already made: "The Giants who formed this world into its sensual existence, and now seem to live in it in chains, are in truth the causes of its life and the sources of all activity; but the chains are the cunning of weak and

[24] Nietzsche, *Ecce Homo*, pp. 138-9
[25] Ibid., p. 141.
[26] Nietzsche, *Beyond Good and Evil*, aph. 201.

tame minds which have power to resist energy; according to the proverb, the weak in courage is strong in cunning."[27] The Church with its moral law represented the triumph of the weak and tame minds; it attacked these "Giants", the primal energies and passions, at their roots and so sought to destroy life itself: "All ancient moral-mongers were unanimous on this point, 'il faut tuer les passions'."[28] The great task which awaited man was to release these passions from their chains, to prepare for a new fullness and abundance of life: "The aim should be to prepare a *transvaluation of values* for a particularly strong kind of man, most highly gifted in intellect and will, and, to this end, slowly to liberate in him a whole host of slandered instincts hitherto held in check."[29]

At the same time as attacking Christian morality, Nietzsche also attacked the Christian God; in fact, he attacked the whole idea of a supernatural: "I conjure you, my brethren, remain true to the earth, and believe not those who speak unto you of super-earthly hopes. Poisoners are they, whether they know it or not."[30] The Christian God was hostile to life. He was a destroyer of life; "The concept 'God' was invented as the opposite of the concept life – everything detrimental, poisonous and slanderous, and all deadly hostility to life, was bound together in one horrible unit in Him."[31] He was a faithful image of the pitiable and pathetic minds which had created Him: "The miserable God of Christian monotono-theism" is a "hybrid creature of decay, nonentity, concept, and contradiction, in which all the instincts of decadence, all the cowardices and languors of the soul find their sanction."[32] He was a negation and denial of life: "With God war is declared on life, nature, and the will to life! God is the formula for every calumny of this world and for every lie concerning a beyond! In God, nonentity is deified; and the will to nonentity is declared holy."[33]

[27] 'Marriage of Heaven and Hell', Nonesuch Blake, ed. Geoffrey Keynes, (London, 1941), p. 187.

[28] Nietzsche, *Twilight of the Idols*, pp. 119-120.

[29] Nietzsche, *Zarathustra*, Prologue, section 3.

[30] Ibid., p. 7.

[31] Nietzsche, *Ecce Homo*, p. 142.

[32] Nietzsche, *Antichrist*, p. 147.

[33] Ibid., p. 146.

And he contrasts the pagan affirmation of life with the Christian denial of life: "*Paganism* is that which says yea to all that is natural, it is innocence in being natural, 'naturalness'. *Christianity* is that which says no to all that is natural, it is a certain lack of dignity in being natural; hostility to Nature."[34]

Nietzsche in fact is basically accusing Christianity of having adopted a form of dualism similar to that which Plato had accepted from Parmenides. On the basis of such a dualism it had erected, he maintained, a life-denying morality whose effect was the suppression of man's instinctive powers. It had split creation in two and had disrupted those ties which link man to the universe. It had regarded as negative and even as evil all that side of man which is chthonic, in which he is joined to earth and to the forces of earth. It had identified what is destructive, irrational and contrary to its conceptions of the spiritual life, with what is evil. It had waged war on the body and on man's eroticism. It had, moreover, identified the source of this ascetic morality with the source of spiritual life itself – with God. It had confused religion with moral teaching. It had, as it were, made God Himself responsible for a life-denying moral code. Thus when Nietzsche took upon himself the role of martyr on behalf of that side of life which, he claimed, Christianity had suppressed – on behalf of the "crucified" passions and the "Giants who formed this world into its sensual existence" – he was forced, in order to attack the Christian ethic, to attack also the whole idea of the transcendent Divinity dwelling in the depths of the human soul. He was forced, in other words, to take his stand at what amounted to the opposite pole of that same dualism by which, he thought, Christianity itself had been dominated, and to cry: "Am I understood? – *Dionysus versus the Crucified*"[35] – "Dionysus" in this context representing all those instincts and energies of life which, in Nietzsche's view, Christianity had either slandered, denied, crippled or otherwise disastrously abused.[36]

[34] Nietzsche, *Will to Power*, I, aph. 147.

[35] Nietzsche, *Ecce Homo* IV.9.

[36] For a fuller account of the import of the Dionysus concept in Nietzsche's work see M. S. Silk and J. P. Stern, *Nietzsche on Tragedy* (Cambridge, 1981), *passim*.

It is easy to point out that, in making his attacks on Christianity, Nietzsche radically ignored many crucial aspects of Christian doctrine and that the very idea of the sacrament, for instance, presupposes an understanding of things entirely at odds with that which he sees as endemic to the Christian mentality. But that being said, it nonetheless remains true that Christian (or what is called Christian) morality, and even Christian anthropology as a whole, have been vitiated by an all-too-negative approach to that side of things which Nietzsche terms Dionysiac. If its theology does not formally stipulate an unbridgeable ontological divide between the ultimate transcendent ground of being and the manifold forms of created life as these manifest themselves in all their munificent abundance, it nevertheless finds it difficult to affirm that the inner immortal Self – the transcendent God – and the source of the great cosmic energies are one and the same, or that the transcendent One and the changing multitudinous world of the senses constitute a single undivided and indivisible reality. This is particularly the case perhaps with regard to its understanding of the sacramental potentiality of the sexual energies: it would be hard to find in the writings of the great theological masters of the Christian tradition anything that even remotely corresponds to the passage on this subject which was cited above from the *Corpus Hermetica*.[37]

It is from this point of view that the criticism of Christianity made by such figures as Plethon, Blake, Goethe, and Nietzsche (to name but those of whom we have spoken here) represents a positive challenge: if the Christian tradition does possess – as it certainly does – a doctrine of creation capable of embracing and validating the integral reciprocity of the two poles of life – the transcendent and the immanent, the One and the many, the intelligible and the sensible – which these critics accuse it of having sundered and opposed so disastrously, then surely Christian theologians should take it upon themselves to reaffirm it with all the rigor and unambiguity for which it calls.

---

[37] See also on this theme my *Christianity and Eros* (London, 1976).

Chapter Six

Christianity and the Religious Thought
of C. G. Jung

Two preliminary remarks must preface this chapter. The first concerns the source material on which it is based. Jung had no "religion" in the commonly accepted sense of the word. He did not belong to any branch of the Christian Church, nor did he affiliate himself to any other explicit religious tradition, like Islam or Buddhism. Therefore on the face of it he did not accept any system of doctrine or dogma based on revelation and elaborated by the spiritual interpreters of the tradition in question. On the contrary, he claimed that he was a natural scientist, and that such religious ideas as he had were developed over the course of his life in relation to his empirical experience as a psychologist and the reading he undertook in order to reach an understanding of what he had experienced.

If this is true, then his religious thought was in a continual state of growth and modification. It was fluctuating rather than stable. What he perceived or believed at certain times might be altered or even reversed by subsequent experience and reading. Therefore, one would risk being unfair to Jung if one were to extract concepts and thought from the developing body of his work and to say that these represent his religious ideas. One would have to make sure that they were concepts or thoughts he maintained up to the end, and did not reject or modify out of recognition. Consequently, for the purposes of this chapter, it has seemed best to confine attention to his autobiography, *Memories, Dreams, Reflections,*[1] put

[1] C. G. Jung, *Memories, Dreams, Reflections,* (London, 1963).

together during the last years of his life and expressing his ideas at their most mature and most intimate level. This has the additional advantage that the English edition at least of this book has been supplied with a glossary giving, through extracts from earlier works, explanations of his central psychological concepts and terminology.

The second remark can be put in the form of a question: to what extent are we entitled to speak of "religious thought" at all where Jung is concerned? Religious ideas normally speaking derive from and refer to a world of truths that are regarded as supernatural or metaphysical. They are to do with metaphysical realities. It is not that Jung refused to discuss problems commonly called religious. It is even stated in the introduction to his autobiography that he "explicitly declared his allegiance to Christianity". But, as the introduction continues, he looked at religious questions from "the standpoint of psychology, deliberately setting a bound between it and the theological approach". In fact, this is an understatement, at least where intention is concerned. Jung not only sought to set a bound between psychology and theology. He denied the very basis of theological statement altogether.

This he did from, as it were, both ends. First, he denied the objective existence of those metaphysical or metapsychical realities which theological statements presuppose, and affirmed that there is no truth but purely subjective truth. "We are still a long way from understanding what it signifies," he writes, "that nothing has any existence unless some small – and oh, so transitory – consciousness has become aware of it."[2] Then he denied – as a necessary consequence, it might be said, of this initial denial – that there can be any statement or comprehension at all other than the psychological. The passage is worth quoting in full, since it shows how far Jung was willing to go in rejecting the validity of the theological standpoint (at least as theologians themselves understand it), and illustrates the contradictions in which he is involved as a result. "All conceivable statements", he writes, "are made by the

[2] Ibid. p. 15.

psyche.... The psyche cannot leap beyond itself. It cannot set up any absolute truths, for its own polarity determines the relativity of its statements.... In saying this we are not expressing a value judgment, but only pointing out that the limit is very frequently overstepped.... In my effort to depict the limitations of the psyche I do not mean to imply that only the psyche exists. It is merely that, so far as perception and cognition are concerned, we cannot see beyond the psyche.... All comprehension and all that is comprehended is in itself psychic, and to that extent we are hopelessly cooped up in an exclusively psychic world."[3] There are, in other words, no supra-psychic realities that man can comprehend, and all so-called theological statements that pretend to derive from and refer to such realities are really no more than psychological statements (if that) invested by their authors with a status which, in the nature of things, they cannot possess.

As is so often the case with those over-anxious to deny a point of view other than their own, Jung in fact is led into a position which contradicts what he wishes to affirm. In saying that "every point of view is necessarily relative", and that "all conceivable statements are made by the psyche", and that "all comprehension and all that is comprehended is in itself psychic",[4] clearly what he wishes to emphasize is that no theological or metaphysical statement has the significance which a theologian or metaphysician would claim for it. It must in the nature of things be subjective, relative and psychic, and refer only to subjective, relative, and psychic realities. We are exclusively doomed to this relative, subjective, psychic world.

Yet if that is the case, Jung's statements themselves are not exempt from these conditions. They too are relative, subjective, psychic. In that case, their categorical appearance is all bluff. Objectively, as enunciations of general truths, they can have no significance. To say that "every point of view is necessarily relative" is virtually a meaningless thing to say, since, taken at its face value, it itself then represents but a relative point of view and so cannot apply as a general statement valid for every point of view. For a

[3] Ibid. pp. 322-3.
[4] Ibid. p. 198.

statement to be valid for every point of view, there must be some point of view which is not relative but capable of embracing all points of view.

Similarly, if all comprehension and all that is comprehended is in itself psychic, then Jung's statement that "all conceivable statements are made by the psyche" is again virtually meaningless. It has no status at all as a general truth, applicable to all statements, but simply represents Jung's own relative and subjective point of view. It could only have a general validity applicable to all statements on condition that it is true in a non-relative and non-subjective manner. But, Jung says, it is impossible for any statement to be non-relative and non-subjective. Why, then, does Jung make this statement in such categorical terms, as if he were making a pronouncement which applies to all statements? Why, in effect, is he issuing a dogma – one, it is true, designed to undermine the traditional basis of religious dogma, but no less a dogma on that account?

The answer would seem to be fairly clear. Indeed, it is precisely this, that he did wish to undermine the traditional basis of religious dogma, as well as of all theological thought of the traditional kind. He wanted to clear the ground, establish a kind of *tabula rasa* on which to build afresh. So long as the great structure of Christian doctrine and dogma, regarded as sacred and inviolate, stood in the way, his own ideas could make little progress. But if he could show that this structure shared in all the necessary limitations of human thought as he conceived them and was in fact essentially subjective and relative and psychic, its authority would be shaken. It would be seen to have no greater claims to validity and belief than any other system of thought. Indeed, it might even have fewer claims than other such systems, since these could often point to what is called empirical evidence in their support, whereas many of the dogmatic formulations of Christianity appear to flout such empirical evidence.

Jung's task had therefore a twofold direction. First, he had to demonstrate that the claim of theology and dogma to possess a kind of eternal and objective status, independent of the judgment and even the consciousness of particular individuals, was ground-less, and that in the nature of things they could possess no greater or more significant – less relative and subjective – status than any other thought-forms or mental formulations; and this he attempted to do, in the way we have shown, by insisting that all statements are made by the psyche and that where our understanding is con-cerned we are hopelessly cooped up in an exclusively psychic world. And second, he then had to create his own system of thought, and to put it forward not as the truth in a theological sense, but simply as a series of tentative, limited observations based upon his purely pragmatic investigations of the human psyche.

In other words, Jung's system of thought could claim validity not because it was metaphysical, but precisely because it was not metaphysical; and he frequently asserts that unlike the theologians he does not overstep the limit, but bases what he has to say, indi-vidual and relative as it is, on solid scientific ground. "My *Answer to Job*", he writes, "was meant to be no more than the utterance of a single individual. . . . I was far from wanting to enunciate a meta-physical truth. Yet the theologians tax me with that very thing, because theological thinkers are so used to dealing with eternal truths that they know no other kinds. When the physicist says the atom is of such and such a composition, and then he sketches a model of it, he does not intend to express anything like an eternal truth. But theologians do not understand the natural sciences, par-ticularly psychological thinking."[5]

This is very disarming, and one might well be taken in by it were it not for the fact that when it comes to the point Jung is quite as capable of making categorical statements lacking all so-called empirical basis as the most dogmatic theologian. Those few already cited could be matched by others occurring throughout the book. Indeed, it is quite clear from a reading of this book that Jung's thought is essentially religious. It may even be said that he regarded himself as the apostle of a new religion, one that should replace for western man the exhausted formulas of Christianity, and one that in this scientific age would stand a far greater chance

[5] Ibid. pp. 206-7.

of acceptance if its own tenets could be presented in the guise of scientific theory, underpinned by solid psychological observation. Moreover, there seems to be little doubt that Jung regarded his mission as God-given. He was, it may be recalled, the only son of a Protestant pastor, and eight of his uncles were also pastors. Religion, one might say, was in his blood.

Yet it was not the religion of his father, or indeed of Christianity as the Church presented it. This religion was in many ways abhorrent to him. In his youth, he tells us, the Church was a place of torment for him,[6] and not until the age of thirty could he confront *Mater Ecclesia* without a sense of oppression.[7] Though greatly traveled, he could never go to Rome, and when in old age he at last decided to make the journey, he had a fainting fit while buying the tickets and had to turn back.[8] But this dislike of the Church and its theology did not mean that he was therefore an atheist. On the contrary – and it is here one can discern to what extent he felt his mission was God-given – he considered that God disliked the Church and its theology just as much as he did, if not more.

When still quite young, he had a terrifying and "sinful" thought. He thought of God sitting high up in the clouds on a golden throne and excreting a large turd which fell on the cathedral of his hometown and shattered it.[9] Later, in relation to this experience, he writes: "Now I understood the deepest meaning of my earlier experience: God Himself had disavowed theology and the Church founded upon it."[10] Therefore in undermining and denying the basis of traditional Christian theology and in propagating his own gospel in its place, Jung did not feel he was acting in an arbitrary and irresponsible or godless manner. He felt he was carrying out the will of God. He had been entrusted by God with this mission: to make clear to men what God had disavowed and why He had disavowed it; to save God Himself, and man with Him, from the theology and the Church which smothered them, and to proclaim

[6] Ibid. p. 55.
[7] Ibid. p. 30.
[8] Ibid. p. 269.
[9] Ibid. p. 50.
[10] Ibid. p. 98.

a new religion of life to take the place of a moribund Christianity.

It is this that entitles us to speak of Jung's ideas as religious without doing them any violence. The main lines of his thought, his central concepts and images, constitute what really amounts to a theology and a mythology. Moreover, he did not himself regard this theology and mythology as anti-Christian. As we have seen, he professed his allegiance to Christianity. He thought Christianity of central importance for western man.[11] But he considered that it needed to be "seen in a new light, in accordance with the changes wrought by the contemporary spirit." Otherwise, he writes, "it stands apart from the times, and has no effect on man's wholeness".[12] In effect, he thought Christianity had concentrated too much on the ideal, bright, and good side of man's nature, and this at the expense of the non-ideal, dark, and sinful side. When he was a young boy he had a dream of a phallus on a throne in an underground cavern. This had made it difficult for him to accept the conventional image of the Christian Savior. "Lord Jesus never became quite real for me," he writes, "never quite acceptable, never quite lovable, for again and again I would think of his underground counterpart, a frightful revelation which had been accorded to me without my seeking it."[13]

According to one interpretation of the dream the phallus represented the dark side of Jesus. Later it was revealed to him as "the breath of life", the "creative impulse".[14] He thought that God, who had disavowed the theology and the Church that had concentrated on the ideal and good side of man, was now wanting "to evoke. . . his darkness and ungodliness".[15] As we had failed, through traditional Christianity, to overcome or escape our anxiety, bad conscience, guilt, compulsion, unconsciousness and instinctuality from the bright, idealistic side, "then perhaps we shall have better luck by approaching the problem from the dark, biological side."[16]

[11] Ibid. p. 200.
[12] Ibid. pp. 200-1.
[13] Ibid. p. 27.
[14] Ibid. p. 36.
[15] Ibid. p. 77.
[16] Ibid. p. 149.

In a way, one might say that Jung regarded it as his task to redeem the devil. The devil in Christian thought had come to represent everything that was evil, godless, instinctive, dark in life. All this was regarded as the opposite of God, who was exclusively good, rational, bright. Consequently, Christians had concentrated on suppressing all these "diabolic" aspects of themselves and on developing only their good, rational, bright aspects. The result had been the warping and sterility of human life. Now these "diabolic" elements needed to be released and integrated into man's experience of himself.

Moreover, these elements must be seen not as belonging to the devil as the enemy of God, but as aspects of God's own nature. What traditional Christianity had foisted on to the devil as a figure diametrically opposed to God and had driven out into the wilderness as a kind of scapegoat, must now be seen to have its source in God. The devil is also God. God is "the dark author of all created things, who alone was responsible for the sufferings of the world".[17] The chthonic spirit, the spirit indicated in the dream of the underground phallus, is the "other face of God", the "dark side of the God-image".[18] It is God who has created the world and its sins,[19] and in failing to recognize this – in failing to recognize that God is the author of evil just as much as of the good – Christianity had promulgated a false idea of God whose acceptance had resulted in the gradual atrophy of man's creative life. Now God was calling for His dark evil side to be recognized and accepted once more, so that the dark evil side of human nature could also be recognized and accepted. Both God and man were seeking to be liberated from imprisonment in the good, ideal, bright, rational side of themselves, so that they could again function in their original wholeness. It was this call for liberation on the part of God and man to which Jung felt compelled to respond. It was this that constituted his religious mission and it was to the realization of this mission that he devoted his creative life and developed his religious thought and mythology.

[17] Ibid. p. 97.
[18] Ibid. p. 163.
[19] Ibid. p. 206.

From an autobiographical and historical point of view, Jung's religious thought may be said to have begun as a reaction against the type of Protestant Christianity represented by his father, and so, by extension, against the extreme rationalism of the nineteenth-century western world. This Christianity seemed to amount to a more or less blind adherence to various articles of faith one never questioned and which effectively cut one off from any real experience either of man or God. "The arch sin of faith, it seemed to me," he wrote, "was that it forestalled experience."[20] Together with the passive acceptance of this untested and unlived religious dogma went an elementary moral code based on a clear-cut and equally unquestioned opposition between good and evil, black and white. Living the Christian life seemed to consist solely in maintaining faith in this abstract bundle of Christian precept by turning a deaf ear to everything that assailed it, and in conforming to the prescribed moral code. It was a mixture of mental bigotry and moral will-power.

Nor did the rationalism of current nineteenth-century scientific thought, against which men like Jung's father were so stubbornly opposed, seem any more satisfactory. This too seemed solely a device for shutting man off from any living contact with real life. The attempt to dominate everything by the reason seemed but to serve the secret purpose of placing one at a safe distance from real experience and of substituting for psychic reality an apparently secure, artificial, but merely two-dimensional conceptual world in which the reality of life is well covered up by so-called clear concepts. Both the intellectual idealism and ethical dualism of Protestant Christianity and the naive rationalism of nineteenth-century science seemed to leave out of account and provide no explanation for those realities of which his youthful vision and experiences had made him aware. They seemed to leave out of account and offer no explanation for the whole irrational, dark, primitive, "evil" side of man's nature.

This Jung was able to perceive more objectively when at a later stage in his life he made a journey to North Africa and came into

[20] Ibid. p. 98.

contact with the Arab world. The passage in which he speaks of this, though it includes expressions and ideas deriving from a more fully formulated phase of his thought, deserves to be quoted because it demonstrates what he must have less explicitly realized when, at the outset of his intellectual development, he reacted against the religion of his childhood and the rationalism of modern western man. "The emotional nature of these unreflecting people [the Arabs]," he writes, "who are so much closer to life than we are, exerts a strong suggestive influence upon those historical layers in ourselves which we have just overcome and left behind, or which we think we have overcome. It is like the paradise of childhood from which we imagine we have emerged, but which at the slightest provocation imposes fresh defeats upon us. . . . The sight of a child or a primitive will arouse certain longings in adult, civilized persons – longings which relate to the unfulfilled desires and needs of those parts of the personality which have been blotted out of the total picture in favor of the adopted persona. . . . The predominantly rationalistic European finds much that is human alien to him, and he prides himself on this without realizing that his rationality is won at the expense of his vitality, and that the primitive part of his personality is consequently condemned to a more or less underground existence."[21]

Since the lifeless abstractions of the Christian faith, though supposedly referring to supernatural realities, and the two-dimensional conceptual world of the rationalists were both creations or at least appurtenances of man's everyday consciousness, and belonged to what he consciously believed or thought, Jung found it convenient to give that primitive part of the personality which modern man had condemned to a more or less underground existence an opposite label and to call it the unconscious. This concept of the unconscious, later elaborated into the "collective unconscious", is crucial to Jung's whole system of thought, so it is important to try to get clear what he meant by it.

This is not an easy task, since in spite of its crucial position in Jung's thought it nevertheless remains a somewhat vague concept.

[21] Ibid. pp. 230-1.

To begin with, Jung seems to have thought of the unconscious as a kind of repository of all those psychic elements and drives which have either not entered man's conscious world, or been driven out of it, suppressed, because of his inability or unwillingness to admit them on the conscious level. He first became graphically aware of it in a dream. In this dream, Jung found himself in a two-story house. He was on the upper floor. He first descended to the ground floor, and then to the cellar, and finally down into a cave cut out in the rock beneath the house, where there were two human skulls lying among scattered bones and broken pottery.[22] He interpreted the dream as a kind of structural diagram of the human psyche. The upper floor where he first found himself represented the consciousness; the ground floor stood for the first level of the unconscious, while the cave itself was the world of the primitive man in every human being. This primitive and deepest part of man's unconscious psyche borders, he writes, on the animal soul, just as the caves of prehistoric times were usually inhabited by animals before men laid claim to them.[23]

According to this interpretation, the dream appeared to postulate "something of an altogether *impersonal* nature" underlying the psyche. This, Jung says, was his first inkling "of a collective *a priori* beneath the personal psyche". He took it to be "the traces of earlier modes of functioning". Later, "with increasing experience and on the basis of more reliable knowledge", he recognized these earlier modes of functioning "as forms of instinct, that is, as archetypes".[24] These archetypes and forms of instinct ("archetype" and "instinct" are synonyms in Jung's terminology, and their sense must on no account be confused with that of "archetype" in the traditional Platonic and Christian meaning of the word) constitute the unconscious. He calls this unconscious "collective" because, "unlike the personal unconscious (represented by the ground floor in the dream), it is not made up of individual and more or less unique contents but of those which are universal and of regular occur-

[22] Ibid. p. 155.
[23] Ibid. p. 156.
[24] Ibid. p. 157.

rence. . . . The deeper 'layers' of the psyche lose their individual uniqueness."[25] The collective unconscious is common to all people[26] and it consists of "archaic psychic components which have entered the individual psyche without any direct line of tradition".[27]

This schematic representation of the psyche in the form of a house gives what one might call its vertical cross-section. But this vertical progression from lower to higher, from the cave to the upper story, has its corresponding horizontal extension in man's actual historical evolution. Although Jung had become aware of limitations in the rationalism of nineteenth-century scientific thought, he did not on that account reject its theories, or at least not all of them; and one of these theories which he accepted totally and interwove with his own thought so intimately that one can say that they stand or fall together, was the Darwinian theory of man's evolution. This theory he married to his own conception of the human psyche, and particularly of the unconscious. That is to say, he thought that the various layers of the human psyche had their counterparts in the various phases of man's evolution through the centuries on earth.

The conscious aspect of the psyche represented man's present phase of evolution; those aspects of the psyche which in the course of his evolution western man condemned to a more or less underground existence correspond to those historical layers in himself that he has overcome and left behind, but that still remain buried within him. Thus it is that the deepest level of the collective unconscious, the deepest part of man's nature, "borders on the life of the animal soul".[28] This correlation of the psyche with man's evolutionary progress led him, inevitably, to reject Christian ideas of man's creation and consequently of the structure of the human psyche, and to substitute his own ideas. "If the unconscious is anything at all," he writes, "it must consist of earlier evolutionary stages of our conscious psyche. The assumption that man in his whole

[25] Ibid. p. 357, note on the *Unconscious*.
[26] Ibid. p. 136-7.
[27] Ibid. p. 35.
[28] Ibid. p. 156.

glory was created on the sixth day of Creation, without any preliminary stages, is after all somewhat too simple and archaic to
satisfy us nowadays. There is pretty general agreement on that
score.... Just as the body has an anatomical prehistory of millions
of years, so also does the psychic stream. And just as the human
body represents in each of its parts the result of this evolution, and
everywhere still shows traces of its earlier stages – so the same may
be said of the psyche. Consciousness began its evolution from an
animal-like state ...".[29]

The Christian idea of man's psyche – that man's consciousness
has its roots in the Divine and that only as a consequence of his
degradation and immersion in earthly and animal existence has it
become obscured – would seem here to be turned on its head:
human consciousness began in the dark sub-human world of the
animals and plants and over the centuries has been gradually emerging into the light of complete evolution. Perhaps nowhere does
Jung's thought appear to be more non-Christian, not to say anti-
Christian, than in relation to this crucial concept, the idea of the
collective unconscious.

Man's psyche, then, is made up of its conscious and its unconscious components; and although fully-evolved consciousness is
the goal towards which man's life is ultimately directed, only too
often his actual state of consciousness, even in this latter-day phase
of his evolution, is pathetically meager. Largely through an over-
development of his reason (though Jung more frequently calls the
reason the intellect, not recognizing any distinction between these
two faculties[30]), and his refusal to admit into consciousness anything which is not rational or capable of being rationalized, he has
driven underground, suppressed, locked up in the unconscious all
those primitive, irrational, instinctive contents of the psyche on
which his vitality and creativeness depend. To such an extent has
he done this that what one may take to be the proper relationship
between consciousness and the unconscious in fully-evolved man
has now been reversed; and far from man being truly aware of

[29] Ibid. p. 320.
[30] For a clarification of this distinction see Ch. 9 below.

what he is, what he thinks he is bears little or no relationship to his total being.

In fact, his true life now is not his conscious life at all, but his unconscious life. "Our unconscious existence", he writes, "is the real one and our conscious world is a kind of illusion, an apparent reality constructed for a specific purpose, like a dream which seems a reality as long as we are in it."[31] The tenacity with which, none the less, modern western man clings to this conscious world – this illusion – at the expense of the unconscious world, results not only in reducing his existence to a kind of shadow-play but also in chronic psychic dislocation. It is in fact the extreme resistance which the consciousness of modern western man offers to the unconscious contents of the psyche that produces the vast range of psychic disorders, both individual and collective, that characterize our time. Modern man has identified himself with what is at best but a superficial aspect of himself, and his real self lies buried within him, in the obscure substrata of the unconscious. It follows from this that if modern man is to recover his psychic health and realize what Jung calls his wholeness or complete form, he must once again allow his submerged, suppressed, unconscious existence to enter his conscious world.

To this process, whereby man bit by bit releases the submerged contents of his unconscious into consciousness and so achieves his wholeness of being, Jung applies the term *individuation*. Individuation, the glossary states, "means becoming a single, homogeneous being, and in so far as individuality embraces our innermost, last, and incomparable uniqueness, it also implies becoming one's own self. We could therefore translate individuation as 'coming to selfhood' or 'self-realization'."[32] It must not on any account be confused with the coming of the ego into consciousness, which results simply in ego-centeredness and auto-eroticism. The self that has to be realized through individuation comprises infinitely more than the ego. The self embraces not only the conscious, but also the unconscious psyche; and it does not simply embrace them, it is the

[31] Jung, *op. cit.*, pp. 299-300.
[32] Ibid. p. 352.

center of this totality, just as the ego is the center of the conscious mind.

The self is the wholeness of the personality,[33] that which we are, the "principle and archetype of orientation and meaning".[34] It is realized through a process of self-knowledge by means of which "we approach the fundamental stratum or core of human nature where the instincts dwell. . . . This core is the unconscious and its contents."[35] Through self-knowledge, the psyche is transformed by changing the relationship between the ego, or human consciousness in the ordinary restricted sense, and the contents of the unconscious. What was before hidden and forced underground is now brought out into the open and liberated.

In this psychic transformation what Jung calls the *anima* (or, in woman, the *animus*) plays a vital part. The *anima* is in a sense the transforming instrument, the go-between operating between the conscious and the unconscious world. She is a kind of psychopompos, establishing the relationship with the unconscious. Related to the unconscious in this way, she has, like the unconscious, a strongly historical character. "As the personification of the unconscious she goes back into prehistory, and embodies the contents of the past. She provides the individual with those elements that he ought to know about his prehistory. To the individual, the *anima* is all life that has been in the past and is still alive in him."[36] She functions thus as a bridge or a door, leading into the unconscious. There, in the unconscious, she produces a mysterious animation, and gives visible form to ancestral traces, the collective contents.[37] Like a medium, she gives these contents a chance to manifest themselves.

This they do in terms of images and myths. Images and myths are not human inventions. They are the spontaneous forms in which the unconscious reveals itself. Projected by the unconscious into the *anima*, they can be grasped by the consciousness. Received in

[33] Ibid. p. 187.
[34] Ibid. p. 190.
[35] Ibid. p. 305.
[36] Ibid. p. 267.
[37] Ibid. p. 183.

the consciousness, and there interpreted, they provide the means through which the contents of the unconscious are released into the consciousness. It is through myth and symbol that individuation is achieved. Through them, man can begin to live all those phases of his evolutionary past that are still present within him. Through them, too, he comes into contact with his primitive instinctive life, with those pre-existent dynamic factors which ultimately govern the ethical decisions of his consciousness.[38] Consciousness and unconscious are thus brought into relationship and harmony. Man reaches the goal of his psychic development, represented by the self. He achieves his wholeness.

These notions of the unconscious, the *anima*, and the process of individuation could be derived, Jung claimed, from empirical observation of his own and other people's psychic activity, although, as he admits, psychology is subject, far more than any other science, to the personal bias of the observer.[39] In fact, he seems to have arrived at them after a lengthy and dramatic confrontation with his own unconscious, a confrontation which lasted over some eight years (1912-20) and on which he embarked after his split with Freud.[40] Hence it could be maintained that these notions are purely scientific notions and do not enter into the sphere of religious ideas at all. But not only are they so embedded in his religious ideas that it is impossible to speak of the latter without including them; they also – and this is more important – presuppose the acceptance of certain ideas which in this context one can only call religious.

This is particularly true where the process of individuation is concerned. The process of individuation, or psychic transformation, through which the contents of the unconscious are released into the consciousness, depends entirely on the understanding and interpretation of the myths and symbols in which these contents have revealed themselves to the consciousness. Their meaning and significance must be known and recognized. If they are not under-

[38] Ibid. p. 305.
[39] Ibid. p. 192.
[40] Ibid. see Ch. 6.

stood and interpreted, there is danger of miscarriage and the whole process of psychic development is in danger of failing or at least of being arrested.

This means that before one can successfully complete the process of psychic transformation, one must already be in possession of certain *a priori* principles of understanding and interpretation in the light of which one can give significance to the myths and images which the *anima* bears from the unconscious to the consciousness. Without these principles, one is simply working in the dark. There is no objective pattern of meaning, nothing according to which one can read the signs in which the unconscious is urgently seeking to transmit its messages. The process of *individuation* therefore presupposes the acceptance of certain ideas, certain principles of understanding, which cannot themselves be derived from empirical observation but which must be applied as it were *ab extra* to the psychological process that is being observed. This is an inescapable condition of individuation. Its implications are considerable. They lead directly into the sphere of what in this context can only be called religious ideas.

Jung already recognized this, though perhaps not clearly, at quite an early stage in his career. His interest in mythology started before his own personal confrontation with the unconscious. It started, he writes, in 1909, when he "read ... through a mountain of mythological material, then through the Gnostic writers ...";[41] and it is evident that already the basic principles according to which he began to interpret the significance of the fantasies he experienced during his long personal confrontation with the unconscious were derived from his reading at this time. But after his personal confrontation, the need to find an objective standard of reference, a structure of *a priori* ideas allowing him to interpret the significance of the myths and images thrown up by the unconscious, became far more pressing. To understand the fantasies arising from this confrontation, he had, he writes, "to find evidence for the historical prefiguration of my inner experience".[42] He had to discover

[41] Ibid. p. 158.
[42] Ibid. p. 192.

where the premises underlying his experiences had already occurred in history. Unless he could do this, he writes, he would never have been able to substantiate his ideas, since a psychologist depends in the highest degree upon historical and literary parallels if he wishes to exclude at least the crudest errors in judgment.[43]

In this crucial quest, Jung once more turned to the Gnostics. Between 1918 and 1926 he again "seriously studied the Gnostic writers, for they too had been confronted with the primal world of the unconscious".[44] Whether it was because they provided a confirmation and elucidation of Jung's own personal experience and intuitions, or whether it was because they consciously or unconsciously began increasingly to condition those experiences and intuitions themselves, there is no doubt that it was in the central religious ideas of the Gnostic writers that he found that objective pattern of meaning, that framework of a priori principles of understanding and interpretation, according to which he evaluated the significance of the myths and images not only of his own and his patients' collective unconscious but also of the various religious systems in which they had in the past been enshrined. They were the historical configuration for which he sought; and having discovered them and accepted them, he applied them with faithful conformity in his interpretation both of the dreams and fantasies he encountered in the course of his professional work and of such Christian and Biblical themes as the dogma of the Trinity or the story of Job. He also applied them in his interpretation of alchemical symbolism.

Jung's interest in alchemical symbolism seems to have arisen directly out of his reading of the Gnostics. Though the Gnostics provided him with his basic theological notions, he felt they were too remote in time to link up immediately with the psychological questions of today.[45] Accepting as he did the Darwinian hypothesis of evolution and applying it to the life of the psyche through pre-historical and historical times, he had to find a corresponding

[43] Ibid. p. 192.
[44] Ibid. p. 192.
[45] Ibid. p. 192.

evolutionary progress in the symbolic patterns in which the various stages of the emerging subterranean life of the unconscious had been reflected during the last two thousand years or so – between, that is, the time when the Gnostics had confronted the unconscious and the years in which he had confronted it. At first he failed to discern this progress, and it seemed that the tradition which might have connected the Gnostics with the present had been severed. Finally however he thought he discovered it, in the works of the alchemists.

Alchemy, he claimed (though his claim is based on little other than his desire to establish the connection), represented the historical link with Gnosticism. "Grounded in the natural philosophy of the Middle Ages, alchemy formed the bridge on the one hand into the past, to Gnosticism, and on the other into the future, to the modern psychology of the unconscious."[46] In alchemy, Jung writes, "I had stumbled upon the historical counterpart of my psychology of the unconscious. The possibility of a comparison with alchemy, and the uninterrupted intellectual chain back to Gnosticism, gave substance to my psychology";[47] and it was through the understanding of alchemical symbolism that he arrived at the central concept of his psychology: the process of individuation.[48]

The chain was – or appeared to be – complete; and to demonstrate it Jung wrote his *Psychology and Alchemy* and his monumental *Mysterium Coniunctionis*. But this seemingly unbroken chain and its demonstration in Jung's works should not blind one to the fact that if it was the understanding of alchemical symbolism that led Jung to the central concept of his psychology, and so appeared to give it an objective authenticity, yet it was on the religious theories of the Gnostics that he based his understanding of alchemical symbolism itself. It was these theories that gave him his doctrinal premises. They are the ultimate key to his psychology and to the significance which he attributed not only to alchemy, but also to human life in general.

[46] Ibid. p. 193.
[47] Ibid. p. 196.
[48] Ibid. p. 200.

We have already glanced briefly at certain of these theories, though without referring to their Gnostic antecedents. Their point of departure in Jung's case would seem to lie in his often repeated conviction that God is the author of evil and suffering as well as of good. Put in Biblical terms, God in His omniscience created everything so that the original parents of mankind – Adam and Eve – would have to sin. It was God's intention that they should sin.[49] This leads inescapably to the conclusion that in the final analysis God is responsible for the sins of the world.[50] The conventional Christian idea of God, therefore, as essentially and exclusively good, and as the author only of what is good, must be modified. God not only includes goodness in His nature; He also includes evil. He is a *complexio boni et mali*.

In fact, not only good and evil are bound together in God; all opposites are bound together in Him. He is female as well as male. This Gnostic idea of a God who is the union of all opposites in a total complex form is at the basis of Jung's religious thought. In its light he refashioned the traditional Jewish and Christian idea of God. The God of the Old Testament is now shown to be a half-satanic demiurge. The Christian Trinity is enlarged to a Quaternity, with the devil as a holy fourth. In the account of Job's sufferings "we have a picture of God's tragic contradictoriness".[51] Job is a prefiguration of Christ. He, like Christ, though to a lesser degree, is the suffering servant of God. Both had to suffer because of the sins of the world. It is God who is responsible for these sins. Because of His "guilt" in creating a world full of evil, God must perform an act of total expiation. This He does in subjecting Himself to ritual killing in the Crucifixion of Christ. It is this act of Christ that individual Christians seek to imitate in their lives. In this manner they help God atone.

From what has been said it is clear that, in spite of his protests to the contrary, Jung oversteps the boundaries between psychology and theology all along the line. His claim to reject the

[49] Ibid. p. 49.
[50] Ibid. p. 20
[51] Ibid. p. 206.

metaphysical and to restrain himself to the psychological is merely a device for attempting to make the psychical the only legitimate metaphysics. His psychology is virtually a new religion. It is true that this religion, unlike the frankly metaphysical religions, is not concerned with the relationship between the human soul and the supra-psychic transcendent Reality that nevertheless acts intimately upon and within the human soul. It is concerned with the relationship between the consciousness and those psychic events which do not depend upon consciousness but take place on the other side of it in the darkness of the psychical hinterland. It is a religion of pure psychic immanence. It is in confronting the soul's own immanent contents that man encounters the Divine. And this soul is simply the soul as it is, the "materialized" soul, not the soul detached and purified from "earthly" influences and contradictions.

There is no question of any birth of the supra-psychical Spirit in the soul. There is only the realization of the psychic self. Again it is true that Jung called this self the *imago Dei* in man. But in its realization, man calls back the projection of his self onto a God outside or beyond him. It is not that this God is explicitly denied. It is simply that He is not any longer regarded, as He is by the metaphysical religions, as the initiator and perfecter through His deifying power of that process of psychic transformation which is completed only when God has *taken the place of the psychic self*. For the practical purpose of the realization of the Jungian self, God is unnecessary. One need neither pray nor have faith nor require the assistance of grace. It is the self alone that is regarded as the unifying, "deifying" power, the regulator and balancer and harmonizer of the conflicting forces in man. The self, in other words, assumes in man the status and function of the Gnostic God. It is the incarnation of this God – a god who unites male and female, good and evil, in a wholeness in which all opposites are integrated. In this way man becomes his own deity. He is the final form of the Gnostic *complexio* – Christ and Satan in one – now destined to appear on the earth as the identity of God and man.

Set in its historical context, Jung's psychology can be seen as a much-needed protest against the simplifications of scientific rationalism. It is a plea for man to face the realities of his own inner world, to take his own path in the fulfillment of his personal created destiny, and not to barricade himself, as is so often the case, behind an abstract structure of religious or metaphysical principles whose only real function is to prevent him from ever realizing who or what he is, to prevent him from ever developing the potentialities of his own unique being. "Anyone who takes the sure road is as good as dead",[52] he writes, and against this death he proclaimed "the risk of inner experience, the adventure of the spirit".[53] He sought to affirm what the mechanistic attitude of the modern western mind ignored or denied – man's deep affinities with the natural world, the world of animals and plants, the beauty of earth and sky. He wished to see the spirit of life recognized in everything, not only in man but also in inorganic matter, in metal and stone; and he held that the phenomena of the natural world were expressions of the same energy – psychic energy, as he called it – as that which underlay the various phenomena of the human soul.[54]

In his study of myths and symbols, he asserted against those who saw in these nothing but futile speculation or childish fantasies their prime significance as the spontaneous irreplaceable language of the human soul. "No science will ever replace myth," he wrote, "for it is not that 'God' is a myth, but that myth is the revelation of a divine life in man."[55] But together with, or in spite of, all this, he accepted that hypothesis of scientific rationalism which perhaps more than any other is inimical and stultifying to man's inner growth – namely, the Darwinian hypothesis of evolution. And he also accepted a "metaphysic" which, by affirming the idea of a purely immanent deity, led inescapably to an idea far more dangerous to human life than atheism itself – the idea of man as a naturally deified or divine creature. Man cannot take the place of God, since man's being can never attain to the essence of

[52] Ibid. p. 27
[53] Ibid. p. 140.
[54] Ibid. p. 201.
[55] Ibid. p. 313.

God. When nevertheless man tries to take the place of God, he steps over into the sphere not of God, but of the infernal powers of his own soul.

In his autobiography, Jung recounts a dream he had quite late on in his life.[65] In this dream, Jung and his father entered a house. They came into a large hall which was the exact replica of the council hall of Sultan Akbar at Fatehpur Sikri. Only, from its center a steep flight of stairs ascended to a spot high up on the wall. At the top of the stairs was a small door, and Jung's father said to Jung: "Now I will lead you into the highest presence." Then he knelt down and touched his forehead to the floor. Jung imitated him, likewise kneeling, but he could not bring his forehead quite down to the floor. Meditating on this dream afterwards, Jung declared that this failure to put his forehead to the floor in the dream "discloses a thought and a premonition that have long been present in humanity: the idea of the creature that surpasses its creator by a small but decisive factor."

In ancient Iranian literature there is a story of a primeval king, Yima, whom the highest god, Ahura Mazdah, sets over the world he has made, to protect it and nourish it. This Yima does. In response to his sacrifices, the gods free man and cattle from death, and water and trees from drought. They give Yima command over all lands, and also over all the demons, so he can free Ahura Mazdah's creatures from evil. But in the course of time the world falls into materiality and Ahura Mazdah says he will send a greater winter over the earth so that no creature can live on it. Yima is told to make a fold, a kind of fortress, and there to gather the seed of all living things. This Yima does as well.

Then, however, Yima begins to extol himself. He begins to think that all that has happened, all the great benefits that have come to the world and its creatures, has happened and have come as a result of what he is and what he has done. He begins to see himself as the real lord of creation, and to ascribe his mastery over all the powers of nature and his own being to himself, and to boast that

56 Ibid. pp. 207-8.

he is the author of life and immortality. At precisely this moment his royal glory leaves him and he falls into the grip of demons who drive him over the face of the earth and eventually destroy him. When Yima regards himself, and what he is in his own created existence, as self-sufficient, and so feels that he is relieved of all need to look for true being beyond himself, he relegates his god and creator, Ahura Mazdah, to the realm of the unnecessary. He virtually proclaims himself his own creator. It is at this point of self-assertion that he falls into the power of the demons that eventually destroy him.

It is difficult to avoid the conclusion that Jung's own thought, culminating in the idea of the creature that surpasses its creator by a small but decisive factor, attains an identical point of self assertion, with all the disastrous consequences this has for the integrity of human life.

Chapter Seven

The Presence of Evil:
Christian and Neoplatonic Views

One of the most difficult and seemingly irresolvable questions facing not only Christians, but all those who would acknowledge that human and other life is inspired and nurtured by some power of ultimate goodness and perfection, is that of reconciling this recognition with the evident and devastating incidence of evil and suffering. How can a God who is essentially good and who out of His goodness creates human and other life permit and even connive in the evil and suffering which are, or appear to be, part and parcel of His creation? If there is such a God, why does He not protect human and other life from these afflictions which invade and disfigure it? Or if He fails to do this, does not this indicate that there is something almost sadistic about Him, in the sense that it is in His nature to visit mankind with these ills, or at least allow mankind to be visited by them? If that is not the case, and still He does not intervene to prevent their manifestation, does not this then signify either that there is some other and equally effective power in the nature of things that is essentially malefic and whose activities God cannot control, or that we are wrong in thinking of God simply as good and must realize that He is also the author of evil and suffering?

This last conclusion was, as we saw in the last chapter, that proposed by Jung. Jung thought that the Christian idea of a God who is wholly good must now be supplanted by the idea of a God who includes in Himself, and hence is responsible for, all those characteristics and functions which Christians have attributed to

Satan. The postulate that "Deus = Summum Bonum" is, he says, naive and false. It has blinded us to the obvious fact that God is ambivalent, that He also has a dark, evil side, and that He alone is responsible for the sufferings of the world. Thus, what theology terms Satan or Antichrist is in reality just "the other face of God". From this it follows that man, as created in the image of God, must recognize that the dark and evil side of his nature is just as God-given, just as much created in the divine image, as his good and bright side, and so must be, not suppressed or purified, but given equal freedom to express itself. Indeed, Jung concludes, since man has not made much of a success of things by approaching them from the bright, idealistic side, he might have better luck if he now approaches them from the dark, biological side.

Such a theological conception, with its anthropological conse-quences, would of course, if accepted, destroy Christianity at its heart – something of which Jung himself cannot have been un-aware and which therefore, despite his declared allegiance to Christianity, must have been part of his hidden ambition. But that this conception, as well as other conceptions that attempt to re-solve the enigma of evil in a way which either directly or indirectly implicates God as its causal agent, or involves positing a power of evil at the basis of things equally as effective as the power of good, are totally alien not only to Christianity but also to any spiritual understanding worthy of the name, is something that it is easier to affirm than to demonstrate. What follows is an attempt not to resolve the problem of evil as such, but to elucidate the perspective within which, at least in terms of the Christian tradition, it must be envisaged if certain other vital aspects of Christian doctrine are not to be violated.

To assist in this elucidation and to throw into relief certain dis-tinctive features of Christian doctrine in this sphere of things, Christian theory will be compared, and here and there contrasted, with a different theory, that which may be called Neoplatonic, since it is in this form that it is most familiar in western tradition. I am of course aware that in applying the term Neoplatonic in such a general way to this theory, I am ignoring distinctions in interpretation among those writers who are classified as Neoplatonists which are of considerable significance. None the less there is, I think, sufficient unanimity among them with respect to this theory to justify my calling it Neoplatonic. At the same time it is by no means exclusively Neoplatonic: to go no further, it has definite affinities not only with Platonic doctrine, as would be expected, but also with Hindu doctrine, something which is not in the least fortuitous. Needless to say, both theories, Christian and Neoplatonic, are equally emphatic that no evil or "dark" side is to be imputed to Supreme Reality itself, whether this Reality is called God, the Good, the One, the Absolute, or the Self.

Clearly, the problem of evil is one that confronts man as an existing being: it is an existential problem, intimately involved with the existence, or apparent existence, of the world.[1] It is therefore intimately involved with the question of how the world, and man as a concrete being in this world, came or appears to have come into existence. Here at once, where Neoplatonic and Christian understanding is concerned, one is faced on the one hand with the theory of emanation (or manifestation), and on the other with the theory of creation. Hence it is to these two theories that we must first give attention.

The theory of emanation is briefly as follows. The One – the Good or the Supreme – is absolute and perfect. As absolute, It must contain in Itself the seeds of everything, the possibility of everything; for if there were some possibility outside It, It would be, not absolute, but limited by this extraneous possibility. As perfect, It must distribute this perfection to the fullest extent possible. Its goodness must be everywhere. For if it were lacking anywhere, or if there were some part of a possible universe from which something of this goodness was excluded, then the One would be failing Its own nature. It would be contradicting Itself, for It would not be as perfect as It could be, and would be admitting a degree of imperfection there where It might impart greater perfection. Thus, not only must the One contain the seeds of everything within

[1] See also Philip Sherrard, *Human Image: World Image* (Ipswich, 1992), pp. 167-75. (Ed.)

Itself, but It must also manifest those which are capable of manifestation. This manifesting activity expresses a necessity:
manifestation is a necessary consequence of the fact not that the
One is absolute, but that It is perfect – that It is the Good absolute.

This necessity of manifestation – this necessary breaking out of
the One from Its self-enclosed isolation – might seem to imply a
contradiction: that which affects the freedom of the One. It would
seem that the One is under constraint, in that It has to bring Itself
forth into manifestation. It has to emanate. But in this case it is
not the One that is Supreme, but this other power according to
which It is compelled to enter into manifestation. Thus, the One,
if It is the Supreme, cannot be under any constraint or necessity to
manifest Itself. So there is the contradiction that as the absolute
Good It must manifest Itself, but as the Supreme It cannot be
under any constraint. This contradiction is further complicated by
the fact that even if It were not under any constraint to enter into
manifestation, still the One could not actualize any of the seeds of
manifestation It contains within Itself. To actualize any of these
possibilities is to admit that there is something other and less than
the One, and that the One is not, in Itself, all-inclusive, or is not
total Reality; and this cannot be admitted. Not only therefore can
the One not possess any possibility of self-determination, but also
It cannot contain the seeds of manifestation in Itself in any actualized state, or in any state capable of being actualized, or in any
state that implies any distinction from or differentiation in Its entirely simple and totally self-sufficient nature.

The One, therefore, in Itself, cannot be the principle of manifestation. What then brings forth or emanates is not the One in
Itself, but its first product, the divine Intellect (*Nous*), or, in the
Platonic sense, pure Being. Intellect or Being is the first determination of the One: and in its turn determines all the subsequent
ranks and conditions of manifestation. This does not mean that it
is the One that determines Being: we have seen that this is an
impossibility, for it would involve the disruption of the absolute
simplicity and unity and self-sufficiency and non-determinable

nature of the One. On the contrary, Being is self-determined. Thus
the One in Itself is exempt from any constraint. It is metaphysically free. Even pure Being, the principle of manifestation, is still
free, even though this manifestation is a necessary act. It is because it is free that it necessarily acts in this way. If it were anything
less than free, it would be constrained to act in some other way. As
it is, being free, it acts what it is: not in accordance with its nature
– which assumes that its action is a consequence of its nature, which
it is not – but as it is. Its action is itself, just as its non-activity is
itself; and both are what it wills, though the willing and the action
and the non-activity are all one.

From the Christian point of view, this theory of emanation appears to leave an unbridgeable gap between the One in Its totally
non-differentiated and self-sufficient unity, and any degree of determination or multiplicity. If the One contains in Itself all the
seeds of manifestation, It must contain them not only in a state
which is not actualized, but also in one which is free from any
possibility of actualization. They must be so identified with the
One, so totally subsumed in Its original nature, that there is no
possibility of any distinction: they are essentially and necessarily
one with Its entirely simple indivisibility. In a way, they constitute
a kind of Godhead without a God. They have no author. And in
so far as they are identified with the One, they cannot themselves
produce or manifest anything. They could only produce or manifest anything on condition that they became distinct from the One,
and this is impossible, since the One, subsuming in Itself total
Reality, cannot admit anything other than Itself. How then does
distinction or differentiation, or even the appearance of distinction or differentiation, first arise? In Neoplatonic theory there is
and can be no answer to this question – or at least no answer which
is not a kind of *deus ex machina* like, for instance, Proklos's theory
of the *henads*, which is an attempt to bridge this gap between the
One and multiplicity, or the appearance of multiplicity, while leaving
unimpaired the perfect unity and non-determination of the One.

In Christian theory – and here reference is above all to Greek
Patristic authors rather than to the Scholastics – God, the Absolute

or the Supreme, is not regarded as the God-Unity of the Neoplatonic tradition. Certainly, God is One, but this unity includes multiplicity; it includes – leaving on one side the whole doctrine of the Trinity – the divine energies and powers. God's Essence is, like the Neoplatonic One, totally transcendent, totally non-differentiated, totally undetermined and incommunicable; but His energies and powers are multiple, creative, communicable. And it must be stressed that though these energies and powers are distinguished in this way from the divine Essence, they are not on that account said to be any less real or less absolute than the Essence. Nor must one think of the Essence apart from the energies and powers, or *vice versa*, in such a way as to conceive of the Essence as unenergized or of the energies as inessential. Nor, finally, is the Essence to be regarded as a superior order of Reality in which the energies and powers are subsumed and lose their differentiation and distinction. God – the Absolute – is not to be identified with His Essence alone, nor is the Essence to be thought of as His superior or more inclusive or absolute nature, and nor are His powers and energies to be identified with His Essence.

It might be said that while in Neoplatonic theory the divine Essence is abstracted from all Its principial determinations, including that of Its Being, and this Essence alone, in Its perfectly undetermined, non-differentiated, and entirely simple nature is thought of as embracing in Itself the totality of the Real, and as Itself constituting the Absolute, so that all determinations – all powers and energies, even pure Being – are in the final analysis seen merely as contingent and relative modes or aspects or attributes of the Essence, in Christian theory it is precisely this act of abstraction that is a primal doctrinal error. Thus, in Christian theory there is no question of how differentiation and distinction arise from the unity of the One: differentiation and distinction are inherent *in an actualized state* in this unity "in the beginning". God – the Absolute – is One-in-Many, simplicity-in-distinction, a divided indivisibility; and, as has been said, to seek to resolve this paradox by appealing to a higher principle in which its contradictory terms are subsumed and reconciled is a basic doctrinal error.

It is because of this paradoxical idea of the Absolute that Christian theory has tended to affirm that the act of creation, in contrast to the act of emanation in Neoplatonic theory, is entirely free and spontaneous, and no necessary consequence of the Absolute being what it is. God creates, brings forth out of nothing, through the spontaneous, undetermined operation of His powers and energies. What He creates – the whole intelligible order, including the intelligible archetypes of the visible world – is not a necessary part of His nature; neither is it to be principially identified either with His Essence, or His Being, or His multiple powers and energies. It is a new mode of reality, not necessary in any way.

In other words, this theory seems to emphasize God's free will – His freedom – in a manner that amounts to an exclusion of the idea of divine necessity which plays so important a part in the emanation theory. God creates because it is His "pleasure", His "glory", to create, and that is all, humanly, to be said. Thus while the emanation theory appears to posit manifestation as a necessary consequence of the absolute goodness of the One, the Christian theory of creation appears to do away with all idea of necessity where the Divine is concerned: it might equally have been God's "pleasure" not to create; He could be God, absolute and infinite Power and Perfection, without showing forth His power and perfection in any creature. He could refrain from creation and still be omnipotent.

Two things may be said in this connection. The first is that, as we have noted, in Neoplatonic theory the necessity operative in manifestation is not at the expense of or incompatible with the freedom of the principle of manifestation: it is because it is free that this principle necessarily acts in the way it does, and does not act in some other way, as it would have to if it were not free. In other words, for Christians to criticize Neoplatonic theory in this respect, on the grounds that it compromises the sovereign liberty of the Absolute, is for them to ignore its full refinement and acumen.

The second – and perhaps more important – thing to be said in this connection is that the Christian tendency to oppose freedom and necessity *in divinis*, as if they were incompatible or mutually exclusive, can lead to a demeaning of creation by reducing it to something accidental or even arbitrary, and hence to a demeaning of the plenitude of God Himself. For it is one thing to say that when one affirms that God does not create the world out of necessity but creates it through an act of sovereign free-will, what one is affirming is that nothing external or extraneous to God compels him to create. It is quite another to say, unreservedly and without considerable qualification, that He does not create according to any necessity.

Of course, necessity does not determine God's being what He is or doing what He does in the sense that He is under constraint in the way stated above: God simply is what He is, beyond any determination in this sense. But this does not mean that He is free from necessity *tout court*. Necessity in God – and this accords with Neoplatonic theory – is the necessity of being what He is: being what He is, He necessarily acts in certain ways. God cannot not be love: to love is a necessity of His being what He is. Similarly, God cannot not be the Creator: to create is a necessity of His being what He is. If God did not, or even could not create, He would be other than He is. Creation is only not a necessity of God's being what He is if God can be other than He is, just as to love can only not be a necessity of God's being what He is if God can be other than He is. If God cannot be other than He is, then to love and to create are inseparably intertwined necessities of His being what He is.

To say this does not – to repeat – imply that there is any external constraint compelling God to do anything. To act according to what one is is to act freely. But this does not make one's actions any the less a necessity of one's being what one is. Freedom and necessity coincide in God: they are one example – perhaps the prime example – of the coincidence of opposites in God of which St. Nicholas of Cusa speaks. If one forgets this, and elevates God's freedom above all and every kind of necessity, one is in danger, as I remarked above, of demeaning the whole mystery of creation, which is to demean God as well; and the converse also applies. Of course, God's Essence itself is beyond both freedom and necessity, as it is beyond all else that can be affirmed or denied about it. Moreover, there is, as will be indicated below, a sense in which the very concept of necessity cannot, in the Christian perspective, properly be applied – as it can in Neoplatonic theory – to the divine realm at all, though by the same token it might be said that in that case the concept of freedom likewise cannot properly be applied to that realm.

Both Neoplatonic and Christian theories agree, then, that manifestation "in the beginning" is good. This goodness is not of course goodness absolute, for this pertains to God, or the Good, alone. It is a relative goodness. Compared with the perfection of God or the Good (if comparisons may be made in this sphere), a degree of imperfection has entered in. But it should be made quite clear that neither in Neoplatonic nor in Christian theory is the presence of evil in manifestation a necessary consequence of this degree of imperfection. It is sometimes argued that in so far as anything falls short of the absolute perfection of God, to that extent it is bound to be implicated in evil. There is, according to this argument, some necessary connection between imperfection, or relative perfection, and evil; they are even in some sense identified, as if they were the same thing. This is not the case with the two theories under review. In neither does a relative perfection necessarily imply the presence of evil: it may imply the possibility of evil, but that is another matter. In both theories, on the contrary, what is relatively perfect may be entirely free from evil. In both theories, manifestation may be free from the actual presence of evil.

This is something particularly emphasized in the Christian tradition. Indeed, in a certain sense, it is at the core of Christianity, being one of the essential aspects of the Incarnation: Christ assumes human nature in every respect except that in Him this human – and created – nature is free from evil. It is from this that derives the Christian promise of a new Heaven and a new Earth – of a created existence, that is to say, which, while not identified with the perfection of God Himself, is none the less entirely free from evil; and it is from this, too, that derives the Christian theory of the sacraments, a theory quite meaningless if evil is necessarily inherent in everything that is created. Hence the actual presence of evil for the Christian is no necessary consequence of creation. If it is a necessary consequence of certain phases of manifestation in Neoplatonic theory, this is not because what is manifest is necessarily imperfect and hence evil. It is because certain "lower" phases of manifestation bring it into contact with evil.

The question of evil in Neoplatonic theory is intimately linked with that of the descent of the soul into a bodily form. The existence of the soul at all is itself a further consequence of the initial necessity of emanation. The first degree of emanation from the One – the Supreme – is pure Being. Being is the first determination of the undetermined One. Pure Being contains all the possibilities of particular beings – all the souls – in a unified state. Just as Being is necessarily determined, so it necessarily determines all its own possibilities – necessarily, because it is in the nature of things for the One to manifest Its goodness in all ways possible. Hence particular beings – souls – receive their particular existence.

Yet these souls must have some activity different from that of pure Being, for otherwise the two would be identical. They must have a different manner or mode of being. This different manner or mode of being involves the assertion of variety and individuality which, since they are possibilities in pure Being, must be made manifest. This outward movement, movement away from the center – the One – must continue without any halt until all possible degrees of manifestation are accomplished and exhausted, or until there is nothing left to manifest. This is a natural and necessary accomplishment deriving from the original nature of the One.

Where, then, into this process of emanation does evil enter? It cannot be imputed to the process itself, since, this process being in the nature of things, to do so would be to impute evil to the originator of the process, to the One Itself; and what is the Good absolute cannot also be the source of evil. Nor can it be imputed to individual souls as such, for these, in spite of their differentiation, are still essentially modes of the intelligible world of pure Being, rooted in the substance of pure Being, and so free from evil. Evil, therefore, enters into the process in some sense from without or, rather, from a sphere opposite to that of Being from which the soul derives, of which it is a mode, and which knows no admixture of anything evil.

This sphere, in Neoplatonic theory, is that of matter. Matter is the total opposite to Being. It is total Non-Being, total lack and destitution, unformed and measureless, having no share whatsoever in Being, so inconceivable in its unreality that it may be apprehended only by a kind of spurious reasoning. But if it has no share whatsoever in Being, and Being is essential goodness, it can have no share in the Good. It is the negation of the Good. It is therefore evil, evil utterly. And it is from its implication in matter that the soul is implicated in evil. In the last phase of its outward manifestation, soul, naturally good, and seeking to distribute this goodness to the farthest extreme, seeks to give matter, essential Non-Being, some share in Being; seeks to confer on it some form. It is from this determination of matter by the outward-flowing soul that bodily forms come into existence, and it is from the soul's commerce with or entry into bodily existence, and hence from its contact with matter, that it becomes prone to evil. It is inherence in a bodily form and a sharing in the body's states that corrupts the soul.

Three observations are relevant here. The first is that in Neoplatonic theory evil is only actively present in the world of corporeal existence. The second is that it is necessarily actively present in this world, for a precondition of this world is the presence of matter, and hence of evil. In soul, free from body and bodily states, there is no evil. The third – and in this context the most significant – is that since a condition of his being at all is the possession of a corporeal nature, man only exists and can only exist in a world in which evil is actively present: as man, he can never be free from evil and the suffering that goes with it. At the same time, since it is in the nature of things that soul descends into a bodily form (for it is a necessary phase of the process of manifestation), it would seem that no blame can be attached to the soul or to man for this actualization of evil: no blame, and hence no responsibility for evil done.

Yet there is another aspect to this descent of the soul in Neoplatonic theory which introduces the idea of definite choice on the soul's part and hence of culpability. On the one hand, the soul's descent is a necessary spontaneous outward movement of its nature. But on the other hand it is a turning away from a greater good to a lesser good. It is a failure to choose what is better. It is better for the soul to remain in the intellectual world, free from the body and its accompanying evils, for this is a better world. At the same time, the soul (the soul, that is to say, whose task it is in the process of manifestation to distribute the Good to the farthest limits) is under compulsion to participate in the sense-world. A condition of its descent is that it in some degree separates itself from its source, becomes self-centered, ignores the Divine, falls into forgetfulness, lapses. Thus, viewed from this angle, its descent into bodily form is a kind of punishment for its failure to choose the Good. It is its nature to enter into the sense-world; its descent – its "fall" – is pre-determined by its allotted task in the process of manifestation; yet the performance of this task involves an apostasy and a degree of self-ownership which brings its own punishment: complicity in evil and in the sufferings that spring from it.

So that in Neoplatonic theory one gets finally a situation something like this: given that the Good is the Good, it is inevitable that certain souls should come into being whose nature predetermines an apostasy from their source. At the same time, this apostasy is a consequence of their own self-will and deliberate choice; the descent which follows on their choice is both an actualization of the choice itself, a punishment for it and, thirdly, a natural fulfillment of the task appointed to that soul in accomplishing the divine purpose in the universe. The Good – the Absolute – is only to "blame" for this descent, and the suffering in which it involves the soul, to the extent that the Good is to blame for being the Good. The alternative would be no Good, no Being, no differentiation, no souls, no sense-world, nothing, absolute blank. If this would be a better state of affairs than the present one, with all its tribulations yet with its real possibilities of release from these tribulations by a return to the Source, then the Good is to blame. If it would not be, then the Good must be absolved: God is blameless, as Plato puts it.

In spite of the assertion of an element of choice in, and hence of responsibility for, the soul's suffering condition in this world, it is difficult to see how, according to Neoplatonic theory, things could have been other than they are; for they are as good as they can be, given the circumstances in which necessarily they must come to be. "Fallen" existence is in the nature of things, and the individual souls present in this existence are present because in this way they fulfill their appointed nature: there are necessarily certain weaker souls predestined to fall, and it would have been contrary to nature, as well as a breach in the divine purpose, for them not to have fallen.

In other words, fallen existence, and man's presence in a world inseparably involved with evil, are perfectly natural, indeed, inevitable, a direct consequence of the Absolute being what it is. This does not make evil any less real, or any less shameful and vicious, or lighten the suffering it entails; but on the other hand it is unavoidable, since it has its roots in a certain lack of Being, a certain lack of Reality, that is inseparable from the sense-world itself and so from created human existence itself. One might say that evil is an accident that occurs not in all manifestation as such, but certainly in all manifestation that includes man as a corporeal being.

The whole of the Neoplatonic theory of manifestation and of the presence of evil within manifestation is, in short, an inevitable development of the introduction of the idea of a necessity – of a logical necessity, it might be said, for that is the way it presents itself to us – operating in the original "*fiat lux*" according to which the first emanant, Intellect or pure Being, is determined. It follows from this necessity that this world is as good as it possibly can be – and must be – in the circumstances under which it has come into existence. This means that there is really very little scope for what one might call moral responsibility on the part of man, or for its correspondent, moral guilt: if someone acts destructively, inflicts deep suffering or murders, he will be punished for his crime by a process of natural retribution (the justice of Adrasteia, ineluctable Retribution) which will keep him bound to the wheel of becoming until he has exhausted the proclivities that attach him to it; yet at the same time if, in committing his crime, he acts truly according to his nature (which he must do, for otherwise he could not act as he does), he is ultimately morally blameless. Evil, as we said, does not cease to be evil, but, first, it contributes to the good of the whole and, second, the individual instrument is not to blame that he or she acts in an evil manner, since the harmony and well-being of the whole demands that this evil should be manifest through him or her: as Plotinus writes, the well-run state has to have an executioner, or from the adultery or the violation of prisoners may spring fine children.

Compared with Neoplatonic theory, the Christian teaching on the "fall" puts far more emphasis on the element of free choice than it does on its being the inevitable consequence of a necessary process. The fall, that is to say, is a consequence of such choice and not something accomplished under the constraint of a natural divine law. There is no need for it to have happened as part of the inevitable process of manifestation. It happened because primal man – Adam – chose that it should happen. This in its turn presupposes two conditions. The first is the possibility, already noted, of a creation, including man, that is free from evil – of a creation whose perfection, though relative (when compared with the perfection of God), does not necessarily entail the presence of evil; and the second is that it is possible for Adam to have chosen not to fall. That both these possibilities are real and not simply ideal, or sentimental, or anthropomorphic, is established for Christians in the revelation of the Incarnate God, the second Adam, who, as man (and not in so far as He is God), and therefore as a created being, is free from sin, and who, again as man, does not succumb to the temptations of the devil in the wilderness. Christ, in other words, fulfills the destiny that Adam failed to fulfill. What from the Neoplatonic point of view is a metaphysical impossibility is thus seen to be the central message of the Christian revelation: that there can be, and is, a created or creaturely existence which is free from evil and suffering; that evil and suffering are no necessary characteristics of material creation as such.

Indeed, where man is concerned and consequently where material creation is concerned, evil is as it were something extraneous, which only gains access through a certain apostasy on the part of man. This of course is mirrored in the Christian myth of man's seduction by the devil in paradise and the fall that ensues. Evil, that is to say, is something that occurs first on the plane not of sensible creation but intelligible creation. This is in contrast to Neoplatonic theory, in which the intelligible realm is by definition impervious to evil, even though the soul that is destined to distribute the Good to the world of matter is said to be guilty of a certain turning away from a greater good to a lesser good.

The principle of evil in Christian theory is, therefore, not in itself that which is total negativity and unreality, as it is in Neoplatonic theory. On the contrary, it is an intelligible power that, having itself chosen to assert a freedom of being outside and independent of divine life and love, and consequently having pledged itself to what is totally unreal, non-existent, dark and negative, now deploys its energy – intrinsically divine and free from evil – to persuade other created beings, first angelic then human (in whom intelligible and sensible mingle and interact), to choose a similar spurious freedom and so give an illusory existence to the same total unreality, non-existence, darkness and negativity as those to which it is itself committed. Acts which we call evil are therefore those of created beings that, having lost the vision of the spiritual intellect and hence the intelligence and purity that is theirs "in heaven", arrogate to themselves what are originally divine powers and use them to serve vicious and violent purposes. Without the vision of the spiritual intellect and its control and balance, such powers can be transmuted, as we are only too well aware, into forms that are as unsubdued and destructive as they are insatiable and rabid.

It might be added, in view of what was said at the beginning of this chapter, that one of the principal means through which we can be induced to submit to diabolic persuasion is by instilling in us the idea that evil, far from being alien and extraneous to our nature, is in fact an integral part of it, so that in expressing our evil proclivities we are being just as natural and true to ourselves as we are when we express positive qualities of goodness and love. If in addition to this we can be persuaded that our evil proclivities are an integral part of our nature because they represent the "dark evil side" of the God in whose image we are created, the situation is infinitely worse: for then in expressing our evil negative proclivities we can claim divine sanction, in that in expressing them we are acting in accordance with the divine nature itself. In other words we are then truly and ineluctably in captivity to the devil, under the illusion that we are irredeemably trapped in the world of evil, since we cannot purge ourselves of it unless we first purge God Himself of His dark side, something which of course would be beyond both our and even God's own power to do. That is why to impute evil to the source of things is to commit one of the most terrible acts of perversion of which the human mind is capable.

From the Christian point of view, then, our fall as well as our consequent implication in evil and suffering are neither necessary nor natural. Or, rather, evil and suffering are a necessary consequence of Adam's choice, but this choice itself is both undetermined and involves us in a state of existence that is not ours by nature. If this is the case, it may be asked, why did God allow it? If He could create a world that is free from evil (not from the possibility of evil, which is another matter), and a human nature capable of resisting the seduction of evil (and that He could is demonstrated by the incarnate life of Christ), why did He permit Adam's fall? And further, since He did permit Adam's fall, must not this fall have been in the original scheme of things, and therefore as much according to nature as the fall of the soul in Neoplatonic theory? In any case, does not Christian theory implicate God one way or another in our fall and fallen state and therefore in the evil and suffering inseparable from it?

The Christian answer to this is again by reference to the freedom in which man (Adam) is originally created. God's intention in creating man is that he should be a creature who, once having been given existence, should be responsible for what he does with it. His freedom to turn to God or to turn away from God, to exist in life or to exist in death (for existence is the one thing he cannot get out of), is therefore an inherent property of his original nature: Adam, unlike the soul that in Neoplatonic theory is predestined to manifest the Good in the sense-world, could have chosen not to fall. If God had created an Adam incapable of falling, or in some way have prevented him from falling, or had abstained from the creation of Adam knowing that he would, certainly or possibly, fall, He would have been frustrated in His purpose.

In other words, from the Christian viewpoint, God is to "blame" for man's fall and the consequent evil and suffering in which it involves him only in so far as He is to blame for wishing to create man free from constraint in his choice of accepting or rejecting His love and life; for wishing that man should participate actively and voluntarily and not merely passively and compulsorily in this love and life. Had He created man in a state from which he had no possibility of falling, man's goodness would have been conditioned in a servile and arbitrary manner and would not be the consequence of any choice or cooperation on his part. One can say that God is at fault in wishing man to possess this freedom; but once it is granted that this freedom is within the intention of God's original creation of Adam, the responsibility for the fall and for all its disastrous consequences lies with man.

Several further distinctions between Neoplatonic and Christian theory are implicit in these primary distinctions. Four seem to be of direct relevance in this context. The first is one about which something has already been said, and concerns the difference in attitude to freedom and necessity. In Neoplatonic theory, the notion of necessity plays a far greater part than it does in Christian theory, where on the contrary, freedom is pre-eminently stressed. But this does not mean that the pre-eminence attributed to freedom in Christian theory, and its reluctance to recognize categories of necessity where the Absolute is concerned, are the result of arbitrary prejudice or sentimentality. The difference between the two theories in this respect derives from their different attitudes to logic and their different understandings of the relationship between logic and metaphysic.[2] The notion of necessity, which involves relating one thing to another (part to whole, effect to cause, and so on) in a purely logical manner, is one that itself can only arise within the logical order. In Neoplatonic theory, it is legitimate to transpose such a notion to the supra-logical order, on the grounds that the laws of logic reflect or correspond to metaphysical realities. In this way, it is legitimate to speak of necessity in connection with the Absolute Itself. From the Christian view-point, freedom – the absence of any constraint, logical or other – is of the nature of the uncreated divine order, while necessity, whose source is in the relative and quantitative sphere of the created order within which logic also arises, merely characterizes certain aspects of this order and its conditions. To apply this notion to the divine order, as if there were a necessary and pre-established analogy between the divine and the logical orders, is to assume a relationship between the two orders which Christianity does not assume.

A second distinction is connected with the first. According to Neoplatonic theory, there is a necessary relationship between man and the One – or, rather, between man's soul and the One. Man's soul, though it adds nothing to the One, is yet the natural and generic offspring of divine Being; it is rooted in this Being, part of the same substance. The soul may go up or down the scale of Being, but it cannot lose its substantial identity as a mode or phase – an emanant ray – of the Divine. This means that the line of demarcation between the Divine and "other than Divine" does not, in Neoplatonic theory, pass between the One and Being on the one hand and soul and sense-world on the other; it passes between soul and the material world *tout court*; or, rather, since soul is a mode of Being, it passes between Being and the whole intelligible world including soul on the one hand, and the world of matter on the other.

[2] See Ch. 4 above for a full development of the theme.

In Christian theory, on the contrary, there is no necessary (natural and generic) relationship between God and man or God and man's soul: man, either as soul or body, or as both together, may participate in the Divine, but there is no substantial identity between his soul and the Divine. Soul and body are created realities, new forms of existence in the presence of God. The line of demarcation therefore, in Christian theory, between the Divine and "other than Divine" does not pass between the intelligible world of Being and the world of matter, but between the uncreated and the created, between God and His Being on the one hand and the intelligible and sensible world considered as a single organic creation on the other. It is because of this that Christian theory is able to envisage a degree of human independence and freedom that is impossible according to Neoplatonic theory.

A third distinction between the two theories is also one that has already been touched on. Both theories agree that evil has no substantive existence: it is a kind of negation, a defect, a total lack of Being. Both further agree that it is not a natural property of all manifestation or creation as such: in Neoplatonic theory the whole realm of Being is free from evil, and in Christian theory both Paradise and the new Heaven and the new Earth are free from evil. Nor is either theory dualistic. But while in Neoplatonic theory evil is necessarily inherent in matter and hence in our existence in the material world, this is not so in Christian theory: evil is not a necessary property of matter, and hence it is not necessarily part and parcel of our existence in the material world.

In Christian theory, both the material world and our life in it become implicated in evil as a result of the fall, which in itself is neither a necessary nor a natural occurrence. Evil is a possibility inherent in creation (a possibility which measures the distance, if one may put it like this, between the uncreated and the created), but one that need not ever be actualized. That it is actualized, through Adam's choice, brings about a rupture in creation. It is not because evil and suffering are a natural and inescapable condition of our created existence that we must sin and suffer so long as we remain existential creatures – a notion which has as its counterpart a theory of deliverance according to which we can only be free from evil and suffering on the condition that we cease to exist as creatures altogether. It is because we have perverted existence that we sin and suffer, and with us the rest of creation; so that deliverance from evil and suffering is not a matter of escaping from the natural and inevitable limitations of creaturely existence, but of restoring or remaking its integrity.

This means that the Christian idea of the fall introduces a tension into fallen human existence quite alien to the life of man as envisaged in Neoplatonic theory. In Neoplatonic theory, everything basically is in its place; it is where it has to be according to its nature, and there is injustice and stupidity in wishing human life, for instance, or existence in general, to be other than it is. It is only possible to find fault with the ordinance of things in the sense-world, and so with human life, on the assumption that everything ought to come into existence in this world with all the perfection of those beings that, since they have remained in the intellectual world, have never known such a coming into existence at all. Such an assumption is ludicrous, for things in the intellectual realm cannot have an unbroken continuity with things in the sense-world. It would be better if things had not come into existence in the sense-world, for the simple reason that this has involved a lapse from the intellectual world, which is a better world. But this lapse has to be because the Good is what It is: the soul guilty of such a lapse is under divine compulsion.

In Christian theory, on the other hand, our existence as we now know it is not as it should be: there has been this breach or rupture in creation, and this, since it has been brought about by us and not by any natural or necessary divine process in which we are inevitably involved, places on us a different kind of responsibility and introduces this tension to which reference has been made.

Moreover, this responsibility incumbent on us extends to our relationship with the whole created world. If the whole of creation is now affected by evil and suffering, this is not because creation is implicated in matter, which can never be given any positive quality or brought any nearer to reality and goodness but must always

remain what it is – total negativity, absolute privation and otherness. On the contrary, the material element of creation is a real
potentiality, and is capable of being transformed and of participating in divine life and hence of being delivered from the sphere in
which it is affected by evil and suffering. But such a deliverance
depends upon us, in the sense that unless we recover the integrity
of our nature, and so raise ourselves – or are raised – to the realm
in which evil and suffering are no longer operative, our own lack
of integrity, which is a consequence of our submission to evil, will
affect the rest of creation as well and implicate it in evil and in the
suffering that accompanies it.

Fourthly, and partly as a consequence of what has been said
immediately above, there is a distinction between the two theories
in their attitude toward time and in the significance attached to it.
In Neoplatonic theory, time is the life of the soul in its various
transmigrations in the world of sense: it comes into being as a
consequence of the soul's descent and its flight from eternity. As
this descent and flight are part of a natural and necessary process,
so also is time. In one sense, time must always exist: intellectual
beings are eternal and as these must necessarily generate their own
likenesses, the images they produce in time must stand for as long
as their archetypes, which is always: the Good ever is, and so must
all that is sequent to the Good ever be. Thus evil, which is inseparable from the becoming-process, is inseparable also from time;
and as the becoming-process is perpetual, so too is the actualization of evil perpetual: there can be no final end of evil, as there can
be no final end of time.

On the other hand, this perpetuity of time is punctuated by a
certain inner cyclic rhythm, and one of the phases of this rhythm
is the return of all things to their pre-manifest source: the becoming-process, and time with it, are brought, for this phase, to a halt;
and consequently, during this phase, evil lies dormant, unactualized.
But this phase is only a phase, for the Good cannot cease from
being the Good and so the necessary process of manifestation must
again be radiated forth. This being so, time is really a function of a
certain lack of true being; it is the movement of the fallen soul, a

kind of fragmentary flight splintering eternity, which eternity can reclaim only by destroying.

In Christian theory, time, like matter itself, is not necessarily implicated in evil and is not the consequence of a certain lack of being or of a flight from eternity. On the contrary, it is rooted in eternity. It is a kind of transmutation of eternity whereby the archetypes of the divine world are made manifest in creation. There is, that is to say, no hiatus or ontological gap between time and eternity, and that we perceive such a gap is due to the fact that we have closed our eyes to true vision, not to any dichotomy in reality itself. It is our lack of true perception that has introduced a kind of unreality into time and that makes us view it as a dimension existing apart from and somehow as set over against eternity. Consequently, time is not something that has to be destroyed in order for eternity to redeem it. As the proper destiny of created human nature is to share in God's uncreated life and love without becoming other than it essentially is, so the proper destiny of time is to share in eternity without becoming other than it essentially is. Both participations – and the one is the condition of the other – require not a change in nature, but a realization of the integrity of this nature, an integrity obscured and disrupted by the fall and its consequences. And this realization in its turn can be brought about only through a victory over evil.

Thus, a condition of the end of the active presence of evil is not the end of time or of created human nature. Time and created human nature are not inseparably linked with evil, or with its consequences. Both, while remaining what they are, and with the limitations of what is created, may be free from evil and its presence: free through ever-increasing communion in the eternal "now" and unconditioned freedom of the inexhaustible depths of God.

Chapter Eight

On Death and Dying: A Christian Approach

Death and dying are, of course, crucial for every form of sacred tradition; and perhaps nothing so illustrates our alienation from the sources of our being and our subjection to the trivial and trivializing norms of modern science than our virtually complete loss of the traditional understanding of their significance and of their relationship with life. Christ calls Himself "life": "I am the life" (Jn. 11:25); and it is the death of Christ, according to St. Paul, that we carry in the body so that this life – which is Christ – can also be manifested in our bodies. Plato calls true philosophy the study of dying, or a meditation on death (*Phaedrus* 81A). And a Japanese Zen master[1] exhorts us

> While living, become a dead man
> Thoroughly dead
> Then do as you will
> All will be all right –

– counsel repeated in the words of Jalāl al-Dīn Rūmī and Angelus Silesius: "Die before you die."

Yet by the eighteenth century, this traditional awareness of the paradoxical oneness in which living and dying are inseparable has given way to a view in which life is distinguished from and opposed to death, and death from and to life, in a more or less absolute manner. Life becomes essentially a this-worldly category, deriving its origin and significance, not from God, but from the world. Seen in this light, it has nothing to do with God becoming flesh and

[1] Shidō Bunan, of the early Tokugawa period.

calling Himself the life to which He summons everyone. On the contrary, life is reduced to a matter of physical survival that is brought to an end by death. In this way life becomes an idol, a caricature, and a blasphemy.

As a result, we have polarized life and death into two irreconcilable categories, and instead of realizing that we are involved at every moment in a living-dying existence in which life and death are two faces of an identical reality, we regard them as contraries, at enmity one with the other, and to all intents and purposes look on death as the end of life. We want to hear as little about it as possible, as though it were something disgraceful and shocking which should be covered up or covered over quickly and unobtrusively. Consequently nearly all of us are simply carted off to the hospital to die, hygienically, in air-conditioned wards, our minds and senses numbed and stupefied by drugs and injections. Doctors – the whole world of modern medical science in general – interfere with the death-process in a quite deplorable and irresponsible manner, blinded by their more or less total ignorance of the significance that death has for life and life for death.

Such ignorance, as our ignorance in practically every other sphere, has been engendered, as I said, by the norms of modern science. Prior to their ascendancy – as in parts of the world still not yet infected by their degradation – there was a far greater, and a far different, knowledge and concern. There was an art of dying as fully comprehensive as any art of living – in fact, the art of living embraced the art of dying, and *vice versa*. We have only to recall, for instance, how important the Eleusinian Mysteries were in the ancient Greek world, and to remember that at the heart of these Mysteries lay a death-rite, to grasp how crucial this art of dying was.

Cicero, an initiate into these Mysteries, writes that, having experienced them, "we at last possess reason why we should live; and we are not only eager to live, but we cherish a better hope in death." Plutarch refers to "the crowd of people who are not initiated and purified, and who throng to the mud-pit [of pleasure in this world] and flounder in the darkness, and through fear of death cling to their woes, not trusting in the bliss of the hereafter." Works like *The Egyptian Book of the Dead*[2] (the correct title of which is "The Coming Forth from Day") and *The Tibetan Book of the Dead*[3] (which is entitled in the original Tibetan "Liberation by Hearing on the After-Death Plane") testify to the universality of this knowledge and this concern.

Is it possible to reassemble any of this knowledge, to make anything coherent out of it? To start with, this can be done only provided that we give our assent to categories of thought which by and large have been eliminated from our consciousness. We have, first, to accept that there is such a reality as that which is designated in western parlance by the word "soul", and that this soul is either immortal by nature or at least possesses immortality as an intrinsic potentiality. It is not subject, that is to say, to the kind of mortality to which our physical, material body is subject. Then we have, second, to recognize that there are two types of dying and death: there is a physical dying and death (which nowadays tends to be the only type we acknowledge), and there is what might be called a metaphysical dying and death, in relation to which our purely physical dying and death are, as it were, incidental.

I use the word "incidental" in this context because, from the point of view of the perspective that I am now trying to clarify, our purely physical death is not regarded as making initially much difference to our life. This is to say that, surprising as it may sound, the form of life we experience anyhow initially after our physical death is very much the same as that which we experience before we die. This may sound surprising since insofar as we envisage the existence of the soul at all, and even acknowledge that it is not subject to the kind of mortality to which our physical material body is subject, we find it difficult to conceive how our physical death cannot make a great difference to the form of life it then experiences.

Yet this difficulty is itself perhaps due to the confusion we have created over our understanding of the nature of the soul, and par-

[2] Translated and edited by E. A. Wallis (London, 1895).
[3] Introduced and edited by W. Y. Evans-Wentz (Oxford, 1927).

ticularly of its relationship to the body. This in its turn may only be another way of saying that it is itself partly due to the confusion we have created over what constitutes the body. We tend for the most part to identify the body purely with its gross material elements, with its bone, flesh, blood and so on as we possess them during our earthly life. Hence when this form of the body disintegrates and corrupts at the end of our earthly life, we are forced to envisage the soul (provided we accept that it survives our physical death) as something bodiless, without any sensitive organism through which it can operate. And this being in a bodiless state must, we conclude, make a great difference to how we experience things after the dissolution of the mortal body.

Yet from the traditional point of view with which we are here concerned, this must be an entirely wrong way of envisaging things. In terms of the Christian tradition, for instance, it is quite clear that Adam in his paradisal, pre-fallen state was fully embodied, and it is equally clear that his body was very different in consistency from his body subsequent to the fall, since it was not subject to corruption. For one of the consequences of the fall was not that man acquires a body, but that his body becomes compounded with denser, coarser, more material elements than those which pertain to it in its pre-fallen state. Our true body, that is to say, or our original, paradisal body is not to be identified with those densely material elements it acquires as a consequence of the fall. It is of a far finer texture, a texture so fine that it can be described as a spiritual body, a *soma pneumatikon*.

Correspondingly, the dissolution and corruption to which the gross material elements compounded with the spiritual body as the result of the fall are subject at the time of physical, earthly death do not mean that the soul is left bodiless. It still possesses after this death a perfectly good body. It still possesses an organism, or a *complexus* of organs, through which it can act or react, can think, see, hear, feel and so on. In other words, the spiritual body possesses in a spiritual form the whole range of senses of which what we call our corporeal senses are, as it were, the reflexes or the prolongations. The life of the eye is not of the material body, but of the spirit. And so it is with all our other senses: their grounds or roots are not corporeal but spiritual.

This means that our animating selves, or what we might call our spiritual-psychic complex with its corresponding spiritual organism, constitute our real or true selves; and that of this true personal identity the dense material body is simply the instrument adapted to the conditions of this world – this fallen world – in which during our mortal life we have to operate. Consequently, when this complex is separated from the dense material body with which it has been compounded – a separation that we describe as death – the real self still lives. It still lives in possession of all its senses. It still sees, hears, thinks, feels, tastes and so on, after separation from the dense material body just as much as – in fact far more than – when in this body.

This is why the form of life we experience, at least initially, after our physical death is very much the same as that which we experience prior to this death. When we die, we simply pass from one state to another; and the conditions we find in this other state are almost exactly the same as those we found in the world we have left. And this, too, is why people who tend to have the idea that after their physical death their souls will be bodiless are often astonished to find on dying that they are still alive, are still men and women equally as before, and can see, hear, speak and so on as before, and that their body has a sense of touch as before, although now all this pertains to another plane of existence. They have lost nothing but their gross material body – and at first they may not even be aware that they have lost this. But in losing the gross aspects of their organs of sense, they have also lost the capacity to communicate directly by means of the senses with those still in the world which they have left.[4]

That what I have been saying accords with the traditional understanding of things is testified to by the account of the

---

[4] Many books have been published in recent decades recounting after-death experiences, perhaps the best known being Elizabeth Kubler-Ross's *On Death and Dying* (New York, 1969) and Raymond A. Moody's *Life after Death* (Atlanta, 1975). A more recent publication is David Lorimer's *Whole in One* (Arkana, 1990). (Ed.)

transfiguration of Christ in the New Testament. As I have explained elsewhere,[5] in revealing His spiritual body to His disciples,
Christ is simply revealing to them the archetypal human body,
that which we all possess but which we fail to perceive because of
the opacity of our senses, as the disciples failed to perceive Christ's
body until He lifted the veils of such opacity from their eyes. In a
similar manner, St. Serafim of Sarov revealed his resurrected[6] spiritual body to his disciple, Nicholas Motovilov, perfect and
unblemished in spite of the many injuries that had crippled his
mortal body, which was all that those about him were able to perceive. As W.B. Yeats says: "The old . . . conception of the individual
soul as bodiless or abstract led to what Henry More calls 'contradictory debate' as to how many angels 'could dance booted and
spurred upon the point of a needle', and made it possible for rationalist [materialist] physiology to persuade us that our thought has
no corporeal existence but in the molecules of the [physical] brain."[7]

Does the fact that the form of life we experience immediately
after our physical death is very similar to that which we experience
prior to this death mean that we go on living always after our
physical death in more or less the same state as we are in earthly
existence? This for some of us might appear to be an attractive
prospect, or something of a relief, while for others it might be an
intolerable prospect. In either case, the reaction is beside the point,
because our life does not go on in the same way.

The immediate post-mortem phase is an intermediate phase. It
is a phase of self-discovery, or of being self-discovered, in which
our true character is revealed. Or it can be called a phase of judgment, in accordance with the scriptural text, "There is nothing
covered that shall not be revealed; nothing hidden that shall not
be made known . . . " (Lk. 12:2-3), or with the other text, "I say to
you that every idle word that men utter they will give an account
of on the day of judgment" (Mt. 12:36). These texts have a quite

---

[5] See my *The Sacred in Life and Art* (Ipswich, 1990), pp. 85ff.

[6] See p. 187ff. below as to the understanding of "resurrected" in this context.
(Ed.)

[7] W. B. Yeats, *Mythologies* (London, 1959), p. 352.

literal application, and they apply to the phase directly after our physical death and the shedding of our gross material body.

To understand what is meant by this, we have to understand certain other factors. The first is that in our immediate after-death state, our bodily form is far more pliable, more subtle and responsive – more fluid or flexible one might almost say – than it is in its mortal state. In its mortal state our body, stamped as it is with so many hereditary and other external features, much like the shell of an oyster, offers considerable resistance to the shaping power of the soul. Although of course it is affected and changed by our inner disposition, by our ruling loves and hates and other passions, it does not reflect them completely: it is not a true mirror of our inner state. One can say that there is a certain lack of correspondence between inner and outer, between our psychic state and our physical state. Our outward appearance by no means reveals what goes on inside. It may even disguise what goes on inside. It allows us to play the hypocrite, to pretend to be, or to feel, that which we are not and do not feel. It gives us ample scope for dissimulation.

After our physical death, however, our bodily form, being far more malleable, does not offer the same resistance to the molding power of the soul. It reflects the soul far more directly. It becomes the mirror of the soul, the mirror of its inner disposition and its ruling passions. One might say that it takes on the form of the soul and becomes its true image. We cannot hide behind or within it any longer. We cannot dissimulate. Instead, what we are is immediately apparent. Our features conform to our true thoughts and feelings, grow beautiful or ugly according to the purity or impurity that animates them.

This is one thing we have to understand if we are to understand the phase of judgment into which we enter immediately after our physical death. A second thing concerns the shaping power of the soul itself, the determining principle of our after-death state. This is more complicated, and is closely linked with all those processes through which the soul acquires its characteristics and which are so minutely analysed by the psychological masters of the spiritual life. It is also something which introduces us to our major theme, the theme of metaphysical death.

What follows must, in the nature of things, be a simplification. But at least it may be said that during our present mortal life the soul, prompted by the passions, forms in itself, or conceives, certain thoughts and images; and that once these thoughts and images have been conceived in the soul, and the soul has attached itself to them, then they develop according to a logic of their own. Such growth may go on, or retain its potential for going on, quite apart from our conscious knowledge, so long as the passions which prompted it are unassuaged or unpurified.

We are always setting these sequences going, these "parasitic vegetables" as Yeats calls them, in our soul. Sometimes we act out the logic of their development in our lives, through an endless sequence of objects which they have suggested to us; and sometimes we cut their development short, forcing them back into the psyche but leaving them still with the full power to develop unless we have also freed the soul from the passion or passions which gave them birth. Indeed, until such time as our soul is freed from the passion or passions which gave them birth, these thoughts or images will continue to haunt us, and will go on breeding these parasitic sequences in our soul until we are free of them.

What has to be grasped is that these mental images or apparitions to which our soul is attached – these thoughts – do in fact constitute for us what we call reality: they constitute our world. That is why at our physical death so little changes for us. We still inhabit, or imagine we inhabit, the same world that we inhabit before our physical death. For the world we inhabit before our physical death is constituted, as I said, by these mental images to which our soul is attached; and this whole psychic complex we carry over with us into the after-death state. And the images that compose it have just as much power over us then as they do now. In fact in some ways they have more power over us then than they do now, because now, as I said, we can through an act of will prevent some of them from developing. We repress them, whereas then they are free to grow in accordance with their own inner logic.

Hence it is that the thoughts or images that occupy us after our physical death, and which constitute reality for us, are those that represent the dominating passions, purged or unpurged, of our lives. They represent our true ruling disposition rather than any disposition which, like a mask, we have been able to adopt and to convince others is representative of our true self during this present life. It is much the same when we dream: we are wholly caught up in the dream, and while we dream it is the dream that constitutes the true world for us. The difference is that in our post-mortal state our dream-reality is more and more determined by those images which reflect our deepest and perhaps most concealed passions.

To illustrate what is being said here, we may cite the case of the lady in one of Balzac's stories who after a life of outward purity is possessed on her death-bed by visions of the lover she had renounced in order to set out on her ascetic path. A desire of whose presence she had become totally unaware had reaffirmed itself, and one can imagine it occurring and recurring with all its anguish and longing after her physical death. Or similarly we can imagine ourselves to be persecuted by demons; while those who for one reason or another are persuaded in this life that there is no life beyond the grave can be so locked in that thought that after their physical death they cannot shake it off, and go on imagining that they are dead and in the grave. Yeats cites the example of a ghost in a Japanese play who is set on fire by an imagined scruple, and though a Buddhist priest explains that the fire would go out of itself if the ghost simply ceased to believe in it, the ghost cannot cease to believe in it.[8]

In a footnote to the Foreword to *The Tibetan Book of the Dead*, Dr. W.Y. Evans-Wentz gives an account of a European planter who died in southwest India and was buried by the local people. Some years later, friends visiting the grave found it fenced in and covered by empty whisky and beer bottles. They asked the local people for an explanation, and were told that the sahib's ghost had been causing much trouble, and that no way could be found to lay the ghost until an old witch-doctor declared that the ghost craved for whisky and beer, long-indulged habits in fleshly life and the real

[8] Yeats, *Mythologies*, p. 353-5.

cause of its separation from its earthly body. The local people, though hostile to intoxicants, purchased bottles of the same brand of both, and with the regular ritual for the dead began sacrificing them to the ghost by pouring them out on the grave. Finding that this kept the ghost quiet, they continued the practice in self-defense.[9]

In our post-mortal state our habits continue, though the means we have for satisfying them are now different. They continue because we are still in the thrall of those images, or apparitions, or fantasies, which fill our soul after our physical death as they filled it prior to this death and which are the progeny of our unpurified ego and our ego-consciousness – images or their corresponding thoughts that are entirely real for us and from which it may not be very easy for us to escape. Hamlet refuses to take his life with the bare bodkin because of the dreams that may come once the mortal coil is shuffled off, for it is in the post-mortal state that we are caught up in those passionate, parasitic sequences of thought and image – those streams of consciousness – which we have set moving in this mortal life through some "vital congruity", as Henry Moore describes it, of our soul and which we are compelled to follow, like a dream, as they unfold in our post-mortal state.

Hence the importance of our life on earth, since it is in our life on earth, through our choice or through our failure to choose, that we set these sequences or these streams of consciousness in motion. How we are in our immediate post-mortal state, and which direction our life takes then, will depend on what direction we have given it here. It will depend on what we have attached to it here, or on what we have allowed to attach itself to us. The judgment we have in this phase is, in this respect, a self-judgment: we are condemned or delivered according to what we have allowed to become our ruling disposition, or our ruling love. In the phase which follows this present phase, we are this disposition and this love in action, free from all dissimulation. Our external form becomes the image of this love and disposition.

---

[9] Evans-Wentz, op.cit. pp. xli-xlii

In this sense it is true that we make our own hell and our own heaven. If at the hour of our physical death we are still caught up in the world of lies and falsities and evil – still enslaved to that bundle of illusions and deceits which St. Paul describes as "the body of this death" (Rom. 7:24) – we are in hell. To the degree to which we have freed ourselves, or resurrected ourselves, from the body of this death we receive the blessings of heaven.[10]

It is here that we encounter the theme of metaphysical death, or of the great death, in contrast to the minor or incidental physical death. In order to grasp the significance of this theme, we have to set it within the perspective of our own existential situation. In so doing, we will to some extent anticipate what is explained at greater length in the following chapter of this book in relation to what – using Christian terms – we may call our fall and our resurrection.

Briefly, in our natural, non-fallen state – the state represented in Christian mythology by the figures of Adam and Eve in paradise – our mind and imagination think and imagine in the mind and imagination of God. The thoughts and images that we then conceive are those that mirror the life and light of God. They are the articulation, on the human plane, of God's outflowing wisdom. We could say that in this state the true subject of all our thoughts, images and feelings is not our own ego, but is the divine Source of all things. Our consciousness reflects and interpenetrates with the consciousness of God. Our consciousness is divinized. It is God who is our true ego, our true self; and what we think or image represents a true knowledge of divine realities.

Yet the human mind and imagination can be misguided, misdirected, and perverted. Like Lucifer before us, instead of thinking and imagining in the mind and imagination of God, we can sunder this state of divine-human interpenetration. We can turn our mind and imagination away from God and divine realities, and can begin to think and imagine within our own independent mind and imagination, putting our own image, or our own ego, in the place of God. The thoughts and images we then conceive will no

[10] St. John Climacus, St. Barsanuphius, and others have testified that there are men dead and already resurrected before the general Resurrection.

longer mirror the realities of the divine world. They will not constitute anything that can be called true knowledge. They will merely
reflect the world of our self-alienation and self-exile, of our self-
will and ignorance.

This is a dark and hellish world, the world of the human ego's
self-deception. It is a realm of illusion in which we vainly pursue
our own desires and fantasies in opposition to the luminous forms
and images of the divine world. This exaltation of our ego-consciousness, and of the pseudo-knowledge that goes with it, are
evidence of the fall: the corruption and perversion of our thought
and imagination. We should be the mirror-images of God. Instead we become enslaved to the figurations and phantoms of
egotism and sin.

The stream of thoughts and images in which we are caught up
when our mind and imagination are sundered from those of God
and subjected to the norms of our ego-consciousness are so many
individual tributaries to the river of hell. Or, conversely, it may be
said that the thoughts and images which fill our mind and imagination when we think and imagine our own thoughts and images
and not those of God have their source in the river of hell.

Sometimes, indeed, these streams or sequences of thoughts and
images – these evil dreams – set moving in a few individual minds
and imaginations can, as it were, objectify themselves, or be objec-
tified, in the form of ideologies to which whole collectivities –
whole societies – become enslaved, with the consequence that in
their name the most appalling brutalization and devastation of
both human and other life become operative and accepted norms,
political, social, and other. One has only to think of the birth and
growth of the progressive, liberal, scientific humanism of modern
times, and of the techno-scientific death-trap, the ensuing ecological crisis and of the inhuman political systems such as
communism that have issued from it, to be aware of how this can
happen. "Fear not those who can kill the body but rather those
who can kill the soul" (Mt. 11:28). For since the consciousness in
which these streams and sequences are set moving is sundered from
God, the thoughts and images that fill it, not being inspired by

God, will essentially be dead thoughts and images, whatever spurious "life" we may attribute to them. They will constitute, as we
said, what St. Paul calls the body of death, the death of the soul.
For Christ says that He – God – is life. Hence what does not have
its roots in this divine life is essentially dead.

Seen from this perspective, then, our true death is not our physical death. It is our self-identification with the illusions, deceits,
and ignorance that constitutes the body of death. It is from this
body of death that we have to be rescued, or saved. Correspondingly, it is our deliverance or rescue from this death that constitutes
our resurrection. "I expect – I aspire to – the resurrection of the
dead." But this resurrection is not of those who have died a physical death, but of those dead in the body of their own vain imaginings
and fantasies and ignorance. When Christ says, "Let the dead bury
their dead" (Mt. 8:22), He is not merely making a rather curt and
dismissive remark to someone who wants to go and bury his father. He is uttering a universal hortation to all those who would
wish to live: that they have to die to and bury their dead selves; for
when identified with these selves, they are as dead. In other words,
what Christ says is the same as that which is stated in those cita-
tions given at the beginning of this chapter: "Become a dead man",
"Die before you die".

It is this dying to the illusion, deceit, and ignorance which compose our body of death that constitutes our metaphysical or our
great death. It is a dying to the proclivities and perversions of our
ego-consciousness and to all the sins that go with them – to all
that we think and imagine when we think our own thoughts and
imagine our own images. It is a freeing of ourselves from attachment, first to an unending succession of objects and then to an
unending succession of such thoughts and images, for we have
identified ourselves with these things and in the process have forgotten our true selves and our true being. "Know thy self" is the
command we are given. But how can we know ourselves when we are
still the victims of an amnesia in which we confuse this self with our
ego-consciousness?

Basically, then, it is a matter of dying to this false self of our ego-consciousness and to its loves and desires, for this self is our dead self. And we cannot say that we are dead to this self until we cease from referring things to ourselves and from seeing them in the perspective of our own likes and dislikes, and refer them instead to God and see them as they are in God. Yet to see things in God, we must first see God. And "no one can see God and not die". This is the death we have to die as a condition of our resurrection: this death which represents a conscious loss of our selfhood.

Here, of course, an apparent absence of passions is no guarantee that we are truly detached from them, or that we have truly purified them. The root of the passions is self-love; and until the self, or ego, has died, they are always capable of springing up, however deep their slumber may appear to be. Nor, on the other hand, is any false modesty to our credit: false modesty conceals a high degree of egotism. And we have always to remember as well that passion denied in the world of objects, or on the physical or corporeal plane, will often in revenge manifest itself on the mental plane: the thought of sense-denying religious types is often full of passion, all the more insidious for taking this more subtle form.

Yet if this dying – this freeing ourselves from our ego-bound consciousness and all its illusions and ignorance – constitutes what I have called our metaphysical death, and is a condition of our being reborn or resurrected, it cannot be accomplished without the fulfilling of another condition: that we continually aspire towards and form links with the divine world, the world of eternity. The purpose of the spiritual life is not achieved through some abstract conception of the Kingdom of Heaven, or even through belief, in the pious sense, in the Kingdom of Heaven. It is achieved only through strengthening our living relationship with the Kingdom of Heaven, and through cultivating in ourselves those organs through which we can experience the life of eternity.

If during our earthly life we have not nourished this relationship or cultivated these organs, or if we have destroyed in ourselves the seeds of spiritual aspiration and the capacities for spiritual growth implanted in us at birth, we will not be able to establish this relationship or suddenly grow these organs when we die our physical death. We will not even want to establish or grow them. We will remain impervious to the light of eternity and to the blessings of the Kingdom of Heaven, locked up in our subjective dreams which are by now second nature to us. Surrounded by the spiritual world – as we are in fact all the time – we will not be aware of it: we will be outside it, exterior to it, in hell.

If at the time of our physical death we have not died to our dead self we will simply continue in our self-love; and the opposite is true as well: there is no breach in consciousness between the one state and the other. There is only continuity. And we will continue in the post-mortal state in accordance with those tendencies and dispositions which we have nourished and cultivated on earth and which consequently give us our tone and direction in the state beyond the grave.

It is here that the ritual and sacramental forms of sacred tradition play such a crucial role. It is through them that this relationship and these organs of spiritual vision may above all be nourished and cultivated. Transmitting as they do a spiritual influence, they awaken and galvanize in us the latent spiritual potentialities of our being, those that foster our rebirth, that allow us to transmute our consciousness, to free it from its hidebound ego-centered state in such a way that it is once again able to perceive and mirror divine realities and to interpenetrate with the consciousness of God. They awaken and galvanize the powers of contemplation through which we uncover our higher self, the self that radiates divine life and light. Figuratively we may say that they are God-given rafts by means of which we "pass over" the river of hell and enter the promised land, the world of paradise, liberated from our subjective dream sequences, our dead body of illusion and deceit. Although our participation in them is no guarantee that we will be rescued or delivered from the "enchafed flood"[11] – for we may fail to cooperate with them – it does contribute beyond measure to the possibility that we will not be engulfed by it.

[11] Shakespeare, *Othello*, Act 2, Scene 1.

Thus, if during our earthly life we have nourished and cultivated this relationship and these organs of spiritual vision – or
have allowed them to be nourished and cultivated within us – and
in this way have been liberated from our subjective dream sequences,
then our physical death will be a further step through which we
enter into a state in which we experience, ever more deeply, that of
which we have already had a foretaste. In this sense we will not see
death – again the phrase is scriptural: "By faith Enoch was translated so that he did not have to see death" (Heb. 11:5) – because
we will have already sundered, in this present life, our links with
everything that is capable of starting up those parasitic thought-
sequences in which most of us are imprisoned. If we have done
this then we do not die: we go to sleep. The Christian liturgical
language makes a clear distinction between physical death and
dormition. They are two things completely distinct, however much
they may appear to be the same to superficial physiological observation.

Those who have died to their false selves during this present
life and who have already experienced their inner rebirth – the
uncovering of their higher selves – do not see death and do not
die: they are resurrected to the life of eternity, that life in which
the here and now of their earthly life has already become their
nourishment and their center. "I no longer live, but Christ lives in
me" (Gal. 2:20). What this state is like we cannot know until we
experience it. But as again St. Paul writes: "The eye has not seen,
and the ear has not heard the things that God has prepared for
those who love Him, and neither have they entered into man's
heart" (1 Cor. 2:9). And Richard Crashaw gives us intimations of
it when he speaks, in his "Hymn to St. Teresa",

> Of a DEATH, in which who dies
> Loves his death, and dies again.
> And would for ever be so slain.
> And lives, and dies; and knows not why
> To live, But that he thus may never leave to DIE.

Yet the lives of many saints bear witness to the solemn joyful-
ness of those who "pass over" into a sanctified state. Often they
reveal this most clearly at the time of their physical death. One
such witness is the great Tibetan saint, Milarepa.[12]

Milarepa was well on in years when his final illness came upon
him. When he became ill, his disciples wished to offer prayers and
propitiatory offerings for his recovery. They also wanted him to
have medical treatment. Milarepa, however, declined this, saying:
"It is commonly the rule that illness befalling a *yogi* is to be looked
upon as an exhortation to persevere in devotion, and he ought not
to have any special prayers offered up for his recovery. He should
utilize illness as an aid to progression on the Path, ever ready to
meet suffering and even death. As for me, Milarepa, I have, by the
grace of my gracious Guru, Marpa, completed all special rites for
overcoming illness . . . and now I need neither forces nor media-
tors. . . . The time has come when the visible, illusory physical
body, the mind-evolved form of the Divine Body, must be merged
into the realms of Spiritual Light."

Shortly after making this statement, Milarepa died – he had
just sung a hymn; and at his death, his biography continues, clouds
of various colors adorned the hills, lovely music sounded, and a
sweet scent filled all the air. "Gods and men," the passage concludes, "met and conversed freely with one another, sometimes
exchanging greetings; so that, for the time being, they were carried
back to the Golden Age." The death of a saint is a kind of rebirth
of paradise: sanctity has the power to change the whole landscape.

Or, in quite another context, there is the physical death of William Blake who, although not acknowledged as a saint, yet gave
his life to the task of opening "the immortal Eyes of Man inwards
into the Worlds of Thought, into Eternity". His death is described
by George Richmond, in a letter to the painter, Samuel Palmer:
"Lest you should not have heard of the Death of Mr. Blake I have
Written this to inform you – He died on Sunday Night at 6 o'clock

---

[12] See *Milarepa, ses méfaits, ses épreuves, son illumination,* traduit du tibélain
par Jacqes Bacot (Paris, 1971).

in a most glorious manner. He said He was going to that Country he had all His life wished to see and expressed himself Happy hoping for Salvation through Jesus Christ – Just before he died His Countenance became fair – His eyes Brighten'd and [like Milarepa] He burst out in Singing of the things he Saw in Heaven. In truth, He Died like a Saint, as a person who was standing by Him Observed."[13]

In this connection, too, one can invoke certain myths present in many of the sacred traditions of the world. One such myth is the Taoist myth of the disappearance of a supreme artist: of his opening of a door in the painting he had just completed and his vanishing into his perfected work. This myth of the disappearance or, rather, the transformation or translation of the perfected being, has its counterpart in other traditions. In the Christian tradition there is the Ascension of Christ, often interpreted in much the same way as Milarepa interprets his physical death, as the dissolution of the "illusory" physical body and its reabsorption into the spiritual body. Or in Indian tradition there is the disappearance of the poet-saint Mānikka Vācagar, of Moses, Enoch, and Elias in Hebrew tradition, and of Elias as al-Khizr in Islamic tradition.

In these cases of disappearance – or of transformation or translation – we are faced with something that has nothing to do with physical death as we understand it, and for which the categories and boundaries associated with such a death have no meaning whatsoever. From our earthly point of view, or from the point of view of the sensible, material plane, here and now, the perfected man, the man who attains complete self-realization, is transformed and invisible, because nothing remains by which his existence can be sensibly registered. We cannot even say of him, as we might say of him prior to his translation, "Behold a dead man walking".

Physical death is something which can take place only on a plane on which it can be sensibly registered. "The death of what is created on the seventh day – the mystical Sabbath on which death dies – introduces the Resurrection of the eighth day." The words

[13] Cited in Bernard Blackstone, *English Blake* (Cambridge, 1949), p. 193.

are those of St. Maximos; and the "eighth day", the "Sunday of eternity", announces the passing beyond the created horizon symbolized by the biblical account of the seven days of creation, and so a passing beyond the horizon to which the senses and their reactions are limited. Thus, too, the "eighth day" – the day into which the perfected man, the saint, has entered – represents the passing beyond the point at which death dies.[14] And "Death once dead, there's no more dying then."[15]

There is one final question. If we have not died during our present earthly life to the false self and its corresponding ego-consciousness, so that in our post-mortal state we still identify ourselves with the illusory bundle of thoughts and images with which we have identified ourselves in this present life, can we ever hope to escape from this condition? Must our post-mortal state, that is to say, continue to be a state of hell for all eternity? There are several things that could be said in relation to this question, but all I will say here is that although in our present earthly life we may not have wholly escaped from bondage to our false selves, we may well have begun to actualize those spiritual potentialities of our being whose full deployment is a condition of our transformation and liberation.

This means that, provided we do not suffer a relapse, we can continue to actualize these potentialities, can continue to free ourselves from ignorance and self-love in our post-mortal state. It may well be that after our physical death we are in need of further purification, further refining, even though we have died in a state of repentance. But God can never cease from pouring out His grace and we can never cease, on whichever side of physical death we may be, from possessing the capacity to receive it. As for the eternity of hell, or for whether we can be in the state of hell for all eternity: to be condemned to be in such a state for all eternity must presuppose either that God's grace can never reach it, or that when in hell, although we possess the capacity to receive such grace, we have

[14] See *Centuries on Theology* I:51-60, trans. in *Philokalia*, vol. 2 (London, 1981), pp. 124-6.
[15] Shakespeare, Sonnet 146.

totally lost the capacity to exercise it. Both these presuppositions represent the worst kind of illusion and absurdity. Also, when we speak of eternity, we are not speaking of a state to which we can apply our categories of time. Hence we are not in a position to say that eternity can last even for a single second.

In any case, whether we are on this side of our physical death or on the other side of it, until we have died the metaphysical or great death, we are involved at every moment in a process in which life and death are inseparable. In this process life is not opposed to death, being to non-being, nor in this present life, while we are still part of that process, do we advance from life to death: the process itself embraces a paradoxical and simultaneous interplay of both life and death, an interplay which can be resolved only when we realize that our living-dying existence is itself death, and that it is from this death that we are summoned to redeem ourselves by awakening to the Life that is the ultimate ground of all things, He who declares of Himself, "I am the life" and that "I am come so that they may have life and have it to the full", and to whom we in our turn can only say:

> For I,
> Except you enthrall me, never shall be free,
> Nor ever chaste, except you ravish me.[16]

---

[16] John Donne, Holy Sonnets XIV.

Chapter Nine

Christianity and the Desecration
of the Cosmos

"For every thing that lives is Holy"[1]

In the opening chapter of this book I said that unless we reverse
the premises of the type of thought and action productive of our
present techno-scientific inferno, we will not escape the disaster
towards which it is ineluctably propelling us; and in this chapter I
want to bring into focus the nature of the main premise that has to
be reversed, and to put it in the context of a drama which is not to
do simply with a phase of our local European history, but is archetypal in the sense that it is intimately bound up with the whole
ambiguity of human existence and the whole dilemma of human
destiny as envisaged in the Christian tradition. It is a drama, that
is to say, which has to do with both our fall and our resurrection;
for the reversing of the premises of the type of thought lying behind our present plight entails no less than the reversing of a process
of ignorance, through which the distortion of our capacity to perceive the reality of things leads to our enslavement to an illusory
world entirely of our own invention; and the reversing of that process is simultaneously the prelude to our regeneration, and such
regeneration is simultaneously a return to a state of being and consciousness which can only be described as paradisal.

I referred just now to the distortion of our capacity to perceive
things truly. What do I mean by this? The answer to that question

[1] Last line from William Blake's "The Marriage of Heaven and Hell," op.cit.,
p. 193.

pitches us into the center of the arena, because it leads us directly
to defining this most pernicious of the premises we are called upon
to reverse. For behind this distortion lies our virtually unquestioned
acceptance of the belief that as we see things so they are, or that
the way in which we perceive things with our ordinary consciousness corresponds to the reality of these things – a belief which we
encapsulate in the phrase, "seeing is believing". And behind this
lies in its turn something more sinister. Behind it lies a particular
mental outlook, an outlook implicit in such statements as that made
by Hamlet, that "There is nothing either good or bad but thinking
makes it so", or as the Cartesian *Cogito ergo sum*" – statements
which, as Shakespeare was well aware but as Descartes appears
not to have been, subsume the distortion about which I am talking. For what is asserted in them is not simply the notion that
human thought is the determining factor of all things, including
our own existence; but also that this thought is capable of providing us with a valid type of knowledge. And it is, finally, behind this
notion that there is or can be a valid type of purely human knowledge that lies the premise to which I have been referring.

I will be more explicit. There are two factors that we have to
grasp if we are to escape from the process of ignorance in which
we are entrapped. The first is that how we perceive things depends
crucially upon the state of our consciousness, and that the state of
our consciousness depends upon the state of our being. This does
not mean that the reality of the things themselves varies according
to the consciousness which perceives them, and still less that their
existence is dependent upon their being perceived. It simply means
that how they appear to us, the kind of reality we attribute to them,
and whether we see them as they are or, as it were, through a distorting lens, have very little to do with the things themselves and
very much to do with the quality of our own being, the purity of
our soul and the level of our intelligence. And this in its turn means
that the way in which we see things may not correspond in the
least to the reality of the things themselves. If our consciousness is
dominated by a host of illusory ideas, then how we perceive things
will be correspondingly illusory. And the fact that the great major-

ity of mankind at a particular period may perceive things in a certain way does not in the least alter this: the mass of mankind may simply be enslaved to a particular set of delusions, and its perception will be conditioned accordingly.

In other words, what we perceive by means of the senses, and how we perceive it, as well as the manner in which we investigate it, are always conditioned to conform to the hidden systems of action and reaction, belief and thought, which at any particular time happen to dominate our consciousness. It is the prevailing conceptual paradigm of our consciousness, and the reality we attribute to it, that determine what we think is real and what we think is unreal. It is this paradigm, in which we believe often without being aware that we believe in it, that constitutes for us the ultimate reference point or touchstone according to which we distinguish between what we regard as true and as not true, relevant or irrelevant, in the data on which we base our theories and actions, and that gives them the meaning they have for us. Even what we call a "fact", far from being self-evident, depends entirely upon a consensus of opinion among those of us who call it a fact, and this consensus depends entirely upon our common subscription to the ideas, beliefs, and values built into such a paradigm. And the particular paradigm to which we subscribe will in its turn depend upon the state of our inner being and hence of our consciousness.

This is why the appeal to what is called empirical evidence – the evidence of the sense-data – is so delusory; for it assumes that our senses can perceive things in a kind of objective manner that is quite independent of our prior subscription to such a conceptual paradigm. Far from this being the case, what we think constitutes empirical evidence, let alone the way in which our senses read it, is already determined for us by our prior commitment to the presuppositions built into the paradigm to which, whether we are aware of it or not, we give our adherence. Hence not only how our senses perceive things, but also what we regard as valid empirical evidence, are entirely dependent upon the state of our inner being and our consciousness. That is why Herakleitos can say that the senses are false witnesses for people with impure souls. Muddied, restless water can never reflect truly. We must always remember that we can see things only as they appear to us after passing through the filter of our own perceptual equipment, and that the degree to which this filter will admit or exclude the reality of what we see, or think we see, will depend entirely upon the modality of our own particular consciousness. And this in its turn will depend upon our state of being, on how free we are from self-deception and illusion.

The second factor that has to be grasped – and it is correlative with the first – is that how we see things with what I called our ordinary consciousness, and might better have called our untransmuted and unregenerate consciousness, is purely subjective. Such a consciousness corresponds to a state of being that is closed in on its own subjectivity, and consequently the way in which it views the world is likewise entirely subjective. On this level of things there is no objective world in the way we so often assume, and no view of the world that is objective, since there is not, and cannot be, any objective observer. When in this state, what we call our knowledge is the result of our attempt to know that which we do not know and which we think is not known. It is the product not of our knowing, but of our ignorance. It is the reflection of our not-knowing, of our non-awareness. And what we do not know and what we think is not known is the reality or the true nature of everything we think we observe and investigate. In fact, did we but possess the clarity of mind of a Socrates we would, like him, recognize that in this state the only thing we can know is that we know nothing, for in this state we are not capable of knowing anything else. Whatever else it is that we think we know is merely surmise and guess work.

Yet even to say this is to attribute too positive a status to what we think we know. For if the way in which we view things is determined by our ignorance, by our not-knowing and non-awareness, so that we cannot see things as they are in reality, we must be seeing them in a false way, in an illusory way; and consequently the knowledge that we think we have of them must also be a false, illusory kind of knowledge. And this must mean that any and every theory we may postulate about the nature of the universe, the structure of reality, or anything else, must not only be surmise and guess work; it must also and inevitably be a false theory. And this in its turn must mean that the state of our being is also in some way subject to self-deception and illusion, and that it is our own self-deception and illusion that result in our self-imposed blindness and the illusory knowledge that it postulates.

If we look closer, must we not realize that this state in which we can never possess any true knowledge – in which what we call our knowledge must inescapably be impregnated with falsehood – is itself the consequence of the fact that we identify ourselves with our ego, and allot to it a purely fictitious autonomy in which we attribute our thought, and our perception of ourselves and of the world, to ourselves, as though they derived from ourselves, and as though our thought was itself the determining factor of all things, including our own existence? In other words, do not our self-imposed blindness, and the illusory knowledge it postulates, stem precisely from that type of mentality which can in all sincerity make the kind of statements that Hamlet and Descartes make – statements behind which lurks the old Protagorean sophism about *Homo mensura*, man the measure of all things, and which anticipate that triumph of the Demos expressed in such clichés as "my view is as good as your view"? Because in the end, for this way of thinking, even the gods are nothing more than ideas in the human mind.

This, however, still leaves the more important question unanswered. For if how we perceive things with our untransmuted and unregenerate consciousness – and I will explain shortly what I mean by this – does not correspond to the reality or true nature of things, but simply reflects the self-deception and illusion that characterize our ego or our selfhood, what is the reality or true nature of things, and how is it that we fail to perceive it?

I should at this point make it clear that when I am speaking of things – of the true nature or reality of things – I am denoting things in the sensory world, visible things, what we call phenomena or appearances, or the world of nature. And when I speak of knowledge, I do not mean information about things; I mean understanding of what or who things are, of why they are, of their true identity and what they signify. And when I further say that our unregenerate consciousness, or what we might call our ego-consciousness, cannot perceive the reality or true nature of these things, I mean by this that the perception of our ego-consciousness is limited to the purely material and terrestrial aspects of these things – to their materiality, to those aspects which can be measured, quantified, reduced to what are thought to be mathematical equivalents or for which there is empirical evidence as these words are understood in the terminology of modern science. It is these aspects of things which our ego-consciousness regards as constituting their reality, and thus as capable of furnishing us with knowledge of the things themselves; whereas in actuality these exterior aspects of things do not constitute their reality and cannot furnish us with a knowledge of them.

To say this, however, is either to say quite simply that visible things possess no reality at all and are totally illusory; or it is to say that their reality is constituted by something quite other than those aspects of them which are accessible to observation when the agent of such observation is our ego-consciousness. But I have already said that things possess their own reality quite apart from whether we perceive it or not. Thus what I am affirming is, in fact, that their reality is constituted by something quite other than anything that can be perceived by our consciousness while it is still in an unregenerate, untransmuted state.

What, then, is this something? To start with, recognition of it demands that we read the book of nature, the *Liber mundi*, in a way totally different from that in which we have been taught to read it. It demands that we read it in a way similar to that in which the great spiritual expositors tell us that we should read the Bible or any other Holy Book, not according to its literal, outward meaning but according to its inner, spiritual meaning. This is to say that we have to learn to look on the world of natural forms as the apparent, exterior expression of a hidden, interior world, a spiritual world: all the phenomena of the world of nature represent or symbolize with things celestial and divine.

In this perspective, natural things are essentially effects, never causes, still less causes of causes. In no way in themselves can they suffice to account for their appearance or mutations, and in no way are they self-sufficient entities or themselves the cause of what they are. Each natural form derives from the cause which it manifests and represents, and is preceded and determined in every way by this cause. Each has its equivalent, or archetype, or Divine Name, on the spiritual plane, and is the external expression, the material extension of this archetype. In the whole visible, natural world there is nothing that does not express or represent something of a higher invisible world, the spiritual world. Without this rootedness in the spiritual world nothing could exist for an instant, for apart from the spiritual world nothing can have any existence at all. No visible thing – nothing belonging to the world of phenomena – possesses existence or being in its own right, and divorced from its inner and spiritual dimension and identity, it possesses no reality whatsoever, whether physical, material or substantive.

At this point I must insert a short parenthesis, to avoid misunderstanding. I said that natural events and phenomena are always effects, never causes, and that the cause of each such event or phenomenon, whether with reference to origin or to temporal permutations, is always spiritual, always supranatural. I emphasize this because our minds have become so dominated by linear thought and its mechanical ramifications that we tend to find it difficult to think in any other way. That is to say, we tend to envisage things, and causation and continuity themselves, in terms of an unbroken linear sequence according to which events and changes in the natural world happen because of other events and changes that have taken place in the past; and this notion of unbroken linear sequences and succession is used to explain the present state of things.

Yet this understanding of things in terms of a sequential cause-effect syndrome operating within linear time represents a total misconception of the structure of reality. In fact, it is not going too far to say that this linear model within which our thought has been conditioned to function is among the chief impediments, if not the chief impediment, to our understanding of anything that happens in the natural world, in the world of nature or of history. Causation and continuity are properties of the realm of archetypes or Divine Names. In the realm of events and phenomena there are connections, not causal relationships. All causality resides in the divine archetypes, in the incessant renewal of their epiphanies from instant to instant. The recurrence of things in the world of events and phenomena consists in the recurrence of epiphanies. Thus the identity of a being, human or other, does not derive from any empirical continuity of its visible presence; it is wholly rooted in the epiphanic activity of its eternal archetype. In the realm of the manifest there is only a succession of likenesses from instant to instant. This of course implies a conception of the relationship between this world and "the other world" quite different from that which we have become accustomed to. For this world *is* the other world. It is already the other world: the other world is perpetually engendered in this world, and from this world, which has no beginning and no end. To unlearn the concept of linear time and the notion of sequential cause-effect that lies at the root of linear thought itself, as well as all that they imply, is a *sine quâ non* of any genuinely scientific understanding of events and phenomena, natural or historical.

All that is in the natural world, then, from its minutest particle to the constellations, the whole and each particular of the animal, vegetable and mineral kingdoms, is nothing but a kind of representational theater of the spiritual world, where each thing exists in its true beauty and reality. Each natural form is the center of an influx coming from its divine archetype or theophanic Divine Name. Thus each natural form is the image – the icon or the epiphany – of its archetype, and by virtue of being such an icon each possesses an affinity with its archetype, it corresponds to it, symbolizes with it. And when I say it symbolizes with it I do not mean that there is any gap or disjunction between it and the archetype it symbolizes with. The one is the other, the archetype is the icon, the icon is the archetype, there is an indissoluble interpenetration of the one by the other. The numinous presence, of which the outward form of things is the image, is also present

within it. Though there is a distinction, there is no dualism between the natural and the supranatural world. The spiritual world
is not another world set apart from the natural world. It inter-
mingles and co-exists with, and constitutes the invisible dimension
of, the natural world. It is another world incorporated within the
natural world. And this takes place, as Jan van Ruysbroeck puts it,
"beyond time; that is, without before or after, in an Eternal Now
. . . the home and beginning of all life and all becoming. And so all
creatures are therein, beyond themselves, one Being and one Life
. . . , as in their eternal origin."

This brings us to the second question: if this is how things are,
how is it that we fail so deplorably to see them as they are? There
are two ways to approach the answer to this question – or, rather,
two modes in which it may be answered. The first we might call
historical, in that it consists in defining the emergence and nature
of that premise which has bedeviled the thought and practice first
of the modern western world and now of virtually the whole world.
The second we might call transhistorical, in that it consists in an
archetypal drama played out on the gnostic and mythic plane of
the human spirit.

To speak briefly of the first. It is connected with certain intellectual developments within the European Christian world which
have to do with changes in the relationship between what one
might call metaphysical knowledge – knowledge of the supranatural
and uncreated world – and physical knowledge – knowledge of
the natural and created world – that took place within the Christian theological consciousness in the later mediaeval period,
particularly in the thought of the Scholastic theologians and philosophers. Or, rather, it might be more accurate to say that they
received explicit formal expression in this period, although they
had been incubating in the Christian consciousness for some centuries prior to this, in both the Greek East and the Latin West.

In very general terms, one might say that these changes represent the displacement of a unitary approach to knowledge by a
bifurcated, dualistic approach. In the unitary approach there is no
division or separation between knowledge of the supranatural and

the uncreated world on the one hand and knowledge of the natural and created world on the other: the two run in tandem, are harnessed together; they constitute a single form of knowledge, a single science. This is because the natural and created world is perceived as the embodiment, the material and visible prolongation of realities that are immaterial, spiritual and uncreated, so that there is no way in which we can understand or possess a true knowledge of the natural and physical world without a prior understanding and a prior knowledge of the supranatural and divine world, for the simple reason that, as I said, divorced from its inner and spiritual dimension and identity no visible thing, nothing belonging to the world of phenomena, can possess any reality at all.

We can attain such an understanding and knowledge of the supranatural and divine world both indirectly and directly. We can attain it indirectly from the Holy Book – the *Liber revelatus*, the Book "descended from heaven". The truths of Revelation, although given form in a particular historical and cultural context – namely, where the Christian tradition is concerned, in the life of Christ as this is shown forth in the Gospels – nevertheless correspond to eternally present divine realities; they are a revelation of the true nature of things, of what is entirely normal, not exceptional. Certainly, these truths have to be unveiled from the literal sense in which they are, as it were, concealed in the Holy Book itself. The objective data are provided by the revealed Holy Book, the revealed and revealing divine Logos; but the question is to know their true meaning, their spiritual meaning, not simply their literal meaning. "The letter kills, but the spirit endows with life."

This is not to invoke the mediaeval theory of the four senses of Scripture, the literal, moral, allegoric, and anagogic. It is, though, to presuppose what one might call a *theosophia*: the gnostic or visionary perception of a whole hierarchy of spiritual universes – universes which are not to be disclosed by means of syllogisms, since their unveiling requires a certain mode of knowing, a *hierognosis*, which combines the reflected knowledge of the data given by Revelation and the most personal inner experience; for without such experience, all that can be conveyed is a mere collection of concepts and abstract formulas, more or less arbitrary and essentially fugitive. One might say that the divine revelation is the light that makes it possible to see, while the inner experiential vision of the gnostic is the light that sees. To ignore the first – the divine revelation – is to remain permanently in the dark. Not to attain the second – the inner experiential vision – is to remain blind.

Here I would like to forestall a possible objection. I said that truly to read the book of nature, we have to read it in the same way as we read the Holy Book, the *Liber revelatus*. This, of course, is to assume that both are read in the light of the *theosophia* of which I am speaking, so that the interpretations which are given of either have a transtemporal or transhistorical validity. This assumption and its rider will be of a kind that the modern scientist cannot accept. But they are also rejected by an increasing number of theologians who, persuaded perhaps by the awareness that all hypotheses postulated by modern scientists as a result of their reading of the book of nature cannot at best be other than purely provisional and non-definitive, are led to apply the same conclusion to the reading of the Holy Book and to assert that all interpretation of revealed scripture must likewise be purely provisional and non-definitive.

They would support this conclusion by saying that just as the way in which the modern scientist reads the book of nature is determined by subjective temporal, contextual, and other parameters, so is the way in which the theologian reads the Holy Book; thus the interpretations of the latter are just as dependent on these parameters as the hypotheses of the former, and both will have a certain working validity only in and for their time. This way of looking at things is reinforced in both cases by the common acceptance of the concept of linear time of which I have already spoken, allied to a corresponding notion that there is a certain evolution of consciousness that tends to be part and parcel of it, making it permissible to use such phrases as "the dawn of human consciousness", "the emerging consciousness of our times", and so on. Man is seen as essentially a temporal being, and his thought as necessarily determined by his place in history, in such a way that it can, with the passage of time, become outmoded or obsolete, in need of replacement by more contemporary types of thought.

This attitude effectively undermines, if it does not negate, the understanding that, just as revelation itself, so its spiritual interpretation or hermeneutic – what we call doctrine – has its origin not in the historical order but in the transhistorical order; that it does not pertain to the domain to which scholars can apply their critical historical criteria; and that it is no more a merely sociological or cultural phenomenon than is a human being. Certainly, such interpretation and its articulation in doctrinal forms do reflect, and so indeed are limited by, the temporal consciousness of those responsible for them – this is one of the reasons why they must always be approached in an apophatic manner. But the divine gnosis of which they are the interpretation and articulation transcends these limitations and is eternal, being as it is the effulgence of divine light and life.

Again, with our current sense of history, as of time, we tend to see the irruption of such gnosis into this world as an event taking place at a certain moment "in the past", once and for all and irreversible. But when truly understood, this gnosis and the anterior realities of which it is the mirror are not, and can never be, "of the past"; they are always "in the present" (*instantem*). Correspondingly, spiritual interpretation of this gnosis can also never be of the past, but must be "in the present", since it transcends time by reattaching all temporal manifestation to its non-temporal source. Thus its articulation has, like the incarnation of the Logos in the historical Jesus, a transhistorical dimension, and for those who have eyes to read it, it can never become obsolete or lose its symbolic function as the authentic expression of divine gnosis.

Admittedly – and here I return to the main theme – the *theosophia* of which such articulation is the expression presupposes both the reality, and the possibility of direct personal perception, of a more-than-human body of knowledge – what St. Augustine calls "Wisdom uncreated, the same now as it ever was, and the same to be for evermore" – which pre-exists all interpretation and articulation. And this in its turn is to presuppose that inherent in each human being is an organ of vision, of intellective or imaginative intuition, which when activated is capable of perceiving and experiencing the realities of the supranatural and divine world.

This organ cannot, of course, be the reason. The reason itself cannot have a direct vision or experience of anything. It can operate only from a given starting point, or from given starting points, which we have to assume as a condition of being able to set the progress of reasoning in motion. So what is implied is that we possess within ourselves an intellective and visionary organ that is superior to the reason, and that it is this organ, or power, that is capable of perceiving the inner and spiritual reality of things.

Such an organ – it may be called the spiritual or angelic intellect – although present within us is initially, and sometimes chronically, present in a latent or potential or passive state – why this is so will also become clear later – so that to all intents and purposes it is not operative within our consciousness until it has been brought from a state of passivity into a state of activity, from a state of potentiality to a state of being fully operative. This is why I spoke earlier of our ordinary or ego-consciousness as being "unregenerate" or "untransmuted"; for what regenerates and transmutes our consciousness is precisely this process of bringing our angelic or spiritual intellect from a state of potentiality to a state of active realization, so that it becomes not merely operative in our consciousness but the determinative and transforming agent of our consciousness, conferring on it the capacity to perceive in things those inner and spiritual qualities to which our unregenerate and untransmuted consciousness is totally blind.

At the same time, this regeneration and transmutation of our consciousness has as a direct consequence the regeneration and transmutation of our sense-organs as well, so that they, too, are changed from being what Herakleitos calls "false witnesses", incapable of registering the spiritual and numinous qualities of things, and become capable of participating in the spiritual vision of our reborn consciousness and of sharing in its now undistorted perception. For as the veils are lifted from our consciousness, so the veils are lifted from our sense-organs; just as, correspondingly, when our consciousness is closed to divine life and light, our senses are impervious to them as well.

This unveiling of our consciousness so that it ceases to be impervious to divine life and light – its transmutation and regeneration – is, as I said, a process that goes hand in hand with the realization or actuation of the potentiality of our spiritual intellect. But this process is far from being an automatic one. On the contrary, as explained in the opening chapter of this book, it can be accomplished only on condition that we pursue a long, strenuous and often extremely taxing course of spiritual practice and purification, inner and outer, mental and physical. Christianity, like every authentic sacred tradition, also possesses its own initiatory and mystagogical discipline, gnostic and ritual; and it is through participation in such a discipline, and only through participation in it (except in the few cases that constitute the exceptions which prove the rule), that we can begin to penetrate into the hierarchy of spiritual universes of which previously we had been totally ignorant or had only accepted "on faith", as a kind of theoretical basis for our deliberations. And the further we penetrate into these realms, and the more our consciousness is opened to the influx of divine life and light, the more we can decipher the spiritual meaning of the data given in the revealed Holy Book, the *Liber revelatus*; and the more we can do this the more we are able to attain a direct perception and knowledge of the realities of the supranatural and divine world.

This means that simultaneously and correspondingly we are also initiated into a true reading of the book of nature, the *Liber mundi*, for these realities constitute the immaterial, spiritual and uncreated realities of the forms of the natural and physical world; they embrace the archetypes of which these forms are the apparent, exterior expression. And because when our consciousness is spiritualized by the reawakening of our supreme cognitive faculty – the spiritual intellect – our senses are also transmuted and spiritualized, this in its turn means that we are able to perceive through our physical eyes the symbolic function that natural things possess by virtue of their correspondence and interpenetration with spiritual things. We are able to perceive their inner and spiritual dimension and identity.

It is precisely our capacity to perceive this symbolic function of natural things – to perceive the numinous presence of which each natural form is the icon – that is increasingly eclipsed by those intellectual developments that took place in the Christian, and hence by and large European, consciousness in the later mediaeval period. These are typified by the invention of a particular concept, the concept of the "double truth" promoted in the thought of Scholastic and subsequent theologians and philosophers. What exactly is this concept?

We have seen that in the unitary approach to knowledge, there is no separation or division between knowledge of the supranatural and uncreated world and knowledge of the natural and created world; no separation between the truth revealed in the Holy Book and the truth revealed in the book of nature: the illumined gnostic, his consciousness transmuted and regenerated, can perceive the same supranatural and divine realities expressed equally in and through both of them, and his knowledge of both of them derives from, and is dependent upon, his perception of the divine realities which they both enshrine.

As a consequence of the intellectual developments to which I have referred, this understanding of things is displaced and rendered existentially ineffective, with the result that unitary knowledge, and the vision of the natural world that is part and parcel of it, are also displaced; for the type of consciousness which they demand is eclipsed, and is replaced by another type of consciousness. For, first, the understanding of man as a triune being of spirit, soul, and body gives way to the notion that he is but a dyadic being of soul and body alone. This in its turn means that the faculty which according to the unitary theory of knowledge constitutes our supreme cognitive faculty – our angelic or spiritual intellect – is no longer recognized as a power inherent in human nature, a power altogether superior to and independent of the reason, since it possesses an intrinsic spiritual potentiality. Now the intellect (the word is still used) is seen as no more than a higher aspect of the reason itself. Essentially intellect and reason now describe one and the same power, there is no spiritual visionary organ in man distinct from his reason, and the mode of knowledge proper to man is reasoning or discursive knowledge, a mode within everyone's scope without the operation of any initiatory grace, for by definition everyone possesses a soul and by definition that soul is a rational soul.

It follows from this that the visionary perception of divine and supranatural realities which is a presupposition of any genuine knowledge of the natural world – for without it we are blind to the inner and spiritual dimension of things – is now regarded as being beyond the reach of the human intelligence. It is true that it is still assumed that natural forms have an analogical resemblance to supranatural forms; but this is not in the least taken to mean that we cannot obtain a knowledge of natural forms simply by studying them in themselves, without any reference to supranatural forms. On the contrary, it is now thought that this is the only way in which we can study them, since any direct knowledge of their supranatural dimension is assumed to be beyond our scope. What is within our scope is said to be limited to a knowledge of natural things as they are perceived in the natural light of the human reason.

What begins as the scholastic assertion – already in itself representing a radical inversion of the norms of knowledge – that the world we perceive through the senses is the primary source of human knowledge (*quod in intellectu est, primo in sensu erat*), is now elevated into the dogma that this world is the only source of human knowledge, a knowledge, moreover, that is thought to be entirely valid. It is the growing ascendancy of this misconceived dogma, first in the European and subsequently in the extra-European mind, that has ensured the progressive materialization of every aspect of our culture.

What, though, in the meantime has happened to that other source of truth, the Holy Book, the *Liber revelatus*? Does the fact that it is now thought that the human reason can obtain a perfectly valid knowledge of the natural world, by abstracting it from the observation of those aspects of this world which we can perceive by means of the senses, imply that the truths of divine Revelation are regarded as superfluous? This is not the case at all. But what has happened is that the whole attitude towards, and understanding of, these truths have undergone a similar change. For these truths, although still regarded as valid (since God has revealed them to us), are now said to be beyond human capacity to know in a direct, experiential manner, through noetic penetration into the spiritual universes of which the literal form of the Holy Book constitutes the outward expression. And they are regarded as beyond human capacity to know, because human beings are no longer thought to possess an organ of vision through whose actuation they can be known. The things of faith – the truths of Revelation – which must be believed by all, are equally unknown by all, and there can be no direct experiential knowledge of them.

This might not have presented a problem had the truths of revelation always agreed with the conclusions which the human reason, now granted a charter to operate quite independently of the truths of revelation, derived by a process of abstraction from the observation of natural phenomena. Unfortunately, however, this was by no means always the case. Hence some way had to be found of accommodating both the conclusions of the reason and the truths of revelation, even when they appeared to conflict with each other; for now both theologians and philosophers were committed to accepting that both sets of truths, even when they appeared to conflict, could be valid.

The only way that could be found to effect the accommodation in question was to divide the sphere of revelation from that of reason, to divide faith from philosophy and science, metaphysics from physics. St. Thomas Aquinas, following on the Jewish philosopher Maimonides and others such as Alexander of Hales, Bonaventure, and Albert the Great, clearly asserts this distinction: on the one hand there is faith, which is assent to something because it is revealed by God; and on the other hand there is science, which is assent to something because it is perceived to be true in the natural light of human reason. The two departments are separate, the truths of the one being valid in one sphere, the truths of the other in another sphere.[2]

It is this concept of the double truth – this duplicity in the true sense of the word, or what we might call "double-think" – that constitutes the major premise that has to be reversed if ever we are to escape from the clutches of our materialist world; for it is this concept that constitutes the bedrock of the major thought-paradigms responsible for shaping the course and character of this world, and that is inextricably built into them. It is the initial bifurcation, or splitting asunder, that has given rise to the whole crisis of fragmentation which now threatens to disrupt whatever is left of anything that can be called civilization. It marks the decisive breakthrough of that type of consciousness I have called our ego-consciousness – the consciousness which, being closed to divine light and life, simply reflects the self-deception and illusion that characterize our uprooted selfhood; and simultaneously it marks the opening of the door to the progressive secularization and profanation of virtually every aspect of our life, public and private, philosophical, scientific, political, social, educational and even domestic.

For when, in obedience to the dictates of a theology that has separated the order of supranatural knowledge from the order of natural knowledge, philosophy and hence science declare their independence of the truths of Revelation – their independence of the Holy Book and the spiritual hermeneutic that unveils its meaning; and when they further declare that the human reason is capable in its own right of acquiring a valid knowledge of things, there can be no preventing the breakthrough of this type of consciousness or the consequences that follow inescapably from its ascendancy.

That the ascendancy of the ego-consciousness is in fact written into the status now accorded to the human reason, and the license assigned to it, is due to the very nature and function of the reason itself. We have already noted that the reason itself cannot have a direct knowledge of anything. It can operate only from given starting

[2] See the author's *Rape of Man and Nature* (Ipswich, 1987), Ch. 2, for a fuller exposition of this theme. (Ed.)

points, and it reaches its conclusions by deducing them logically from these starting points. If these starting points are provided by the understanding of reality that accords with the type of perception intrinsic to our spiritual consciousness, the conclusions that the reason will reach with regard to the forms of the natural world will be of one kind; if these starting points are provided by the understanding of reality that accords with the type of perception intrinsic to our ego-consciousness, its conclusions will be of a totally different order. This is to say that a science of the natural world can be termed rational only in so far as its conclusions follow logically from the premises that constitute the starting points from which the reason operates, irrespective of the type of consciousness that determines these premises and therefore its whole subsequent structure, theoretical and methodological. There is no science that is rational as such, or that is more rational if it takes as its starting points one set of premises rather than another set. Nor can the human reason in itself establish these premises, or their rationality, or their truth or falsehood, nor can it acquire a knowledge of the natural world. There is no way in which the natural light of human reason can in itself attain a knowledge of anything. This is why the concept of the double order of truth, promoted by the Scholastic and other philosophers and subsequently built into virtually every aspect of our intellectual and other life, represents such a distortion of things.

This being the case, what precisely is involved in promoting the idea that the human reason is perfectly competent to investigate things without reference to any Holy Book or to its corresponding spiritual hermeneutic, and that it possesses in its own right the capacity to obtain a valid knowledge of the physical world? What is involved in claiming that it is perfectly legitimate to separate the sphere of reason from that of revelation, physics from metaphysics, science from faith? As I have already indicated, what is involved is a radical inversion, not to say perversion, of the norms of knowledge. For now it is no longer recognized that in order to formulate a genuine knowledge of things the reason has to accept as its starting points propositions that accord with the perception of our spiritual consciousness. On the contrary, it is now asserted that the reason can formulate an equally valid knowledge of things by taking as its starting points propositions that accord with the perception of our ego-consciousness, a perception which simply reflects the limitations and characteristics of our unhallowed, self-enclosed selfhood. This means that the premises now effective for philosophy and hence for science are no longer those of the *hierognosis* or *theosophia* of unitary knowledge; they are merely those which the human mind, cut off from a direct perception of spiritual realities, happens to invent or adopt in a purely arbitrary and subjective manner. Given that such a mind is by definition in thrall to self-deception and illusion, and is exposed to every kind of distortion, the conclusions of the reason that operates in accordance with the premises it invents or adopts will be conditioned correspondingly.

In other words, to the purely subjective and unsanctified human consciousness is attributed an autonomy that establishes it as the determinative factor not only of the norms of knowledge, but even of the norms of human existence itself: we are back where we started, with that type of mentality which can in all sincerity make the kind of statements that Hamlet and Descartes make, or that Protagoras makes, and with the agnosticism and materialism which are part and parcel of it. That an agnostic and materialistic science of nature is a contradiction in terms, and that its findings will necessarily correspond to the living reality of nature as little as a corpse corresponds to the living reality of a human being, will be clear from all that I have already said; just as it will also be clear that our tragedy, and the tragedy of the world we live in, are due to nothing more, or to nothing less, than that we prefer the desolation of our own destruction to having to expose ourselves to the trials, dedication and love that are the touchstones of our regeneration.

For it is because we have chosen and continue to choose to live according to this delusion of the double truth that we have ended up by shattering our ancestral universe, our spiritual cosmos, into a thousand fragments and have ejected ourselves into a world that is as nightmarish as it is artificial. It is this duplicity or double-think that lies at the root of what has now become our endemic state of schizophrenia. It is this that permits us to say that we are Christians, or Moslems, or Buddhists, or whatever, and yet to live according to values and standards and ideas that not only have nothing to do with any religion but are entirely contrary to every form of spiritual life and practice. It is this, finally, that allows us not simply to tolerate, but actively to promote, a type of science that inevitably desecrates every area of life on which it impinges because desecration is written into the very view of nature according to which it operates; for this view is itself the progeny of this same misbegotten concept of the double truth which would have us believe that nature is a self-subsistent reality, independent of God, with nothing holy or sacred about it, and that it is quite possible to acquire a valid form of knowledge by investigating it as such.

So long as we fail to realize that this view of nature is a complete misconception, and that what we call our empirical and experimental knowledge of facts is itself an essential part of our ignorance, we will continue to desecrate the earth and everything on it without even the slightest awareness of what we are doing or why we are doing it. And we will go on failing to realize that this view of nature is a complete misconception for so long as we also fail to realize that the words of Christ, "In so far as you did it to one of the least of these my kindred, you did it to me" (Mt. 25:40), apply not simply to his human kindred, but to every natural form of life and being. For every natural form of life and being, down to the most humble, is the life and being of God.

Moreover, the fact that we have been increasingly persuaded over the last centuries, by our submission to the norms and propaganda of the modern scientific mentality, to regard as knowledge only that which has direct reference to those aspects of the natural world that are accessible to the senses has meant that we have become progressively dominated by an insatiable craving to experiment in ever more extreme and demented forms of sensation. For this scientific mentality and its propaganda have not only stimulated our purely profane curiosity beyond all measure, human or divine, but at the same time they have compelled us to accept as axiomatic that such curiosity can be satisfied only by an experimentalism which involves testing hypotheses against what is called empirical evidence, the evidence of the senses.

This cult of experimentation pervades virtually the whole scholarly world, in one form or another. Yet it is a singularly inept cult. For in so far as it is practiced as a means of assessing an hypothesis by testing it against empirical evidence, it simply engages its votaries in the specious rite of arguing in a circle. This, as I have pointed out, is because what a scientist, as anybody else, will think constitutes empirical evidence is already determined for him by his prior commitment to the presuppositions built into the conceptual paradigm that happens to dominate his consciousness. But it is precisely these presuppositions, and his commitment to them, that also determine the formulation of the hypothesis which he now wishes to assess by checking it against this evidence. Yet because of the prestige accorded to this cult, the addiction which it represents is more sinister than most of the other forms of addiction by which our contemporary society is afflicted, for it lies at the root of virtually all of them.

In addition, it has to be remembered that the kind of specialization that characterizes virtually every form of mental activity deployed in the modern world, and especially every form of mental activity deployed in the world of modern science, requires the exercise of only a fraction of our intelligence; the greater part of our intelligence, never called into operation, simply deteriorates or atrophies. As a result we are by and large incapable of entering into realms of thought which lie beyond the extremely narrow scope to which our intellectual understanding, and hence our lives, are now confined, so we cannot but react negatively when we are invited or challenged to enter into those realms, and may even pretend that such realms are non-existent or belong to the world of fantasy. In one sense this is our major problem – how to reactuate powers of our intelligence that now lie dormant, so that we can once more become aware of those realms of thought, and of the realities they mirror, which are now excluded from our field of vision. All that can be said here is that the first step towards such a reactuation would have to be the unlearning of much of what is now called knowledge, and the freeing of ourselves from the presuppositions on which it is based.

No one – or at least hardly anyone – wants to know of such things, and one is regarded as slightly barmy or hysterical when one points them out, and one will get little thanks for so doing. Yet whether we recognize it or not, the truth is that we are involved in a drama that is first of all a spiritual drama, an eclipsing of our spiritual vision; and it is this self-imposed blindness that has resulted in the whole process of disintegration of which the intellectual developments of which I have just been speaking, as well as their consequences in every sphere of our life, are the outward manifestations and symptoms. To conclude, I will say something about the nature of this drama – something that will represent in gnostic and mythic terms a recapitulation of what I have already said.

* * *

At the beginning of this chapter, I remarked that the reversing of the premises of the type of thought lying behind our present plight entails no less than a reversing of a process of ignorance; and that this reversing of a process of ignorance is in its turn the prelude to a regeneration which itself is a return to a state of being and consciousness which can only be described as paradisal. What is this paradisal state, and what does it signify to be exiled from it?

In its simplest terms, to be in a state of paradise is to be free from bondage to self-deception and illusion, and to perceive things, ourselves included, as they truly are, and not as they appear to be through the distorting mirror of our unregenerate minds. This, as I have already explained, means that our perception of sensory things – of created things – will simultaneously embrace the perception of their divine and celestial reality, so that what we see with our eyes when we are in this state are celestial beings, living manifestations of divine life.

At the same time, in the paradisal state, although we possess this spiritual perception of things, we are aware that the Subject active in all our acts of knowing and perceiving is not our own selfhood, but is the Divinity Itself, is God Himself. Or rather, we might say that in this state our personal selfhood is conscious of itself as inseparable from the divine Principle. Our selfhood is transparent to this Principle: its life and light are the life and light of God Himself.

Paradise – the garden – is, then, divine inspiration flowing into us directly and without intermediary. It is knowledge in the true sense, pure spiritual science. This means that when we are in this state of being, we are not simply *in* paradise: we *are* paradise. We are the state in which we are; our state of being – our *modus essendi* – corresponds to our state of knowing – our *modus intelligendi*. Paradise is, then, our inner state; and what this inner state – our mode of being – allows us to experience is an infinity of perceptions derived from the divine Principle active in us. That is why even if we are in paradise, and even if we are paradise, paradise is not ours, for all our perceptions are activated in us by God.

The loss of this inner state – of this paradisal state – is described in Christian terms as the "fall", an event not of the past but one in which we are involved at every moment of our lives. To see what is meant by this, we have to remember that there is a vital distinction between our true being and what we become when we identify ourselves with our own selfhood. Our natural state is our paradisal state, with the consciousness and knowledge that go with it; and we saw that in this state we are conscious that our personal selfhood is rooted in its divine Principle, and that this Principle is the subject of all our acts of knowing and perceiving. But we also possess the possibility of taking another path and of regarding ourselves as existing independently of God: we can assert the autonomy of our selfhood and identify ourselves with that. We can think that we are ourselves of and through ourselves, as self-subsisting beings. We can think that we are the agents of our own lives and of our acts of knowledge and perception. We can become the victims of the terrible illusion that one's own self is sufficient to itself in order to be itself. Swollen like Faustus "with cunning of self-conceit", we, like him, can claim that our souls are our own.

Yet on the day that we do this – on the day on which we assume that we can perceive and know things by ourselves and can investigate the secrets of our own being and of the natural world by ourselves – we die to our celestial nature and to the knowledge and consciousness that go with it. For once we attribute our perception of ourselves and of nature to ourselves, as though it derived from ourselves, we will automatically and inevitably close our consciousness to the influx of divine light and life. God will cease to be the active Subject of our acts of knowing and being, our celestial perception of things will be destroyed, and we will substitute for it, as the purveyor of what we now call knowledge, a perception that can see in things nothing more than their purely psychic and material aspects.

When we become attached to our selfhood as a dissociated, independent reality, two things happen as a consequence. The first is that we cease to realize the difference between our natural state – our paradisal state – and the fictitious autonomous state which we now attribute to ourselves and with which we now identify ourselves. One could put this in another way and say that we cease to identify ourselves with our real being and identify ourselves instead with that which we think we are. That which I truly am – my real identity – is always full and complete and indestructible. That which I think I am when attached to my selfhood is nothing more than an invention of my own mind, an illusion to which I attribute reality and regard as a concrete entity. It is nothing more than a certain bundle of mental and physical accidents, thoughts and feelings and sensations, derived from heredity, education, environment, and a thousand other transient influences and activities, temporarily brought together but changing in such a manner that there is never a moment with reference to which I can say of myself that it is myself: for as soon as I ask what it is, it has become something else. There is in fact on this level no true entity I can call myself; and my ego-consciousness, according to which I regard my ego as an entity, is itself as fictitious as the ego to which it attributes reality, since it is merely a sequence of reactions in whose current we are immersed and by which we are endlessly swept along.

Thus when we assert our independence of God, what we are really doing is centering our attention on a purely fictitious self and attributing to it a reality, and a permanence, which it does not and cannot possess. And it is this false self, or ego, the constantly renewed creation of our ignorance, that becomes the focus of all our illusions, our passions and, it might be added, our sins. It is the independence and autonomy we ascribe to our selfhood that is the crux of our aberration; for this selfhood, being itself a deception, is also the agent of every kind of trickery and falsehood. And it is our attachment to it that precipitates our fall.

The second thing that happens as a consequence of such an attachment to our selfhood corresponds to the first: we cease to be able to perceive the true nature of things, their spiritual and celestial reality, and we identify them instead with what we think they are. But to identify them with what we think they are is to project onto them the same kind of fictitious and illusory identity as that with which we have already identified ourselves. In the end, we cease wanting to know of the existence of what is spiritual and celestial, whether in ourselves or in anything else, and we even deny that we or anything else can possess such qualities. Indeed, we reach the point of thinking that the world of three dimensions which we perceive with our ego-consciousness and with the aid of our five senses is the natural world and that it possesses its own self-subsistent existence.

Our fall, then, is our sundering of our links with the divine and an increasing attachment to the norms of our non-spiritual, non-spiritualized selfhood. It is a limiting of ourselves to our selfhood, a falling in love with ourselves, our surrender to an auto-erotic concupiscence, to an obsessive narcissistic psychosis. We commit, in short, a kind of suicide. And as a consequence, we are expelled from the garden – the paradise – that was, and is, ourselves, in our true being, in our state of transparence to the divine. And since we were – since we are – this garden, our expulsion from it, self-induced, is nothing less than expulsion from ourselves, alienation from our inner being, the despiritualization of human existence, a lapse into a sub-human state. And this expulsion is in its turn an

entry into a state of profound illusion. For although the dissociated, fictitiously autonomous selfhood with which we now identify
ourselves appears to us to be real, it is, as I said, essentially unreal
and illusory, so that our subjection to it inevitably leads, as I have
also said, to our enslavement to an illusory world entirely of our
own invention. And there can be no more abject and degrading
situation in which to find ourselves than that of being enslaved to
our own inventions. To be in such a situation is in truth to be in
hell, for in that situation we have lost our reality, and that precisely
is hell.

In the light of what I have been saying, we can see why it is that
the fall may best be understood not as a moral deviation or as a
descent into a carnal state, but as a drama of knowledge, as a dislocation and degradation of our consciousness, a lapse of our
perceptive and cognitive powers – a lapse which cuts us off from
the presence and awareness of other superior worlds and imprisons us in the fatality of our solitary existence in this world. It is to
forget the symbolic function of every form, and to see in things
not their dual, symbiotic reality but simply their non-spiritual dimension, their psycho-physical or material appearance.

Seen in this perspective, our crime, like that of Adam, is equivalent to losing this sense of symbols; for to lose the sense of symbols
is to be put in the presence of our own darkness, of our own ignorance. This is the exile from paradise, the condition of our fallen
humanity; and it is the consequence of our ambition to establish
our presence exclusively in this terrestrial world, and to assert that
our presence in this world, and exclusively in this world, accords
with our real nature as human beings. In fact, we have reached the
point not only of thinking that the world which we perceive with
our ego-consciousness is the natural world, but also of thinking
that our fallen, subhuman state is the natural human state, the
state that accords with our nature as human beings. And we talk of
acquiring knowledge of the natural world, when we do not even
know what goes on in the mind of an acorn.

This dislocation of our consciousness which defines the fall is
perhaps most clearly evident in the divorce we make between the

spiritual and the material, the esoteric and the exoteric, the uncreated and the created, and in our assumption that we can know the one without knowing the other. This is to say that if we acknowledge the spiritual realm at all, we tend to regard it as something quite other than the material realm and to deny that the Divine is inalienably present in natural forms or can be known except through direct perception which bypasses the natural world, as though the existence of this world is, spiritually speaking, negative and of no consequence where our salvation is concerned.

This other-worldly type of esotericism only too often degenerates into a kind of spiritual debauchery, in the sense that it has its counterpart in the idea that it is possible to cultivate the inner spiritual life, and to engage in meditation, invocation and other ritual practices, whether consecrated or counterfeit, while our outward life, professional or private, is lived in obedience to mental and physical standards and habits that not only have nothing spiritual about them but are completely out of harmony with the essential rhythms of being, divine, human and natural. We should never forget that an authentic spiritual life can be lived only on condition, first, that the way in which we represent to ourselves the physical universe, as well as our own place in it, accords with the harmony instilled into its whole structure through the divine *fiat* which brings it into, and sustains it in, existence; and, second, that in so far as is humanly possible we conform every aspect of our life, mental, emotional, and physical, to this harmony, disengaging ourselves therefore from all activity and practice which patently clash with it. If we offend against the essential rhythms of being, then our aspirations to tap the wellspring of our spiritual life are condemned to fruitlessness, or, in some cases, may even lead to a state of psychic disequilibrium that can, in truth, be described as demonic.

Correspondingly, the divorce between the spiritual and the material means that material forms are regarded as totally nonspiritual, and thus either as illusion or as only to be known through identifying their reality with their purely material aspects. Such a debasement of the physical dimension of things is tantamount not only to denying the spiritual reality of our own created existence, but also, through depriving natural things of their theophanic function, to treating a divine revelation as a dead and soulless body. And in this case it is not only of a kind of suicide that we are speaking; we are also speaking of a kind of murder.

It is just as dangerous to think we can attain a knowledge of God while ignoring, or even denying, His presence in existing things and in their corresponding symbolic rituals as it is for us to think that we can attain a knowledge of existing things while ignoring, or even denying, the divine presence that informs them and gives them their reality. In effect, there cannot be a knowledge of the outward appearance of things – of what we call phenomena – without a knowledge of their inner reality; just as there cannot be a knowledge of this inner reality which does not include a knowledge of the outer appearance. It is the same as with the Holy Book: the integrality of the revelation cannot be understood simply from its letter, from its outward literal sense; it can be understood only when interpreted by the spiritual science of its inner meaning. At the same time this inner meaning cannot be perceived except by means of the letter, of the outward literal sense. There is an unbreakable union between the esoteric and the exoteric, the feminine and the masculine, between the inner reality of a thing and its external appearance. And any genuine knowledge of either depends upon both being regarded as integers of a single unified science.

Such knowledge is not therefore independent of the exoteric aspect of things. It is not a superior, esoteric doctrine which does not need to take into account the outer appearance. It is knowledge of the invisible dimension of things through which alone their outward appearance can be rightly understood. To attempt to attain a knowledge of either inner or outer as if the one were or could be independent of the other is to condemn oneself to an ignorance equivalent to that of Adam and Eve when, exiled from paradise, they knew themselves to be stripped bare of their natural vestments of intelligence and wisdom. Not to understand this is again to succumb to the lie of the double truth – to the lie that has vitiated our whole culture and has brought us to the edge of nemesis. And unless we overcome this lie, all our other efforts to escape that nemesis will be in vain.

This means that we have to disabuse ourselves of the idea that what we have been schooled over the last centuries to regard as knowledge does in fact constitute knowledge, as well as of the idea that knowledge can be obtained in the ways in which we assume we can obtain it. True knowledge can in no way be the acquisition or discovery of an individual, or of a group of individuals. It cannot be found through experiment (which always means treating things with violence), or through research (which always means interfering with nature), or by following the analytical path, for it has nothing to do with anything that can be chopped into pieces, split into sub-divisions, dissected, or broken down into constituent parts, or that assumes that things have to be compartmentalized or fragmented in order for something to be known about them. It cannot be investigated, or pinned down, or classified, or formulated into laws as Newton formulated the law of gravity, as if the earth was something to which we are bound because an impersonal objective force compels us to be so. Nor can we possess true knowledge unless we have personal experience of it; and it totally eludes every form of specialization, as it does any attempt to infer it from the observation of many particular instances.

For, as I said at the beginning of this chapter, the so-called knowledge we think we can obtain by such means is the result of our attempt to know what we do not know and what we think is not known. It is a product of our not-knowing, of our ignorance, and our ignorance is inextricably built into it. And this ignorance that is built into all our so-called knowledge, and which prevents us from seeing things as they really are and from perceiving their true nature and identity, ultimately has its roots in our ignorance of who we ourselves are, and of what constitutes our true nature and identity; for, clearly, unless we first know who we ourselves are, we cannot know what anything else is either. And knowledge into which such ignorance is inextricably built cannot by definition constitute true knowledge. It must inevitably be tainted with this ignorance and hence with falsity. And knowledge tainted with falsity cannot constitute true knowledge. In other words, the human mind, without enlightenment from a more-than-human source, cannot attain a valid form of knowledge.

This in its turn means that if we are to see things as they are, we have to free ourselves completely from this kind of pseudo-knowledge and from the methodologies that go with it. We have to free ourselves from all that we think we know, empty our minds of all that we think we know, of all the conceptions we have formed as a result of going in pursuit of a knowledge we think we can obtain by any of the means of which I have just spoken. We have to become ignorant of all knowledge we think we have obtained through our own efforts. For true knowledge cannot be acquired by any of these means, and still less can it be confirmed or verified by any such means. Anything we can discover for ourselves by such means is pseudo-knowledge, non-wisdom. True knowledge has its source in the wisdom that is the lifeblood of all things and where everything is already known. It is not therefore something that is not known. It is not even something that we do not know. We do know it – it is our lifeblood – only we have forgotten it and lost it, just as we have forgotten and lost our own reality. If we can recover our own reality we will also recover this knowledge, for the two go hand in hand, this knowledge is part and parcel of who we are, in our true being. If we recollect who we are, we will also recollect this knowledge.

True knowledge, then, is something that is given to us, but we can perceive it only when we are in a condition to perceive it. It is not in any way subject to our will, we cannot capture it, we can only be suffused with it, embraced by it, immersed in it. It is a light that dispels the darkness of our ignorance, but a light that remains invisible to those who have eyes but cannot see. And we will never have eyes that can see while we are still dazzled by the glare of pseudo-knowledge. We cannot go on chasing the sirens and will-o'-the-wisps of pseudo-knowledge, let alone conforming our everyday life to its fallacies, and at the same time expect holy Wisdom to make us her tabernacle. For this to happen, we have to attain a new state, a state of unknowing which, contrary to the negative not-knowing, frees us from bondage to our ego-consciousness and to its stream of hallucinatory and dismembering thought, and allows us to perceive the seamless robe of nature in all its pristine integrity. Only then, through this act of self-recollection – which is also an act of re-membering – will Wisdom reveal herself, will she unveil her presence in every natural form of life and being. Only then will we begin to see the beauty at the heart of things. And this is the road to the recovery of paradise. This is itself the overture to paradise.

Chapter Ten

The Meaning of Creation *ex nihilo*

This short chapter is a kind of codicil to the preceding chapter, in that it attempts to answer a question latent in the premise which, I argue, opens the door to the mentality that has produced our secular and materialistic world. How, it might be asked, could it come about that such a bifurcated, dualistic approach to knowledge as that represented in the theory of the double order of truth could so displace the unitary theory of knowledge in the Christian consciousness that it was accepted, and still is accepted, as a valid theory? How could the Christian consciousness accept the idea that it is quite possible to obtain a knowledge of the natural world without basing it on the spiritual hermeneutic of this world? How came it that *theosophia* was regarded as referring to one sphere of reality, and the natural sciences to another sphere, a dichotomy that results in the denigration of the created world to the degree that permits it to be regarded as virtually lifeless, soulless and without any direct participation in the Divine? How was it possible for Christians to embrace a cosmology of this type?

Perhaps the first thing to be said here is that this type of cosmology appears to reflect an almost pathological fear of what the theologians who espouse it tend to call idolatry or pantheism. Mindful of St. Paul's warning (Rom. 1:25) about the fate of those who worship what is created rather than the Creator, they have felt that the only way to avoid a similar fate is to deny that there is any natural relationship between God and the world He creates. This means that they have to reject the idea that God creates the world within Himself – *ab intra* – for if He does this, inevitably there is a natural, even congeneric relationship between God and the world He creates. In some way, in fact, if God creates in this manner God must actually be that which He creates; for He must be the all in all of that which He creates, even if that which He creates is not in the same condition or state as He is. Such an understanding appears to lead so directly to pantheism, and thus to the crime of idolizing what is created rather than the Creator, that these theologians feel that it must be misguided, not to say heretical, and they reject it accordingly.

This radical exclusion of the idea that God creates the world within Himself means that these theologians are forced to assert that God must create the world outside Himself – *ad extra* – for otherwise He could not create it at all. But here they encounter another difficulty. For if God creates the world outside Himself, this could imply that there is something – some matter – outside Himself out of which He creates it. To admit this would be to admit that there is from all eternity something in the universe that is not God, that is a distinct and independent substance in its own right, over which God may exercise His power but which has no inner roots in His own Being. Yet if this is the case, God is not infinite: there is this other substance in the universe by which His infinity is limited. There is an absolute dualism built into the very nature of reality. To admit this would be to embrace a heresy even more sinister than the pantheism these theologians are so anxious to shut the door on.

This posits something of a dilemma. On the one hand it cannot be accepted, in this view of things, that God creates the world within Himself, and on the other hand it cannot be accepted that He creates it outside Himself if this implies, as it appears to imply, that there is a substance or matter independent of God and not deriving from His own Being out of which He can create it. Out of what, then, can He create it?

Faced with this dilemma – which, it may be said, was entirely of their own making – the theologians in question thought they could resolve it by positing the conception that God created the world "out of nothing", *ex nihilo*. It should be stressed from the start that this conception has nothing to support it in the Gospels – it is not a *datum* of Revelation. It is formulated solely with a view to escaping from the dilemma we have described.

It is thought that it provides such an escape, first, because if God creates the world not out of Himself but "*ex nihilo*", then the idea that there is any natural or congeneric relationship between God and the world can, it is argued, be excluded. It can be asserted that the Divine is not intrinsically present in the world He has created; and that therefore to regard the world as if God were intrinsically present within it would clearly be to commit an act of idolatry.

At the same time it is thought that it provides such an escape because, while closing the door to idolatry, it does not open it to the equally dangerous "heresy" of positing a radical dualism at the basis of creation. For, it is said, this "nothing" – *nihil* – out of which God creates the world possesses no substantive existence and so cannot be invoked as positing a reality outside or independent of God, or as in any way implying that His infinitude is limited. This "nothing", they claim, is nothing in the absolute sense: it is a kind of absolute vacuum, totally privative of all life, being, consciousness, and of anything else one can think of – a total blank. Thus it cannot constitute a reality eternally outside and independent of God, a kind of second universal principle.

In other words, in positing this conception of the creation *ex nihilo*, these theologians imagine that they escape both the Scylla of recognizing that the Divine is intrinsically present in Creation, a recognition which, they again imagine, would lead directly to the kind of pantheism by which they are so alarmed; and that at the same time they escape the Charybdis of a radical dualism, in that they assert that absolutely nothing existed prior to creation out of which God could have created the world.

It is the ascendancy of this conception of creation *ex nihilo* in the Christian consciousness, both in Eastern and Western Christianity, that underpins and makes possible the whole theory of the double order of truth. At the same time the formation and acceptance of the theory of the double order of truth mark, as we have seen, a definitive step in the fostering of the mentality that promotes the appalling desecration of the created world which is now reaching its climax. From this point of view, consequently, it can be categorically affirmed that the conception of creation *ex nihilo* lies at the root of our contemporary ecological crisis. Correspondingly, it can equally be affirmed that as this conception was formulated and promoted by theologians whose claim to be Christian theologians has not been disputed by the Church, the Christian Church, at least as represented by those responsible for its major dogmatic, canonical and conciliar orientations and decisions, bears a direct and incontrovertible responsibility for the desecration of the cosmos. It is absolutely no accident that a purely materialistic view of nature first arose not within the Hindu, Buddhist, or Islamic world, but within the Christian world. It is absolutely no accident either that the official responses of the Church, whether in the Christian East or Christian West, to what we call the ecological crisis have been, as I have already said, lamentable: the "official" theology of the Church being so hamstrung by precisely those conceptions that have directly promoted this crisis, it is hardly surprising that the pronouncements are as vapid as they are ineffectual.

This being the case, we should scrutinize the conception of creation *ex nihilo* more carefully, since clearly a conception which has such disastrous consequences should not constitute a part of Christian doctrine. As we have seen, one of the main purposes of this conception was to exclude all access to the idea that, prior to creation, something existed outside and independent of God out of which He created the world. It was intended to exclude, for instance, such ideas as that there was a kind of formless matter to which, in creating, God gave form. Yet the attempt to exclude such a possibility in this way leads, in fact, to precisely the kind of dualism that such a conception is intended to deny.

If the statement that God creates the world out of nothing is taken to signify that absolutely nothing existed prior to creation, then the question is posed as to whether this nothing existed or did not exist prior to creation. Was there nothing prior to creation, or was there not nothing? If the answer is that there *was* nothing prior to creation, then this nothing would in fact have been a kind of something, a positive vacuum, a kind of non-I in relationship to God, or a non-God; and at the basis of creation would lie an irresolvable dualism between God and non-God of a type equally as radical as the dualism which the statement in question is attempting to exclude.

If, on the other hand, it is said that this nothing did not exist prior to creation, so that prior to creation there was no relationship between God and this nothing such as would posit an absolute dualism at the basis of the world, what we are asked to give our assent to is a kind of absurdity. For how can there be a denial of relationship before there is such a thing as relationship, or a privation of existence before there is any existence? The notions lack all meaning.

Moreover, the term "prior" employed in the phrase "prior to creation", presupposes a temporal dimension. But time characterizes exclusively the created world and thus there can be no such thing as "prior", in so far as this word possesses a temporal connotation, until creation has appeared. From this point of view, then, to attempt to clarify whether the "nothing" did exist or did not exist prior to creation is a completely pointless endeavor.

Thus the term "nothing", if it is interpreted as denoting an entirely negative category, does not refer or correspond to any reality, either metaphysical, logical or physical. It refers or corresponds only to a negative and entirely hypothetical figment of human thought. It is unlikely, to say the least, that God creates the world out of such a figment.

The fact that, none the less, this figment of human thought leads directly to the formulation of its conceptual counterpart, the theory of the double order of truth, and hence opens the door to those developments which have issued in the ecological crisis, is not difficult to explain. For it posits the existence of two orders of reality, the supranatural and the natural, between which there may be an analogical resemblance but between which there is certainly no actual interpenetration such as would permit it to be understood that God is intrinsically present in everything that He creates, while everything that is created, simply by virtue of that fact alone, participates, though it may be in a potential and not in an actualized manner, in the Divine.

It posits the existence of these two non-interpenetrating orders of reality, between which there is not and cannot be any natural or congeneric relationship, because if the world is created out of nothing conceived in this purely negative and privative sense, it must be created outside God. For clearly this nothing is not a quality of God's own nature and reality – on the contrary, it is entirely privative of God. Nor can it ever become a quality of God's own nature and reality in such a way that it could be said that there is a natural relationship between God and the nothing. Hence the world that is created out of this nothing must exist outside God, and there can by definition be no natural or congeneric relationship between God and that which is outside God.

God can neither be intrinsically present in that which is outside Him, for then it would not be outside Him, and nor correspondingly can that which is outside God simply by virtue of the fact that it is created be said to participate in the Divine, for such participation presupposes the indwelling presence of God, and in this view God cannot be intrinsically present in that which He creates simply by virtue of the fact that He does create it. He can be present in that which He creates, and that which He creates can participate in Him, only on condition that through a sacramental action in which man is the sole bond or synthetic link between God and nature, that which pertains to the world of nature is raised out of its natural state and is transformed by the intervention of grace that is extrinsic to it but is now superadded to it. Unless there is such sacramental action, that which is created will remain non-divine, non-divinized, simply godless raw material, deserving of respect perhaps, because it is created by God, but essentially neither holy, sacred, nor ensouled.

As to why this conception of the two orders of reality, the supranatural and the natural, with the natural order being assigned the character which is assigned to it, should inevitably result in the formulation of the idea that there are two corresponding orders of truth, this must be obvious. Once the existence of two such non-interpenetrating spheres of reality, each with innate characteristics and qualities that the other does not possess, has been posited in this way, it is quite clear that the laws pertaining to the one sphere cannot be those that pertain to the other sphere. And this is only another way of saying that the truths pertaining to the one sphere are not those that pertain to the other sphere. There is, in other words, that double order of truth of which I spoke in the last chapter.

It is not difficult to see how the view of the natural world implicit in this understanding of the *nihil* – a view in which nature is seen as entirely dependent on man for its rescue from its godless, unhallowed state – would inevitably invite man to become the predator of the natural world, and even to become its predator with the conviction that, by interfering with it, he is conferring on it some benefaction or even blessing of which without his interference it would be for ever deprived. For according to this view, man is the sole channel through which any benefaction or blessing can be bestowed on it, and thus his interference in nature is a *sine quâ non* of its ever transcending its godless, unhallowed state. Nor is it difficult to see how, by embracing and fostering such a cosmology, and the interpretation of the *nihil* – the nothing – out of which God created the world which it presupposes, the Church stands directly responsible for the desecration of the cosmos.

Fortunately, this type of cosmology is not the only cosmology that the Church and the Christian tradition have to offer. The phrase, "God created the world *ex nihilo*" – or, rather, "God creates the world *ex nihilo*", for He creates it at each instant *ex nihilo* – may be interpreted, and has been interpreted by Christian theologians (one may specify St. Gregory of Nyssa, the author of the *Corpus Dionysiacum*, and John Scottus Eriugena among them) in a way totally different from that of which we have already spoken. According to this different interpretation, the term *"nihil"* or "nothing" does not denote an absolute blank, the privation of every quality or an entirely negative category. It is not a mere figment of human thought that does not correspond to any reality whatsoever. On the contrary, it is a positive category. It denotes the absence of all space, time and matter, or of everything extended in space and time – the absence, that is to say, of all that can be called a "thing". It thus denotes a realm of divine interiority in which there is "no thing". It refers to that in God which is free from all form, material or non-material, and which to us presents no identity because it is beyond the capacity of our minds to grasp it. In so far as we can envisage it at all, it may be envisaged as the fathomless, incomprehensible ground or depths of God's uncreated energies and possibilities, the pre-ontological "*nihil*" from which all things proceed. In this way it refers not to something that is outside or privative of God, or that is void of His presence. It refers to what is within God.

This interpretation of the term '*nihil*' in its turn permits a type of cosmology totally different from that which results from the interpretation that would equate the "nothing" with a mere negative category. Creation out of nothing means, simply, creation out of God, God being "no thing". To speak of what is "prior" to creation is not, therefore, to refer to a time that precedes creation, a conception which, as we have seen, is meaningless. It is to refer to the ontological and pre-ontological realms of the Divine that stand, in a vertical hierarchy, prior to the realm of creation.

Similarly, to say that the world has a beginning, and to mean by this that it has a beginning in time, or a temporal beginning, is likewise meaningless. For what meaning can it have to assert that the world has a beginning in time or a temporal beginning when time has no existence apart from the existence of the world? Something can have a temporal beginning or a beginning in time only on condition that time pre-exists it, and time does not pre-exist the world. The world cannot have either a beginning in time or an end in time. This does not mean that the world does not have a beginning. It does have a beginning, but in a totally non-temporal sense: its beginning or origin lies in God's transcendent creative power.

Within the perspective, then, opened up by this interpretation of the term *nihil*, God creates the world not outside Himself (*ad extra*) but within Himself (*ab intra*). The original act of creation is that of the differentiation of the forms of all things from the un-differentiated unknowable ground – the *nihil* – of the Divinity. The only *nihil* that can conceivably correspond not to a meaning-less figment of thought but to a meaningful reality is the latent state of beings prior to differentiation – and even in that state, hidden in the pure unrevealed potentiality of the Divine, in Non-Being itself, beings possess from pre-eternity a positive status.

Thus, creation is not the separation or projection of an extra-divine world or of the extra-divine beings that constitute that world; nor is it emanation in the strictly Neoplatonic sense. It is theophany, differentiation by increasing incandescence from within. It is a process through which God reveals Himself to Himself. It is an act of self-revelation through which God not only knows Himself in created beings but also is known by them, there being basically no difference between these two acts of knowing: our knowledge of God is also God's knowledge of Himself, or in and through us God becomes aware of Himself.

This means that every created being is a one-in-two, an *unus ambo*. It is both, and simultaneously, its being in the divine uncreated dimension and its being in the created dimension. These two as-pects form a single whole, and both are essential to every created being as such: the one is never not two, and the two is never not one. In creation the spirit never exists without matter, and matter never exists without spirit. And just as the Divine can be known only in the concrete dimension which is the theophany of the Di-vine, so a divine archetype can be contemplated only in its concrete created image, by means of which it is outwardly and visibly per-ceptible.

Thus nature – the created world – is a mode of discourse or the revelation of God to man, communicating to him the mystery of the unity in the variety of all things. It demonstrates the dialectic of the unity in opposites. God and His creation are related both by difference and similarity, by opposition and antagonism as well as by affinity and complementarity. Of creation's two poles, spirit and matter, matter is characterized by attraction and repulsion, while the spirit is characterized by its upward transforming and reconciling impulsion. The logic of the unity in the duality of spirit and nature is the logic of a non-dualist spirituality that denies the monist single principle of ultimate explanation as well as the dualistic two principles. It reunites sameness and difference, proximity and distance.

The world of phenomena is the theophanic world. This world is that world. It is not simply a reflection of the theophanic world in the sense that there is a relation of parallelism or mutual analogy or correspondence between them. All nature, from beginning to end, constitutes a single icon of God. Underlying the whole cosmos and its minutest particles, God is active in nature and nature in God from eternity through all time to eternity. The cosmos is the other self of the Absolute.

Does this mean that we end up with that kind of idolatry and pantheism which the other negative interpretation of the term "*nihil*" was meant to exclude so drastically? Perhaps the first thing to be said here is that most forms of what is called pantheism do not involve the worship of nature. They involve the worship of God in and through nature, in and through His creation, which is a vastly different matter. Even the Pauline warning about the fate of those who worship creation rather than the Creator does not exclude pantheism, in so far as this is experienced as the worship of God in and through His creation. In other words, pantheism is not in the least synonymous with idolatry. If I worship God in the form of a flower, or even in the form of a drop of water in the flower, I am not committing an act of idolatry so long as I remember that if God is a flower, or a drop of water, He is also not a flower and not a drop of water.

Moreover, the fact that every particle of created existence is an image of its divine prototype, and enshrines and participates in that prototype, does not mean that we are led to worship creation: the icon enshrines and participates in the holiness of its prototype without this meaning that we worship it – we simply venerate it as sacred, as we should venerate as sacred every particle of created existence. In any case it must surely be more in accord with God's bounty that we should worship Him in and through His creation than to regard creation as deprived of the divine presence, or to worship a God who is regarded as so divorced from creation that creation can be viewed as existing, to all intents and purposes, outside God and independent of Him.

In fact, and paradoxically, it is those who reject pantheism who are far more likely to end up as idolaters than confessed pantheists. When I understand, *not* that nature is God or that creation is the Creator, but that God is nature and the Creator is that which He creates, then there is no danger of my worshipping nature or creation more than God, or instead of God, or to the exclusion of God. There is a danger of my doing this only when I *fail* to understand that God is nature and that the Creator is that which He creates; for then I can set nature or creation over against God, as something other than God, and can worship it as something independent of god, or to the exclusion of God: I can, that is to say, make a God of it. This is why the negative understanding of the term, *nihil*, opens the door precisely to the kind of "heresy" against which it is assumed to close it. Whenever there is a kind of dualism, one must be on one's guard, just as one must be when there is a hint of monism.

From what has just been said, it should be clear that the identifying of the *nihil* out of which God creates the world with the undifferentiated *ground* of the Divinity does not mean that one ends up with a pantheism that so confuses the concept of God with the concept of the world that, to all intents and purposes, the two concepts are interchangeable. The distinction between the two concepts remains: the Creator is that which He creates, but creation is not the Creator. Nor does it mean that pantheism itself is anything more than an initial phase of the contemplative path, whose goal is not so much to see God in all things as to see all things in God – not so much pantheism as *panentheism*. To stop at this phase of the contemplative path is to abort the whole process of spiritual realization – it is in this sense, rather than in any other sense, that pantheism can represent a possible danger.

In addition, the fact that God is present in all things simply by virtue of their being created, and hence that no special sacramental activity is needed in order to imbue them with divine grace, does not mean that man has no priestly role as mediator between God and creation. That God is present within all created things, and that all created things are therefore intrinsically holy, and should be treated as such, does not mean that this divine presence is always actualized in all things, or *in actu*; it can equally be latent in all things or *in potentia*. Thus there is the need of sacramental activity in order to bring His divine presence, whether in man or in other created things, from a latent to an actualized state.

It is precisely in relationship to this sacramental activity that man possesses a mediating role. Yet if the paradigm of such sacramental activity is represented in the central sacrament of the Christian Church – in the Eucharist, that is to say – then we must not forget that if man possesses a mediating role between God and creation, creation equally possesses a mediating role between God and man; for it is by means of the created elements of wine and bread that man communes with God in the Eucharist. From this point of view, we can say that if the actualization of the image of God in creation depends upon man, the actualization of the image of God in man depends upon creation; and that if man is the bond between God and creation, creation is equally the bond between God and man.

As it has been the concern of this chapter to emphasize, there is a relationship of interdependence, interpenetration, and reciprocity between God, man, and creation; and it is the loss by the Christian consciousness of awareness of the full significance of this relationship that is a basic cause of today's ecological crisis. Correspondingly, if the Christian Church is to offer a positive response to the challenge of this crisis, it can only be through reaffirmation of the full significance of this relationship, a reaffirmation which is no more, if no less, than a reaffirmation of the full significance of its central sacrament, the Eucharist, with all that that means with regard to the miracle of creation and to man's responsibility for fulfilling it.

Yet the reaffirmation of this relationship in its turn means that the Christian consciousness has to overcome its continuing adherence, conscious or unconscious, to the idea that the *nihil* out of which the world is created is a kind of negative, privative category, rather than the unknowable ground of the Divinity from which eternally proceed the inexhaustible sacred presences of creation. A consciousness blind to the presence of the Divine in every created form is a consciousness that is radically distorted, and the type of theology it represents and promotes will be equally distorted, whatever authority it appears to represent. It is not too much to say that this question of the meaning of the *nihil* constitutes the most crucial theological – and existential – issue that we confront today; for on the answer we give to it will depend both our anthropology and our cosmology – in fact our whole attitude to life. If we continue to adhere to the first, the negative interpretation, we will continue to nourish the cankers of nihilism, meaningless violence and despair which our bondage to it has already nourished in our souls. If we can espouse the second we will at least make it possible for ourselves to set out once more on the path that brings us to experience in our own being the revelation that "every thing that lives is Holy".[1]

---

[1] For other expositions of this argument see also the author's review of Met. John Zizioulas' *Creation as Eucharist*, in *Epiphany*, Vol. 13, No. 3, 1993, and in *Phronema* 9 (1994); his *Human Image: World Image* (Ipswich, 1992) pp. 151-67; and with respect to the problem of evil, creation and pantheism, *ibid.* pp. 167-75. (Ed.)

Chapter Eleven

The Renewal of the Tradition of Contemplative Spirituality

The injunction, "Know thyself", inscribed above the entrance to the temple of Apollo at Delphi, proclaims a standard that we fail to honor only by betraying the norms of an authentic human life. For an individual to know himself means much more than simply being aware of his weaknesses and limitations. It means to know his true identity and being. If the injunction is taken to posit a condition that has to be fulfilled before one is worthy of entering the temple itself and of confronting the "God within", then to know oneself may be said to be a condition of knowing God. It may even be said that what is implied is that our true identity and being *is* the God within, or at least that one cannot know oneself without simultaneously knowing the source of one's being, and that this source is no less than the God within. In other words, if one cannot know God without knowing oneself, one also cannot know oneself without knowing God. To be ignorant of oneself is thus to be ignorant of the divine source of one's being. If to be ignorant of oneself is to fail to achieve an authentic human life, then by the same token to be ignorant of God is to fail to achieve an authentic human life.

It is also to fail with respect to what must be regarded as a further qualification for living an authentic human life: the ability to know things other than oneself and hence to act towards them in a way that takes account of their true nature and identity, and that does not violate or abuse them. Clearly, unless one first knows oneself, one cannot know anything else either, and in that case one is bound to act towards other things in a way that will violate and abuse them. But knowing other things means much more than being aware of their physical appearance, just as knowing oneself means much more than being aware of one's body. Ultimately to know other things involves the same condition as knowing oneself: that one knows the source of their existence, which is no less or other than the source of one's own existence. To possess a true knowledge and understanding of things is thus to know their inmost divine reality and identity. It is to know the divine essences of things.

When in Genesis it is said that we shall have dominion over things, what is meant is not that we can lord it over things in an autocratic way, or that these things are at our disposal to use as we want and to satisfy our own selfish needs and proclivities. What is meant is that, by entering into a knowledge of our own divine origin, we can also enter into a knowledge of the divine essences of other things as well, and thus can see them and act towards them in a manner that accords with their true nature and identity. Short of that, we inevitably violate and abuse both ourselves and *a fortiori* the things with which we come into contact. Creation is the act of God's self-knowledge. God's act and self-knowledge are ultimately one. They should ultimately be one in man as well, for only then can he be said to possess an authentic human dignity.

What the Delphic injunction proclaims, therefore, is that a condition of achieving such a human dignity is that we give priority to contemplation and gnosis – to following a contemplative and gnostic way – for contemplation is essentially the action through which we are led to a knowledge of our true identity and being and hence of the true identity and being of other things as well. The Greek word for contemplation is *theoria* – vision – and vision is knowledge. It is not that contemplation is opposed to action: not only is it in itself a form – the highest form – of action, but also unless all our other actions are informed by the knowledge that it embraces they will be performed in ignorance; and ignorance by definition can lead only to destruction and vice. To act well, we must first know. Thus, while contemplation and action are complementary, they are not on an equal footing: contemplation must precede action. Correct action depends on a correct mode of being: without *being* good, we cannot *do* good. And a correct mode of being – to be in a state of grace or goodness – requires that we first return to and know, in an active and not merely a passive way, the source itself of being and goodness that is, at the same time, the source itself of our own inmost being and identity.

Each spiritual tradition has, as it were, consecrated one or more ways – ways of contemplation – through which we can accomplish this return to the center and source of our being, with all the consequences that that will have for the living of our daily lives. One of the main such ways within the Christian tradition is that practiced in the East Christian world and known – from the Greek word ἡσυχία (*hesychia*, meaning stillness) that denotes the inner state it induces – as the way of hesychasm, or the hesychast way.

Hesychasm resumes some of the great themes of Greek patristic anthropology. True human nature is "recollection of God" – "recollection" in the ontological and Platonic sense of ἀνάμνεσις, a "remembering," that implies direct participation in an immanent divine principle. This state of recollectedness, in which the mind is free from distracting thoughts and is present to God as God is present in it, has been lost, or obscured, as a consequence of the "fall". As a result, we have become the victims of a host of indiscriminate, largely valueless thoughts and opinions. No longer concentrated in and on the Divine, we turn towards these mental and sensory images, which lead us outside ourselves, away from our true unity and integrity, and into a void in which we finish by destroying ourselves or by being destroyed by the fabrications of our own fragmented, dislocated and deluded mind.

The initial stage of hesychast practice consists therefore in reversing this process of dispersion and self-destruction; and it is to this end that a whole art and science of "recollection" is elaborated. Through a rigorous method of vigilance – watchfulness – in which the root of each thought is scrutinized and assessed, it becomes possible to strip the mind bare and to awaken a true understanding by freeing it from the thoughts and images that usually possess it and prevent it from seeing and experiencing its own inner reality. It is only then that we are in a position to recover our natural state, to breathe once again the air of divinity and to enjoy the peace we lost through turning our attention outwards, away from ourselves, on to the world of things and objects.

It is here that we encounter the hesychast thesis of the union of the mind – or more exactly the intellect, *nous* – with the heart. Like the Bible and other sacred texts, the hesychasts employ a symbolic physiology, a physiology of correspondences: there is a participative correspondence between visible and invisible, the created and the uncreated, the human and the divine. The physical heart, because it is the principle of the life and warmth of the body, is on that account also the spiritual center of human nature, the receptacle of grace, the "place" of the presence, real but unapprehended, of divine life, where we encounter God and in union with God become integrated and transfigured beings. The art of the spiritual life is therefore to become conscious of the "treasure hidden in the heart" – to become conscious of the real but unapprehended presence of God in the heart; and this art is effectuated by inducing the intellect, freed from extraneous thoughts and images, to "descend" into the heart and so to become conscious of the divine presence hidden there. Thus, this descent presupposes the accomplishment of the initial stage of the hesychast way, whereby the intellect, through rigorous watchfulness, has been cleansed of all that is alien to it and has been restored to its original purity.

The descent itself of the intellect into the heart is consummated above all by means of the invocation of the divine name, in the form known as the "Jesus Prayer". Just as there is a correspondence between the heart as both physical and spiritual center of the human organism, so there is a correspondence between the physical breath, which gives rhythm to and sustains life, and the divine Breath, by means of which God operates and sustains the diastolic and systolic rhythm of the universe, the complementary and simultaneous movements that constitute the epiphany and resurrection of all created things. Thus by linking our breathing to the cosmic and metacosmic divine Breath – by "breathing in God" – we imitate within ourselves, and hence participate in, the *fiat lux* and the return to the source that consummates the life-cycle of the universe and of each distinct and particular thing in the universe.

This linking of the human breath to the divine Breath is itself effected by associating each act of breathing with the invocation of the divine name. In this way the in-breath, led downwards into the heart, acts as the vehicle through which the intellect descends into the heart, becomes conscious of the divine life hidden there, and brings us into union with the source of our inmost being and identity; while the out-breath vehicles the divine grace with which it is now infused to all our members and by extension to the world of living things about us. It is thus that the invocation becomes truly the prayer of the heart.

It is thus, too, that the hesychast – his vital energy, perverted and hardened by the misuse of the passions as a result of the fall, now metamorphosed by the divine light that floods heart and mind – becomes an active agent in the transfiguration, not only of his own soul and body, but also of the world about him: he becomes a living holocaust of divine and spiritualizing energies. But he becomes such an active agent because through the act of invocation he is able to transcend his own limitations as agent through the action itself: by returning to his source by means of the invocation he induces and permits God Himself to become the agent of the invocation, in such a way that it is now God Himself who prays in and through him. It is thus God Himself that in and through him transfigures His own creation. The Logos invoked in prayer is not only the Logos in whom all things are created; He is also the Logos through whom all things are brought back to their source, are resurrected.

Invocation, therefore, is far from being a passive form of mysticism. It is the height of active contemplation and contemplative action, in which the adept, by entering into a knowledge of his own divine origin and by uniting such knowledge with his own existence, enters also into a knowledge of the divine essences of other things as well, perceiving them and acting towards them in a manner that accords with their proper identity and vocation. When he himself is resurrected into his own true being, he is able to be an active agent in the resurrection into their true being of other things as well.

* * *

I said that this hesychast way of contemplation is that practiced in the Eastern Christian world. This statement itself will, to some extent, be qualified in what follows below. But setting aside for the moment the question of the degree to which it has been and still is practiced in this world, what is clear is that it is a way of contemplation that until relatively recently has been virtually unknown in the world of Western Christendom. Yet its discovery by, and impact on, the western world during the last century or so may be said to constitute what is potentially one of the most significant events in the intellectual and spiritual life of this world. It is to identifying the major factors contributing to this discovery, and to exploring in some measure their significance, that the remainder of this chapter is devoted.

The discovery itself has passed through two major stages. The first relates to the rediscovery in the West of the writings of the Greek Fathers and of the Greek patristic tradition, for it is these writings that furnish the theological presuppositions of hesychasm. More specifically, this rediscovery may be traced back to the publication and exploration in the first decades of the twentieth century of patristic texts relating more or less directly to the hesychast way of life.[1] But here the approach was largely one of scholarship and research, and such scholarship and research cannot in the nature of things embrace a spiritual tradition that depends so largely on lived experience and a form of transmission that relies more on

[1] Mention should above all be made of the Assumptionist Fathers of *Échos d'Orient* and the Jesuit Fathers of *Orientalia Christiana* and of the *Revue d'ascétique et de mystique*, as well as of the comprehensive publication, initiated in Paris in 1942, of patristic texts under the collective title of *Sources Chrétiennes*. Also to be noted are the works of Hans Urs von Balthasar, particularly his study of St Maximos the Confessor, first published in German in 1941 with the title *Kosmische Liturgie. Maximus der Bekenner* (Fribourg-Brisgau, Herder).

personal relationship – on the *charisma* of spiritual paternity – than on impersonal and so-called objective criteria. Moreover, the approach was dominantly historical, in the sense that it tended to envisage hesychasm as a purely historical phenomenon, confined both chronologically and geographically. It did not view it as a permanent manifestation of the inner life of the Orthodox Church, as intrinsic to it as the sacraments, constituting as it does a kind of sacramental interiorization of baptismal and eucharistic grace. In other words, there was little attempt to view the hesychast way of life within the context in which its invisible and trans-historical character could have revealed itself more adequately, that is to say, in the part it has played and continues to play in the Eastern Christian world.

The descholasticization and dehistoricization of the approach to hesychasm, and the corresponding recognition that it is a living tradition permeating every aspect – liturgical, iconographic, personal – of the inner and intimate life of the Church, mark the second major stage in its discovery in the modern period. Here one must single out the important part played in this second stage by the translation from Russian into western European languages – German (1925), French (1928), English (1930) – of a remarkable document written by an unknown Russian in the nineteenth century and published in Russia in about 1865. This document – its English title is *The Way of a Pilgrim*[2] – was remarkable in this respect on two counts.

First, it brought to the attention of western readers the fact that the practice of the hesychast way of life, and above all the practice of the Jesus Prayer which lies at its core, were not limited either to the past or to a specifically monastic context: their presence is revealed in the heart of the Orthodox Christian of no matter what time or place, and of no matter what outward circumstances. Second, it brought to the notice of these same readers the existence of a book – regarded by the Russian pilgrim with a reverence usually reserved for the Bible alone – that appeared to explain, step by step, the stages of the mysterious spiritual journey on which the

[2] *The Way of a Pilgrim*, trans. by R. M. French (London, 1954).

pilgrim had embarked, and to lay down the guidelines as to how these stages were to be traversed.

To a West in which the split between abstract theology and individualistic "mysticism", gnosis and eros, knowledge and method, had long since undermined the contemplative tradition, and in which many were beginning to turn to the non-Christian religions of the East for guidance as to how the prophetic way of actual experience could be embraced in the light of doctrine, purifying and liberating the intellect, *The Way of a Pilgrim* came as a revelation. It was perhaps the first intimation of, and introduction to, a "secret science" ($\varkappa\varrho\upsilon\pi\tau\acute{\eta}\ \mu\varepsilon\lambda\acute{\varepsilon}\tau\eta$) of prayer and spiritual wisdom communicated in the form of a tradition organically attached to the integral tradition of the Christian Church and set forth in a work that the pilgrim could carry in his knapsack.

The work in question went by the title of the *Philokalia* and consisted of a series of texts that together constitute a manual, guide and companion to the hesychast prayer of the heart and the following of the hesychast way. In fact, the title itself – *Philokalia* – was a venerable one. It was first applied in the fourth century to a selection of ascetic and mystical texts made by St. Basil the Great and St. Gregory of Nazianzos from the works of Origen. At a time when the notion of "philosophy", although never denied, was too directly associated with "the wisdom of the world" to describe the Christian aspiration to perfection, the term "philokalia", love of the beautiful, was an obvious alternative.

Yet it was more than simply an alternative. For if in the Greek context – and especially in the Platonic and Neoplatonic context – Beauty is the principal attribute of the Good, nevertheless it is the aspect of Beauty which the Greek compilers of this anthology wished to emphasize. Needless to say, they have in mind less the visible and created appearance of Beauty than its invisible and uncreated presence: that presence in which the Light of Truth, transcendent source of life and desire of desires, is at one with divine Love in a union that gives birth to the inner peace and stillness denoted by the word *hesychia* itself.

Several smaller *Philokalias* were compiled during the centuries which followed that of the great Cappadocians. Although these were intended above all for private use or for the instruction of an intimate group of disciples – one has in mind the compilations of a Theodore of Edessa or of a Nikiphoros the Solitary (d. ca. 1340) – they all bear witness to the uninterrupted current of contemplative life present in the depths of the Church. In other words, one is confronted by a tradition, a living transmission or *paradosis*, that sustains this current through history. Yet at the same time one cannot with any certitude trace the itinerary of this tradition – the hesychast tradition – as it follows its historical course, if for no other reason than that those who have enshrined it have renounced the world in order better to serve it, and have already in this life disappeared from the stage of history. The hesychasts are God's dead, self-effaced so that they may unveil the countenance of the Invisible from Whom they and the world they have renounced receive their new life. One can consequently only read the history of this tradition in the signs it leaves of its presence in various other forms, in icons, in the lives of the saints, in the writing and translation of spiritual texts.

Thus it has been possible to attest its convergence on Mount Athos in the final centuries of the Byzantine period and above all in the fourteenth century. It was then that its crucial doctrinal thesis – that although in His essence God is unknown and imparticipable, He can none the less be known and participated in through His uncreated and deifying energies – was re-affirmed by an Athonite monk, St. Gregory Palamas (1296-1359), subsequently Archbishop of Thessaloniki; and it was then, too, that its more personal and specific character as a way leading to spiritual realization was magisterially delineated by St. Gregory of Sinai (1265-1346), who also spent some years on the Holy Mountain. And although in the following centuries there may have been a certain decline, it was on Mount Athos some four centuries later, towards the end of the eighteenth century, that the events decisive for the whole hesychast renewal in the modern world were germinated. Among these events pride of place must be given to the compilation of the *Philokalia* in a form that has become classic.

The date, as we said, is the latter half of the eighteenth century. In the thought of the West, that breach between God and the world, grace and nature, soul and body, already implicit in the Augustinian disjunction between the order of salvation and the order of nature and enlarged by the Scholastics, has now been more than consolidated by figures like Francis Bacon, Descartes and the other *buccinatores novi temporis* who accomplished the scientific revolution of the sixteenth and seventeenth centuries. Nature, whose law in Western theology had tended to be scarcely other than the law of sin, is now stripped of all positive qualities and regarded as so much dead matter, subject to purely mechanistic processes that can be discerned and, it was assumed, ultimately controlled by the human reason; while God, having set the cosmic machine in motion, has now so far retreated from it that for all practical purposes He need no longer be taken into account.

Under this new dispensation, man is seen as a semi-autonomous figure whose well-being can be secured through the acquisition of political and economic liberty: the American War of Independence is one expression of this supposition on the plane of history, as the French Revolution is to be another. Indeed, history itself is increasingly being regarded as an infinite and progressive external power, with whose self-determined dialectic man can cooperate on condition that he gives priority to action rather than to being, or, more explicitly, sees his being validated only in so far as it externalizes itself in terms of action; while this action itself, in conformity with the new dispensation of which we have spoken, is increasingly conceived solely as political or socio-economic action, as the writings of Marx will presently confirm. The consequence of this way of viewing history as action in time and on time entails of course a further lapse: that of man into the world of concepts and things, since to act in the sense envisaged requires something immediately visible and rationally controllable. We are in the sphere of the presuppositions that underlie the burgeoning of our modern technology and the relegation of anything that surpasses them to the status of being mere sub-products of illusory imagination.

One might have thought that the remote tongue of land reaching out into the Aegean from the seaboard of northern Greece, and still entitled the Holy Mountain of Athos, would be immune to the secularizing spirit of enlightenment sweeping across Western Europe and the United States of America. But Greek intellectuals, nourished in the same schools and universities as their western counterparts, were already seeking ways in which they could propagate the new philosophy in their own country, and so prepare for a revolution by means of which their fellow countrymen could achieve a form of national independence established on the basis of the same rationalist ideologies.

In fact, one of the most persuasive and progressive of these intellectuals, Eugenios Voulgaris (1716-1806), had secured appointment as director of the Athonite Academy situated on Mount Athos itself; and it was his presence, and the nature of the ideas that he was trying to instill into his pupils, that perhaps more than anything alerted the monastic Elders to the threat to their own tradition which these ideas signified and gave them intimations of further depredations to come. At all events, it was at this time that they undertook to reaffirm their tradition in a manner which, if it does not constitute a direct response to the thought-forms whose ascendance was to determine the immediate future of western civilization, at least reflects an awareness of them.

At the center of this activity was the monk St. Nikodimos of the Holy Mountain (1749-1809), and it was largely due to his intensive labor that the revival of hesychast spirituality was set within the context of the whole theological, liturgical and canonical tradition of the Orthodox Church. He wrote, translated, or compiled, singly or with others, some twenty-five large volumes covering virtually every aspect of this tradition, while the total number of his published and unpublished works is said to come to over a hundred. He was among the first after the fall of Constantinople in 1453 to undertake a systematic investigation of Greek patristic manuscripts, and he prepared for publication unpublished works by both St. Symeon the New Theologian and St. Gregory Palamas. Moreover – and this demonstrates a surprising catholicity of mind for the age and circumstances in which he lived – he also translated, adapted, and published *The Spiritual Exercises* of Ignatius Loyola and *The Spiritual Warfare* of Lorenzo Scupoli, thus pointing, already in the eighteenth century, to the continuing presence in the West of a current of spiritual understanding and practice still capable of converging up to some point with that of the Orthodox tradition.

Yet in the context with which we are here concerned, it was his compilation, in collaboration with St. Makarios of Corinth (1731-1805), of a collection of texts written between the fourth and the fifteenth centuries by the spiritual masters of the hesychast tradition that is his masterwork. For it is this anthology – *The Philokalia of the Neptic* [watchful] *Saints gathered from our Holy Theophoric Fathers, through which, by means of the philosophy of ascetic practice and contemplation, the intellect is purified, illumined and made perfect*, published in Venice in 1782 – that constitutes the major event in the hesychast renewal in the modern period.

For with this work, St. Nikodimos brings the hesychast tradition into the play of history. He not only stresses in his introduction that the prayer of the heart should be practiced equally by laymen and by monks; he also presents to a modern world increasingly to be dominated by a philosophy of action in and on time, the alternative of a contemplative knowledge of man's destiny and a way of remembrance whose consummation presupposes a reinsertion into the origin of time itself. Yet although the center of Nikodimos's activity was Mount Athos, the immediate impact of the *Philokalia* both on Athos and in Greece as a whole was less than might have been expected, although a new edition of the work was published in Athens in 1893.

Nevertheless, it is worth noting that the movement associated with it did spread beyond monastic circles and that its influence may be discerned in the works of the greatest writer of imaginative prose in modern Greece, Alexandros Papadiamantis (1851-1911); for these works, like those of Dostoyevsky, receive their power from the fact that they are written with the knowledge that it is only in the mystical light of Mount Tabor – the light of the Transfiguration – that human life can be truly perceived and given meaning. Yet it is outside Greece that the renewal of which St. Nikodimos is such a crucial instrument was soonest to bear fruits.

Here the focus is, first of all, on the Romanian world and the figure of a remarkable *staretz*, Paisii Velichkovskii (1722-94). Fr. Paisii was born in the Ukraine and became a monk at an early age. After serving his spiritual apprenticeship in a hermitage situated on the borders of Moldavia, he departed for Athos, to deepen his knowledge and experience of the hesychast way of life. After sixteen years on the Holy Mountain he returned to Moldavia, first as Abbot of the monastery of Dragomira, then of that of Seculu and finally of that of Neamtzu. It was at the last monastery that he accomplished the great work of his life, a work that in many ways parallels that of St. Nikodimos. He re-established the monastic rule, corrected the Church office, organized a printing press and began to translate and publish the works of the Greek Fathers. But above all it was while at Neamtzu that he translated a selection of the texts of the Greek *Philokalia* into Slavonic. It was published, with the title *Dobrotolubiye*, in Moscow in 1793 and reprinted in Moscow in 1822. This was the translation carried by the pilgrim in *The Way of the Pilgrim*, and indeed its influence on the piety and cultural world of Russia in the nineteenth century was immense, as the works of Dostoyevsky, to go no further, are there to testify.

This flowering of hesychast spirituality in Russia, stimulated both by the publication of the *Philokalia* and by the arrival of many of Fr. Paisii's own disciples, and associated especially with the *startzy* of the famous monastery of Optina, is a theme that, however important, lies outside the scope of this chapter. Suffice it to mention here that a translation of the *Philokalia* into Russian was made by Ignatius Brianchaninov (1807-67) and published in 1857; while a further translation into Russian was made by Bishop Theophan the Recluse (1815-94), who included several texts not in the original Greek edition and deliberately omitted or paraphrased certain passages in some of the texts in the Greek edition. Bishop

Theophan's translation was published at Moscow in five volumes, the first appearing in 1877.

Like Nikodimos of the Holy Mountain, the *staretz* Paisii considered that the practice of the prayer of the heart could also be entrusted to laymen and that even the higher forms of contemplation were not incompatible with a life lived in the world and in the context of a certain degree of cultural activity. Yet perhaps the main feature of his teaching is his emphasis on the idea and practice of spiritual paternity. His purpose here was to safeguard the personal character of the spiritual life, to protect this life from the vagaries of individual interpretation and disposition, and to prevent its dissociation from the liturgical life of the Church and the heritage of the Greek Fathers. At the same time, fidelity and unquestioning attachment to the institutions and forms of the Church did not mean that Fr. Paisii and his disciples aspired to salvation through social institutions or identified the victory of the Lamb with the concept of a Christian civilization. By definition, the hesychast lives the eschatological mystery of the Church, something that presupposes his capacity ultimately to transcend the forms of civilization, whether Christian or non-Christian, and even time itself. As a hesychast aphorism puts it, his purpose is to circumscribe the incorporeal within the house of his body.

In Romania itself, the work of Fr. Paisii was continued by his disciples, in whom he had instilled a love for the ascetic Fathers and a desire to see their writings made available in Romanian. Indeed, the first half of the nineteenth century saw the creation of a veritable patristic library on Romanian soil. It was as if Romania stood on the brink of an integral patristic and hesychast revival or, what amounts to the same thing, as if the Orthodox Church in Romania was about to manifest the plenitude of its spiritual tradition. If it is possible to say that such a revival and the manifestation of the spiritual plenitude of the Orthodox Church amount to the same thing, this is because a condition of the Orthodox Church being what it is lies in its fidelity to the Fathers, whose living heritage does indeed constitute the texture of this Church, with all its strengths and weaknesses. In this sense the Fathers are always contemporary with the life of the Church, integrated to it above all through that magnificent instrument of creative contemplation, the Orthodox liturgy, as well as of its auxiliary forms, the iconography and the hymnography.

In fact, the religious revival, of which the signs in Romania in the first half of the nineteenth century were so positive, was interrupted in the 1860s and later, as Romania became subject to a process of secularization on western lines similar to that which had already overtaken Greece and was soon to overwhelm Russia. But not all was lost: the tradition of the prayer of the heart was continued in the shadow of certain monasteries, the liturgy was still celebrated, the Fathers of the Church still remained the supreme criterion of Orthodox theology and practice. And towards the middle decades of the present century, in conditions that might appear even less propitious, the seeds sown in the first half of the nineteenth century and secretly nourished in the interior of the Church, entered a new phase of maturation.[3]

In this phase, it is once again the *Philokalia* that is to play a central part. In a theological atmosphere in which the historical mentality had blunted the sense and scope of a spiritual theology actually lived and experienced, Fr. Dumitru Staniloae (1903-93), in the years immediately preceding the Second World War, embarked on the task of reaffirming the primacy and indispensability of the hesychast contemplative tradition. To this end he undertook the translation into Romanian of the 1893 edition of the *Philokalia* of St. Nikodimos, although he also decided to include additional material and to supply new biographical notes and extensive commentaries on the texts. The first volume of the Romanian *Philokalia* was published in 1946, by the year 1991 twelve volumes had appeared. The bulk of the new material is devoted to St. Maximos the Confessor, St. Symeon the New Theologian and St. Gregory Palamas.

Moreover, the translation itself of the *Philokalia* into Romanian

[3] For the hesychast revival in Romania, see: "Un Moine de l'Église Orthodoxe de Roumanie, 'L'avènement philokalique dans l'Orthodoxie roumaine' ", *Istina*, 1958, nos. 3 & 4, pp. 295-328 and pp. 443-74.

was carried out not simply in the hope that it would counteract the dominantly historical approach to theology then prevailing; it was carried out also in direct response to a thirst for genuine spiritual values among members of the laity. In other words, if it did not signify simply an act of pious devotion and theological culture, but represented an awakening of ecclesial consciousness on the part of the faithful, which is always a condition and a sign of authentic spiritual regeneration, this was because it coincided with a parallel renewal of the hesychast way and the life of prayer. That this quest for the prayer of the heart should have meant the recovery of a line of filiation stemming directly from the *staretz* Paisii is, of course, not accidental. Nor is it accidental – though this is a theme that also lies outside the scope of this chapter – that the Paisiian pattern should have been followed in the sense that, just as Fr. Paisii's disciples had carried the benediction and teaching of their *staretz* into Russia, so there is a direct line of filiation between the hesychast renewal in Romania and the resurgence of the hesychast way in certain Orthodox Monasteries in the Middle East.

* * *

This brief account of the hesychast renewal in the Orthodox world of Eastern Europe, of which the *Philokalia* has been so to speak the testimony, took its start in a description of the stages through which the non-Orthodox western world began to discover the hesychast tradition, a discovery associated initially with the work of Roman Catholic scholars. Consequently, it might be thought that the renewal of this tradition in the West itself would have taken place first of all within the Roman Catholic world, especially as figures like the Cistercian monk Thomas Merton (1915-68),[4] to mention but one example, would seem to indicate the possibilities that lie in this direction. But the fact that what has become the official doctrine of the Roman Church does not harmonize with hesychast spirituality, while its liturgical texture is

---

[4] See Thomas Merton's homage to Mount Athos, "L'Athos, République de la Prière", *Contacts* no. 30, 1960, pp. 92-109.

not patristic in the way that that of the Orthodox Church is, has in practice impeded, if not prevented, such a renewal; for, as we have repeatedly stressed, hesychasm is essentially an ecclesial tradition whose authenticity depends upon its integration with the whole doctrinal and liturgical tradition of the Church. Hence if there are more positive indications of a genuine hesychast renewal in the West, they are to be found within the Orthodox Church.

In effect, the Orthodox presence in the West as a decisive spiritual factor, although not to be identified with the great Russian emigration provoked by the Communist revolution in Russia, was considerably strengthened by it; and this is particularly true with reference to what one might call the preparation of the theological ground for the emergence of an authentic hesychast spirituality. Having said this, however, it must at once be remembered that one of the most influential Russian writers in this connection had already settled in Paris prior to the Communist takeover. This was Myrra Lot-Borodine (1882-1957), whose article "La doctrine de la déification dans l'Église grecque jusqu'au XIᵉ siècle", published in the *Revue de l'Histoire des Religions* in 1932-3, was the first authoritative presentation of the major doctrinal thesis of the hesychast tradition to be published in the West. She followed this article with a series of other works on themes related directly or indirectly to the hesychast way, culminating in a study of the fourteenth century hesychast master, Nicolas Cabasilas,[5] published after her death. But apart from her example, the main thrust of the renaissance of an Orthodox patristic consciousness in the West has been promoted above all, though by no means exclusively, by figures connected with the Russian *diaspora*.

In this respect – since it is impossible to mention by name all who have been associated with it – one must single out, first, the writings of Vladimir Lossky (1903-58), whose *Essai sur la théologie mystique de l'Église d'Orient*, published in Paris in 1944 (English translation London, 1957), has virtually become a classic,[6] and,

---

[5] Myrrha Lot-Borodine, *Nicolas Cabasilas* (Paris, 1958).

[6] Vladimir Lossky, *The Mystical Theology of the Eastern Church* (London, 1957;

second, the magisterial study of St. Gregory Palamas and the translation into French of one of his major hesychast works, *Defence of the Hesychast Saints*, both undertaken by Fr. John Meyendorff (1926-92) and both originally published in 1959.[7] Alongside this purely literary preparation for the emergence in the West of an authentic hesychast spirituality one cannot underestimate the part also played, again above all as a consequence of the Russian *diaspora*, by the presence of the Orthodox liturgy, so deeply impregnated as it is with the theology of the Fathers, as well as by that of one of its integral elements, its iconography: the recognition of the icon as the art form *par excellence* of the Christian tradition has not been the least of the factors contributing to the awakening in the West of a genuine patristic consciousness.

This awakening of consciousness to a theological perspective, in which it is stressed again and again that theological knowledge unaccompanied by personal experience of spiritual realities through a life of prayer and contemplation is little short of vanity – "Our devotion lies not in words but in realities", St. Gregory Palamas was to insist, reformulating the Evagrian aphorism, "If you are a theologian, you will pray truly. And if you pray truly, you are a theologian" – could not but lead to increasing demand among the Orthodox Christians in the West for deeper instruction and guidance on how such experience could best be attained. In other words, in the context with which we are here concerned, it could not but lead to a demand for access to the *Philokalia* translated into a contemporary Western language.

The first response to this demand was the publication, in London in 1951, of *Writings from the Philokalia on Prayer of the Heart*, translations into English made, not from the Greek original, but from Theophan the Recluse's Russian version. This was followed, in

St Vladimir's Seminary Press, New York, 1976); other works by Lossky include *The Vision of God* (London, 1963) and *In the Image and Likeness of God* (London/ Oxford, 1975; St Vladimir's Seminary Press, 1985).

[7] John Meyendorff, *A Study of Gregory Palamas* (London, 1964; St Vladimir's Seminary Press, New York, 1974); *St Gregory Palamas and Orthodox Spirituality* (St Vladimir's Seminary Press, New York, 1974).

1953, by the *Petite Philokalie de la Prière du Coeur*, published in Paris, and in 1954 by *Early Fathers from the Philokalia*, again translated from Theophan's Russian version and published in London.[8] The reception with which these publications met, and the further demand that they stimulated, led in their turn to the initiation, both in France and in England, of a translation from the original Greek of the entire *Philokalia* of St. Nikodimos and St. Makarios. The fruits of this initiation began to be published in the French and English languages in the late 1970s and the work is nearing its completion.[9] Concurrently, a number of Orthodox monasteries have come into being, both in western Europe and in America, where the hesychast way of life can be practiced more intensely.

Thus, into a modern western world dominated for centuries by an activist time-bound mentality that is anti-metaphysical, anti-contemplative and anti-symbolic, has been squarely placed the alternative of what we have called a contemplative knowledge of man's destiny rooted in a way of life in which theory and practice, wisdom and method, are inextricably interlocked and whose fulfillment requires a surpassing of all worldly categories, social, political, economic – in short, of that whole realm of the temporal to which the frenetic activity of modern man is confined. Assuredly, behind this antithesis lies another, namely that between opposed theological and consequently between opposed anthropological orientations. For at the origin (both metaphysical and chronological) of the activist bias of the modern world lies a sys-

---

[8] *Writings from the Philokalia on Prayer of the Heart*, tr. from the Russian text *Dobrotolubiye* by E. Kadloubovsky and G. E. H. Palmer (London, 1951). *Early Fathers from the Philokalia*, tr. from the Russian text *Dobrotolubiye* by E. Kadloubovsky and G. E. H. Palmer (London, 1954). The French translation was made by J. Gouillard.

[9] *The Philokalia*. The Complete Text compiled by St. Nikodimos of the Holy Mountain and St. Makarios of Corinth tr. from the Greek and edited by G. E. H. Palmer, Philip Sherrard and Kallistos Ware, Vol. 1 (London, 1979), Vol. 2 (London, 1981), Vol. 3 (London, 1984), Vol. 4 (London, 1995), Vol. 5 forthcoming. The French translation has been undertaken under the direction of Boris Bobribskoy, *Philocalie des Pères Neptiques* (Bagrolles-en-Magues, 1979–); to date, seven of eleven planned volumes have been published. A second two-volume French edition has also been published (Paris, 1995) under the supervision of Jacques Touraille. (Ed.)

tem of thought, delineated in the preceding two chapters, which turns God into a transcendent and unknowable essence that, although responsible for setting the cosmic process in motion, does not interiorly penetrate creation in all its aspects, invisible and visible, incorporeal and corporeal, intelligible and material, but leaves it to follow its own course as though it were a self-subsistent autonomous reality. The corollary of such a conception is that the mind of man, equated now with its purely rational function, is itself regarded as something sovereign, cut off from the divine and capable of resolving and determining the destiny of man on earth independently of all revelation and of all grace.

In radically condemning such a system of thought, hesychasm affirms what one might call the bipolarity of the divine; for if it continues to maintain the idea of God's transcendence, it no less insists on His total and ineradicable presence in man and in every other form of created existence. In other words, it affirms that God breaks through the wall of His transcendence in order to make Himself both the active source and the true existential subject of everything created, down to the least particle of matter itself: a source and subject who not only can be known by man, but who must be known by man as a condition of man himself possessing anything more than a distorted knowledge of his own being and of the world in which he lives. Such distorted knowledge is of course quite inadequate to serve as a guide to any truly constructive action, whatever the goodwill or humanitarian feeling that may lie behind it.

In this respect, hesychasm not only rejects the profane humanism which divinizes man as an autonomous being, as well as all those concomitant ideological structures whose aim is to establish the just society in terms of this-worldly categories alone; it also rejects the belief, now so common among Christians themselves, that the Christian life can best be lived in terms of human love and of service to one's fellow beings, especially in some collective form. This is to say that of Christ's two commandments, love of God and love of neighbor, it gives priority to the first and affirms that the love or service of mankind, or indeed any desirable activity on the level of this world, can be effective, both as a means of salvation and as a truly constructive expression of charity and compassion, only on condition that it springs from a prior love of God actualized in the most literal sense of the word.

To act in ignorance of this love and apart from its existential actualization is to divorce what one tries to do from its empowering source and so to fall into a kind of idolatry – the idolatry that consists precisely in valuing things apart from God as if they were self-created and self-subsistent. Hesychasm by no means scorns or undervalues human love and service. It is emphatically not "otherworldly" as this term is usually understood. On the contrary, it insists, as we have seen, that the whole of creation is impregnated with God's own life and being and that consequently there can be no true love of God that does not embrace every aspect of creation, however humble and limited. Its purpose is not to abandon the world to annihilation and self-destruction, but to redeem it.

It is to redeem it by transfiguring it. But for the hesychast, this transfiguration presupposes the transformation of human consciousness itself, so that it becomes capable of perceiving the divinity that lies at the heart of every created form, giving each such form its divine purpose and determining its intrinsic vocation and beauty. In other words, he will consider that the way for him, as for any other man, best to serve, at least initially, his fellow men and all other created beings, will be to bring the love and knowledge of God to birth within him; for until that has been achieved, his outward actions, instead of being the necessary expression of this love and knowledge, will be tarnished both with self-love and with the idolatry of which we have spoken.

This will make it clear why hesychasm is, and must be, first of all a way of contemplation. For it is only through the contemplative life in all its aspects – ascetic watchfulness, prayer, meditation, the whole uninterrupted practice of the presence of God to which the *Philokalia* is the guide – that we can actualize in ourselves the personal love and knowledge of God on which depend not only our own authentic existence as human beings, but also our capacity to cooperate with God in fulfilling the innermost purposes of creation.

* * *

What, finally, of Mount Athos itself, from the depths of whose solitudes issued, now over two hundred years ago, the *Philokalia* whose subsequent itinerary, both as a document and in terms of its significance in the intellectual life of the modern western world, we have been tracing? We noted that during the nineteenth century, although monastic life in its hesychast form continued on Athos without interruption, its presence and radiation as a dynamic force was modest; and although towards the end of the century an enormous influx of monks from Russia added a new impetus, transplanting as it did the inheritance of Fr. Paisii Velichkovskii associated with the monastery of Optina and *The Way of the Pilgrim* on Athonite soil,[10] the effects of this had so diminished by the middle decades of the present century that Athos appeared to be threatened with a decline from which recovery might well prove impossible. Moreover, the theological mentality fostered in Greece by the schools and universities was, if not overtly anti-monastic, at least so historicized and abstract that it failed totally to stimulate any aspiration for the contemplative life.

Yet, perhaps partially as a consequence of the renewed interest in the West in the Orthodox and particularly the hesychast tradition, Greeks themselves, in the decades following the Second World War, began to take fresh stock of this precious heritage, so much of whose literature was written in the Greek language. During the years 1957-63 a new edition of the *Philokalia* was published in five volumes in Athens, and this was accompanied by the publication of other related works, including *The Way of the Pilgrim* in a Greek translation. As in Romania some twenty years previously, the publication of this literature not only provided an antidote to the hidebound historical approach to theology then prevailing; it also represented both a response to and a further inspiration for a growing desire for genuine spiritual values and for the life of prayer. The consequence of this has been a veritable resurgence of mo-

---

[10] Staretz Silouan (1866-1938) was a representative of this inheritance on Athos. See Archimandrite Sofrony, *The Undistorted Image* (London, 1958); revised and enlarged edition, *St. Silouan the Atonite* (Tolleshunt Knights, 1991)

nastic life, of which the Holy Mountain has been the center. Moreover, in this resurgence many Orthodox, often converts, from other parts of the world have joined their Greek brethren, so that Athos is rapidly acquiring, or reacquiring, the pan-Orthodox character which is its birthright.

One cannot predict the dimensions that this hesychast renewal on the Holy Mountain, and in the world outside, may assume during our entry into the third millenium and beyond. Yet it may be said that through the seeds of the contemplative life sown in this Garden of the Mother of God for more than a thousand years, and now taking root elsewhere, the past is becoming the enriching experience of the future, while from the end of time the light that transfigured Christ on Mount Tabor continues to dawn in the hearts of those whose vocation, now as always, is to be hidden witnesses of Him Who is and Who is not, the Alpha and the Omega, the Origin and the End.

Index

Abraham 56
Adam 9, 58, 68, 72, 153, 171, 173, 174,
    176, 183, 190, 226, 228
Adonis 64
Agnosticism 34
Albert the Great 216
Alchemy 151, 152
Alexander of Hales 216
Anacreon 64
Anselm, St. 112
Antichrist 131, 159
Antonios, Patriarch of Constantinople 38,
    45
Aphrodite 125
Apollo 245
Apostles, Holy 31, 34
    Acts of, 55, 61
Aquinas, St. Thomas 114, 115, 216
Aristotle 6, 64, 115, 116, 117
Aristotelianism 89, 116
Asceticism 118, 127
Atheism 116, 139
Athos, Mount 253, 255, 256, 257, 260,
    266, 267
Attis 64
Augustine, St. 5, 7, 28, 29, 57, 112, 127,
    211

Bacon, Sir Francis 254
Balthasar, Hans Urs von 250
Balzac 188
Barnabas 55
Barsanuphius 190

Basil the Great, St. 252
Bernard, St. 7
Beyond Good and Evil 130, 131
Birth of Tragedy, The 129
Blackstone, Bernard 197
Blake, William 48, 69, 118, 128, 130, 133,
    196, 200
Bobribskoy, Boris 263
Boethius 114
Bonaventure, St. 112, 216
Boniface VII, Pope 51
Book of the Dead, Egyptian 182
    Tibetan 182, 188
Brahmin 62, 102
Brianchaninov, Ignatius 257
Brothers Karamonzov 47
Bruno, Giordano 41, 128
Buddhism 59, 62, 75, 77, 134, 220, 235
Bunan, Shidō 180
Byzantium 115, 116

Cabasilas, Nicholas 116, 261
Caesar 31, 32, 43, 45, 47
Charybdis 234
Chittick, William 54
Christ *passim*
    Ascension of 197
    Crucifixion of 72, 153
    Incarnation of 72, 104, 166
    Transfiguration of 257
Cicero 181
Clement of Alexandria 29, 56, 61, 116
Constantine the Great 33, 35, 37, 45, 46

Constantinople 39, 114, 127
    Patriarch of see Antonios
Corinth 117
Corinthians, 1st Letter of Paul to 55
Corpus Dionysiacum 238
Corpus Hermeticum 122, 123, 124, 125, 126
Crashaw, Richard 195
Crusades 41
Cyril of Alexandria, St. 29
Cyril of Jerusalem, St. 58

Dante 29, 43
Darwin, Charles 145, 151, 155
Delphi 245
de'Medici, Cosimo 114
Demos 204
Descartes 9, 201, 204, 219, 254
Dionysios 63, 129, 132
Dionysios the Aeropagite, St. 6, 29, 116
Divine intelligence 6, 8, 9, 161
Doctrine 14, 15, 17, 22, 34, 35, 46, 53, 56, 58, 62, 64, 68, 73, 76, 78, 80, 85, 86, 87, 88, 98, 102, 104, 105, 107, 112, 115, 134, 137, 152, 160, 162, 211, 235
    Metaphysical 91, 96, 97, 98, 100, 101
Dogma 35, 54, 134, 137, 142, 151
Domitian 32
Donne, John 199
Dostoyevsky 47, 48, 256, 257

Ecce Homo 130, 131, 132
Ego 109, 147, 148, 191, 192, 193, 194, 205, 212, 217, 218, 225
Eleusis 29, 63, 181
Elias 197
    as al-Khizr 197
Elijah 56
Eliot, T.S. 27
Endymion 64
Enoch 195, 197

Epimenides 63
Eriugena, John Scottus 238
Eros 124, 125
Essenes 28
Eusebius 28
Evans-Wentz, W.Y. 182, 188, 189
Eve 68, 153, 190, 228

Faustus 224
Ficino, Marsilio 117, 128
Florence 114, 116, 117
Forister, E.M. 114
Freud 149

Galatians, Book of 195
Galilee 32
Gemistos, Georgios see Plethon, Georgios Gemistos
Genesis 20, 246
Gennadios, Patriarch 127
Gethsemane 32
Gnosis 14, 15, 17, 30, 35, 52, 60, 108, 110, 122, 150, 151, 152, 153, 252
God passim
    Activity of 33, 236, 237, 239, 240, 241
    Manifestation of image or nature, to man 31, 70, 71, 73, 75, 96, 110, 122, 126, 131, 141, 153, 154, 155, 158, 160, 161, 162, 163, 164, 165, 190
    Presence of 49
    Relationship of, to man 120, 121, 153, 176,
    Relationship of, to the world 232, 233, 234, 236
    Reunion with, man's 36, 38, 248
    Revelation of, to man 19, 62, 70, 122, 123
    Spiritual vision of, man's 17, 18, 124, 193
    Will of 38, 139, 164, 165
    Worship of 55, 126
Godwin, Jocelin 79

Goethe 118, 128, 133
Gregory VII, Pope 40
Gregory Nazianzen, St. 29, 252
Gregory of Nyssa 116, 238
Gregory Palamas, St. 116, 253, 255, 259, 262
Gregory of Sinai, St. 253
Guénon, René 76-101, 104, 105, 106

Hamlet 189, 201, 204, 219
Hebrews, Book of 56, 195
Hellenism 117, 120, 124, 125, 126
Herakleitos 4, 5, 28, 56, 111, 119, 202, 212
Heresy 35, 56, 59
Hesychast 247-253, 255-266
Hinduism 59, 75, 160, 235
Holy Mountain see Athos, Mount
Holy Spirit 22, 30, 54, 57, 58, 61, 72
Holy Trinity 83, 84, 85, 86, 87, 111, 112, 151, 153

Idolatry 105
Attitude of 34, 35, 36
Inquisition 41
Irenaeus 57
Islam 31, 59, 75, 134, 235
Israel 55, 56, 57, 73
Italos, John 116

Jerusalem 32
Joan of Arc, St. 41
Job 151, 153
Job, Answer to 138
John, Gospel of 180
John the Baptist, St. 58
John Climakus, St. 190
John of Damascus, St. 116
Judaism 28, 55, 61
Julianos 66
Jung, C.G. 134-157, 158, 159
Justin Martyr 56, 61
Justinian 116

Khodr, Georges 54
Kübler-Ross, Elizabeth 184

Lawrence, D.H. 16
Lemnos 29
Lewis, C.S. 27
Life After Death 184
Logos 4, 6, 8, 9, 10, 13, 24, 26, 56, 57, 58, 60, 61, 62, 75, 121, 209, 211, 249
Lorimer, David 184
Lossky, Vladimir 261
Lot-Borodine, Myrra 261
Loyola, Ignatius 256
Lucifer 190
Luke, Gospel of 185
Lystra 55

Magarshack, David 47
Maimonides 216
Makarios of Corinth, St. 256, 263
Malatesta, Sigismondo Pandolfo 114
Marx, Karl 254
Matthew, Gospel of 31, 185, 191, 192, 220
Maximos the Confessor, St. 5, 7, 57, 61, 116, 197, 250, 259
Memories, Dreams, Reflections 134, 150
Merton, Thomas 260
Meyendorff, John 262
Milarepa 196, 197
Mirandola, Pico della 128
Mistra 114
Moody, Raymond A. 184
More, Henry 185
Moses 197
Moslem 62, 117, 220
Motovilov, Nicholas 185
Mysterium Coniunctionis 152

Nasr, S.H. 54
Nazianzen, St. Gregory see Gregory Nazianzen, St.
Neoplatonism 28, 66, 106, 116, 118, 119, 159, 160, 162-167, 252

Nero 32
New Testament 27, 55, 185
Newton, Sir Isaac 229
Nicaea, Council of 45
Nicholas of Cusa, St. 165
Nicodemus 73
Nietzsche 118, 128, 129, 131, 132, 133
Nikiphoros the Solitary 253
Nikodimos, St. 255, 256, 257, 258, 259, 263

Occult 77
Oceanus 64
Old Testament 55, 59
On Death and Dying 184
Origen 29, 57, 61, 116, 252
Orpheus 63
Othello 194

Paganism 28, 131
Paisii, Velichkovskii 257, 258, 260, 266
Palamas, St. Gregory see Gregory Palamas, St.
Pallis, Marco 77
Palmer, Samuel 196
Pantheism 242, 244
Papadiamantis, Alexandros 256
Parmenides 119, 124, 132
Paul, St. 32, 55, 56, 180, 190, 192, 195, 232
Peloponnesos 114, 117
Perry, Whitall N. 76
Peter, St. 39
Peter the Great, of Russia 45
Phaedo, Phaedrus 119, 122, 125, 180
Philokalia 252, 253, 256, 257, 259, 260, 262, 263, 265, 266
Photios 116
Plato 4, 5, 28, 64, 66, 116, 118, 119, 120, 122, 124, 125, 170, 180
Platonism 116, 127, 128, 160, 161, 247, 252

Plethon, Georgios Gemistos 114, 116- 119, 127, 128, 133
Plotinus 115, 124, 126, 171
Plutarch 181
Polytheism 128
Porphyry 114
Proklos 66, 76, 162
Protagoras 219
Psalms, Book of 124
Psellos, Michael 66, 116
Psychology and Alchemy 152
Pythagoras 64, 118

Rape of Man and Nature 49, 217
Reformation 9
Renaissance 2, 9, 114
Repentance 74
Republic, The 119, 122, 125
Revelation, Book of 55, 209, 217
Richmond, George 196
Rimini 114
Ritual, importance of 20, 21, 63
Romans, Epistle to 32, 190, 232
Rome 40, 139
Rûmî, Jalâl al-Dîn 180
Ruysbroeck, Jan van 208

Salvation 23, 39, 44, 51, 53, 54, 56, 57, 59, 61, 74
Samothrace 29
Satan 159
Savonarola 41
Scupoli, Lorenzo 256
Scylla 234
Serafim of Serov, St. 185
Shakespeare, William 194, 198, 201
Shankara 101
Silesius, Angelus 180
Silouan, Staretz 266
Socrates 56, 129, 203
Spirit, Holy see Holy Spirit
Staniloae, Fr. Dumitru 259

Stoddart, W. 54
Stoicism 121, 125
Sufi 54
Symeon the New Theologian, St. 61, 116,
    255, 259

Tabor, Mount 256, 267
Taylor, J.W. 116
Theanthropos 104
Theodore of Edessa 253
Theophan the Recluse, Bishop 257, 262, 263
Theophany 19, 34, 60
Timaeus 119, 120, 123, 125
Transfiguration 60
Trinity, Holy *see* Holy Trinity
Twilight of the Idols 129, 131

Upanishad 101, 102

Vācagar, Mānikka 197
Vasili I, Grand Prince of Russia 38
Vatican Council, First 51
Vedanta 66, 76, 101, 102, 103
Velichkovskii, Paisii see Paisii, Velichkovskii
Voulgaris, Eugenios 255

Ware, Bishop Kallistos 263
Way of the Pilgrim, The 251, 252, 257, 266
Whole in One 184
Wicksteed, Rev. Philip H. 29
Will to Power 129, 132
Woodhouse, C.M. 116

Yeats, W.B. 48, 185, 187, 188

Zarathustra 131
Zen 180
Zeus 63
Zizioulas, Met. John 244
Zoroaster 118

Made in the USA
Lexington, KY
18 May 2012